ENGLISH
PEOPLE
in the Eighteenth Century

By the same author

EIGHTEENTH CENTURY ENGLAND

A volume in the series

A HISTORY OF ENGLAND

General Editor: W. N. Medlicott

ENGLISH PEOPLE
in the Eighteenth Century

by

DOROTHY MARSHALL

LONGMANS

LONGMANS, GREEN AND CO LTD
48 GROSVENOR STREET, LONDON W1
RAILWAY CRESCENT, CROYDON, VICTORIA, AUSTRALIA
AUCKLAND, KINGSTON (JAMAICA), LAHORE, NAIROBI
LONGMANS SOUTHERN AFRICA (PTY) LTD
THIBAULT HOUSE, THIBAULT SQUARE, CAPE TOWN
JOHANNESBURG, SALISBURY
LONGMANS OF NIGERIA LTD
W. R. INDUSTRIAL ESTATE, IKEJA
LONGMANS OF GHANA LTD
INDUSTRIAL ESTATE, RING ROAD SOUTH, ACCRA
LONGMANS GREEN (FAR EAST) LTD
443 LOCKHART ROAD, HONG KONG
LONGMANS OF MALAYA LTD
44 JALAN AMPANG, KUALA LUMPUR
ORIENT LONGMANS LTD
CALCUTTA, BOMBAY, MADRAS
DELHI, HYDERABAD, DACCA
LONGMANS CANADA LTD
137 BOND STREET, TORONTO 2

First Published 1956
New impressions by photolithography 1961, 1962

*Permission has been given for this book to be transcribed into Braille by the
National Library for the Blind*

MADE AND PRINTED BY OFFSET IN GREAT BRITAIN BY
WILLIAM CLOWES AND SONS LIMITED, LONDON AND BECCLES

To

DAVID EDGE MARSHALL

PREFACE

IT MAY be wiser to begin this preface by saying what this book is *not* about. It is not intended to be a text-book on eighteenth-century England. In its pages the reader will not find the causes of the Seven Years War or the American Revolution, though they do contain pointers to some of them. Questions of the relationship between the Imperial Parliament and the colonies, between George III and the politicians are not my concern, nor, indeed, are any of the famous personalities of the age, except in so far as they illustrate some point which I wish to make. For such matters readers must look to the work of Professors Butterfield, Namier and Pares, and to the monographs of the constitutional and political specialists on the period. Nor am I attempting to write yet another history of the Industrial Revolution, but am content to refer them to Professor Ashton's *Industrial Revolution* for a brief and brilliant analysis of that movement.

The problem with which I am concerned is the social structure of England just before and just after the first wave of mechanical invention, which in the next hundred years was to transform Great Britain into an industrial nation, struck it. Here I have raised certain questions, while realizing that their complexity makes any fully satisfactory answers unlikely. The first of these is, how powerful were the merchants? To what extent were they capable of shaping colonial and foreign policy to suit their own interests? Were they the tail that wagged the dog? Next, to continue the metaphor, what was the main body of the dog like? Chapter II tries to answer this second question by giving some analysis of the composition of the various groups within the country. Chapter III deals with the extent to which this social structure is reflected in constitutional and ecclesiastical arrangements: it is not an attempt to describe the constitution as a whole. The next two chapters are mainly descriptive of the way of life, the satisfactions, etc., open to the nobility, gentry, middle classes and the labouring poor. In them I try to show from contemporary material what it meant to the English men and women of the time to be a member of one of these classes. In the second half of my theme, and in the last two chapters, I discuss the extent to which economic developments (which I outline briefly) were just beginning to set the stage for new social groupings and how far these were already discernible by the close of the century.

It may be objected that to stop in the middle of the French wars is arbitrary and unsatisfactory and to some extent this is true. The alternative, to continue this study into the middle of the nineteenth century until the first wave of the Industrial Revolution had been spent, would be a very lengthy business. It seemed to me, therefore, better to take the story of eighteenth-century social structure to the eve·of the great changes, to indicate the forces that were beginning to shape them, and to leave their subsequent development to another pen or another time.

What I have tried to do is to write a 'background' book. Of late years there has been an increasing interest in the way of life of our forefathers and a growing awareness of the importance of the eighteenth century as the threshold of modern England. History, after having been the somewhat arid preserve of the specialist, is once again attracting people who read for enjoyment: even the historical novel is regaining something of its old popularity. It is my hope therefore that those people who are interested in this fascinating period, whether they are readers of its literature, of its rich biographical material, or merely of novels set against the eighteenth century scene, will find some pleasure and a little profit in my attempt to put together some pieces of the jig-saw and to construct, as a background for these diverse interests, a picture of the social pattern of the period. I also hope, though they may not be reading primarily for pleasure, that undergraduates, and many sixth form pupils, who are reading history, or economic history in connexion with economics, or eighteenth-century literature, will find it useful, stimulating and not too heavy going. It is not intended as a substitute for lectures or for the private reading of standard authorities, but as a supplement to them, since it is now increasingly recognised that neither economic, constitutional nor political history can be studied in a vacuum. I do not pretend that I have answered satisfactorily all the questions that I have raised, or that readers will necessarily agree with my interpretation. But if I have succeeded in making some of them feel that these questions are important and lie behind many of the political and constitutional problems of the age, I shall be content.

CONTENTS

CONTENTS

PLATES

Chapter One

THE COMMERCIAL FRAMEWORK

IT IS customary, if hackneyed, to describe the eighteenth century, and particularly its closing decades, as an age of transition, and, because it has seemed to usher in the type of industrial civilization with which we are so familiar to-day, much attention has been focused on it. Detailed studies of its political life, its constitutional development, its social and economic activities, are all available. In consequence it is now possible to ask some questions about this period as a whole with a reasonable hope of obtaining at least tentative answers to them. What, for instance, were the essentials of the social and economic structure of the country before the impact of technological change produced the movement we know as the Industrial Revolution? What were the dominant influences in this society? Or in other words who were pulling the strings? What was it like to be an Englishman then? How far were the satisfactions which Society offered to him dependent on the class structure and how rigid was this structure? How closely did social and economic factors influence constitutional arrangements and the formulation of public policy? What were the new forces modifying this picture? How far had it changed by the close of the century?

Kipling's lines: 'What should they know of England who only England know' might have been written with special reference to these questions. Any attempt to understand Hanoverian England must start with a study of its relations, cultural and economic, with its European neighbours and with both America and the East. Its domestic policy, the modification of its class structure, the growth of industrial change were all influenced by these factors. In these circumstances the merchants are of particular importance. They were the channel through which outside forces permeated this country. Comparatively few in number, the merchants were of quite disproportionate significance. Their wealth, their interests and their commercial philosophy were

2

among the most active formative influences of the time. Not without justice has the eighteenth century been known as the age of Mercantilism; indeed, its parentage might be set down as out of 'Landed Gentry' by 'Overseas Trade'.

Important though the merchants were, our contacts with Europe were far from being purely economic. Despite our long rivalry with France we were deeply influenced by her culture. The glories and pageantry of Versailles could hardly be reproduced by British kings, who had at their disposal so much less of the wealth of their country than their French fellow monarchs, but the manners, the fashions, the dress of the French Court set the tone equally for polite society in England. Young gentlemen improving their minds spent more time travelling in France and Italy than imbibing the learning of their own universities or in exploring the beauties of their own countryside. Then, as now, the Englishman liked to bring back trophies of his travels, and as English purses were well furnished much that was beautiful and valuable found its way to this country. It was in this century that the foundations of so many famous collections of French and Italian painting, sculpture, and furniture were laid. Although for much of the century France and Britain were at war, either openly in Europe or informally overseas, this had no great influence on private and personal relationships. Wars were fought for matters of material interest, not for ideologies. In consequence there was little of that bitterness that comes from the clash of opposing ways of life and thought: between the ruling classes in both countries the cultural connexion was close.

Though the aristocracy was under the sway of French ideas, the solid, wealthy merchants looked to Holland. In the seventeenth century it had been her wealth that aroused their greatest envy. Culture was only one of the trimmings of life, suitable enough for those who could afford it, and, like other fripperies of fashion, no doubt best obtained from France: but from Holland we strove to get the knowledge of how best to develop our resources and increase our wealth. This desire to emulate and copy the Dutch is to be found in every sphere of economic activity, in every project put forward by pamphleteer and politician alike. The Dutch owed much to a prosperous fishing industry: we must foster ours by every encouragement that ingenious minds could devise. They were pre-eminently the carriers of Europe: England, too, must build up her merchant navy and endeavour to seize the carrying trade. If this could not be accomplished by skilful competition then regulation and prohibition must be used. To effect this, English merchants and shippers could rely on such support as popular prejudice might be able to afford. If the Navigation Acts were not quite such a single-minded expedient to increase British shipping as to uninformed public opinion they seemed to be, ordinary men could hardly be expected to perceive the ingenuity by which monopoly profits were diverted to private pockets.

Just as we envied Dutch maritime power so we envied their agriculture, which in the early eighteenth century was still considerably in advance of our own. Lord Auchinleck, writing to Boswell in Holland in 1763, bade him 'see the method the Dutch manage their cattle, and take notes of it,'[1] and it was from Dutch sources that the ideas which were to revolutionize British agriculture often came. In consequence, though the rivalry between the two countries was very bitter this very rivalry brought Britain still more closely under the influence of the United Provinces, as by imitation we tried to penetrate the secrets of her success. Bitterly, therefore, as we fought for markets, and deeply as we were involved in the politics of Europe, yet our debt to the countries that we fought was heavy and permanent.

Even more influential than the borrowing of foreign cultures were the consequences of the tangled knots of trade ventures and interests that bound us to the markets of the world. At every stage our advancing standard of life has been bought by our expanding trade. It was the foreign demand for our agricultural products, and above all for our wool, that had levered us out of the rut of a medieval local organization. Already by the sixteenth century the liquid capital of the nation was being concentrated in the hands of the merchants, and the ramifications of their business spread far and wide. Our cloth found buyers alike in Baltic countries, in the great markets of the Netherlands, and in Italy and the Levant, as well as in France, Portugal and Spain. Nor, though it grew in volume, was the character of our European trade to change much in the succeeding centuries, since it was

[1] *Boswell in Holland.* Edited by F. A. Pottle (1952), p. 52.

based on the fundamental needs of the countries concerned. Political patterns might vary. The emphasis in public discussion which took place might be laid now on one branch and now upon another, so that, to the casual observer, the appearance of instability and of variety was produced. Underneath it all certain essential features remained.

Outstanding among these was the importance of the Baltic trade. The northern countries with their bitter winter climate and their totally inadequate textile industries provided excellent markets for the cheap and crudely finished cloth of the North of England. These markets were of particular value because in return the Baltic countries supplied the naval stores which from the sixteenth century were becoming vital to our existence. From the accession of Elizabeth until the 'wooden walls' disappeared, the growing timber shortage was a haunting dread to English statesmen. Required as it was for building, for domestic furnishings, for industrial uses, for the increased smelting of iron and for the needs of a growing navy and mercantile marine, home supplies were neither adequate nor always suitable. It was the pine forests of the North that could provide the great masts needed for the ships-of-the-line and the roving frigates. Such vital naval stores were often in short supply, so that strategy after a battle, or often even before it was fought, depended more than is always realized on the reserves available in the naval yards to replace the wastage of war.[1]

Nor was it only a matter of timber, vital as this was. The Baltic countries also supplied other important naval stores, pitch and hemp for cordage, and material for sail cloth. All these were essential commodities for any seafaring nation. Therefore, at all costs the Baltic trade had to be kept open. British anxieties were doubled by geographical difficulties: if control of the Sound fell into unfriendly hands a critical position might easily develop. In this region, therefore, politics could never be allowed to take their course. Even when political skies were fair, economic difficulties remained. The toll levied on British ships passing through the Sound was always a matter of considerable moment to both the profits of the merchants and the expenses of the Admiralty.

---

[1] R. G. Albion: *Forests and Sea Power; the timber problem of the Royal Navy*, (1926) *1652–1862, passim.*

If naval stores could be procured elsewhere it certainly seemed to be in British interests that alternative sources of supply should be developed. In addition to hemp we imported considerable quantities of flax and of linen yarn, for the Irish production was far from adequate to supply the growing demand. Furs, too, came from the great forests, and potash, while the agricultural population sent hides and tallow from their beasts. From Sweden we drew much-needed ores, particularly copper and first-class iron. Until the technical changes of the eighteenth century made it practicable to use coal for the smelting of the ore, our crippling lack of timber made it impossible to produce iron on a large scale, and we were forced to import from Sweden, whose possession of rich deposits, combined with her vast forests, placed her in an exceptionally favourable position. For all these reasons it is clear how important the proper management of this Northern trade was to the smooth working of the British economy.[1]

But the most important ingredient in English prosperity was to be found in her export of textiles. Of these, woollens still took the first place, even as late as 1785, when Macpherson estimates that some £16,000,000 worth were being exported every year. A considerable amount of raw silk was also being worked up which, although it lacked the finish of the best French manufacture, nevertheless found a ready market. Cotton goods were increasing rapidly, both in volume and in variety, but before the inventions of the second half of the century, they still lagged behind the production of woollens. As long as England concentrated on the manufacture of cloth she was still bound to her traditional markets, the Low Countries, the German states, Spain and Portugal.

The importance of our trade with Spain lay not so much in the demands of her internal, domestic market, as in the fact that through it we could command a channel by which the New World could be supplied with goods of British manufacture. In theory the trade between Spain and her colonies remained a monopoly for the Mother Country: in practice the output of Spanish industry was quite inadequate to supply the needs of South America. British merchants found a most profitable outlet in meeting this

---

[1] *Vide* Charles Wilson: 'Treasure and Trade Balances: The Mercantile Problem' *Econ. Hist. Rev.* (1949), 3rd series, No. 2.

deficiency and acting as wholesalers to Spanish colonial exporters. This trade was considered particularly desirable because Spain and the Spanish colonies were unable to pay for goods with goods and the gap in the balance of payments was accordingly bridged by exports of bullion, the produce of Spanish American mines, to this country. Without the Spanish trade it might have been difficult for British merchants to have procured enough of the circulating medium to manage profitably the Indian trade, which needed to be fed with considerable supplies of silver, or the vital trade with the Baltic countries. Spain and her colonies, therefore, both provided an excellent market for our manufactures and replenished our stocks of the precious metals. It is not surprising that some of the oldest and best established mercantile houses were those that concentrated on the Spanish trade.

By the eighteenth century the growing capacity of our colonies both to supply us with raw materials and to absorb our manufactures, was making us less dependent on our European trading connexions. The importance of the colonial trade is an outstanding feature of Hanoverian England. In it great fortunes were made. Like our trade with Europe it had a long history. The early projects, however, never got beyond the experimental stage, and all Raleigh's gallant efforts ended in failure. He bequeathed to England not a colony but a dream and a name, Virginia. It was left to the seventeenth century to turn the aspirations of the sixteenth into facts. The real foundations of English overseas wealth were laid by her merchants. By the seventeenth century they had accumulated sufficient capital to be anxious to find profitable investments. As Adam Smith observed, 'Money, says the proverb, makes money. When you have got a little, it is often easy to get more. The great difficulty is to get that little'.[1] By the seventeenth century this necessary minimum had been obtained and the merchants of both London and the West Country were eager to get more. In 1606 charters were granted to two companies of merchants, the London Company and the Plymouth Company, allowing them to establish colonies in North America.

To these merchants the new colonies were investments, designed to make returns directly by way of quit rents and dues,

---

[1] Adam Smith: *An Inquiry into the Nature and Causes of the Wealth of Nations.* Edited by E. Cannan (1904), Vol. I, p. 94.

indirectly by giving their promoters control over raw materials and markets. They had no intention of playing any personal part in the life of the colonies. Plantations were a speculation, just as coal mining was a speculation, and, like many speculators, the early investors lost money over them. No gold mines were found to bring in quick profits, while the discovery of suitable staple crops, the clearing of the ground, the importation of sufficient labour, all took time. But, although returns might be slow and individual investors might burn their fingers, the merchants of England as a whole were shrewd enough to see that eventually money could and would return to them as a result of colonial investment. In this they were true prophets. Despite the fact that early companies were wound up and the Crown resumed the charter of the Virginia Company in 1623, the settlements themselves grew and prospered. As a consequence, the cultivation of staple crops, first tobacco, then, as the colonies spread through the south and into the West Indies, other tropical crops such as sugar, cotton and rice, brought to the merchants of the eighteenth century an ample reward.

In the East, also, the enterprise of seventeenth-century merchants was equally profitable to their eighteenth-century successors. It had been the wealth of the East that had first acted as a magnet to draw explorers into unknown oceans, and by uncharted coasts. It was in the discovery of new trade routes that Spain and Portugal had received the recompense for their expeditions. Their monopoly had soon been challenged by the Dutch, who, between 1595 and 1601, sent no less than sixty-five ships, organized in fifteen different expeditions to explore the riches of this new market. In Europe the demand for the products of the East, its spices and its silks, promised a rich reward to merchants who could transport them in bulk. Previously the difficulties of the overland route had restricted such merchandise to the most expensive kinds, and therefore limited effective demand. By the end of the sixteenth century, England, too, incited by the example of the Dutch and in difficulties with her Levant trade, began to turn to the possibilities of this Eastern trade. After spasmodic attempts a charter was obtained and the East India Company created. During the seventeenth century, amid vicissitudes abroad and political difficulties at home, it gradually took shape. Dutch enmity drove it from the East Indies, but on the mainland it slowly acquired stable trading posts, Madras, Calcutta and, on Charles II's marriage with the Portuguese princess, Bombay. By the eighteenth century, backed by a parliamentary charter, it was exceedingly wealthy and powerful, representing one of the great vested interests of the time.

By the accession of George I, therefore, British merchants had interests and connexions in all parts of the known world. Though the export of woollen goods was still important and the traditional course of trade profitable, these older connexions were made the more fruitful because English merchants were now also able to distribute colonial and Eastern products. England henceforth acted as an entrepôt for tobacco, sugar, rice, hardwoods, for the gay textiles of India, and, particularly after 1784 when the duty was reduced, for tea. Thus British trade fell into two interlocking parts; the export of finished goods and the re-export of colonial and Eastern products. Each had its profitable extensions. The colonial exporters of raw materials bought the manufactures of the Mother Country, which in its turn exchanged colonial products for the specialized merchandise of its European customers. From Portugal came wine and oil, fruit, anchovies, dyestuffs, soap and wool; from the northern countries timber, iron, copper, hemp, flax, linen yarn, tallow, hides, furs and potash. The German states sent tinplate, skins, linen yarn and some linen goods, while France supplied luxuries like laces and brocades, velvets, wines and brandy. It is little wonder that the British merchants were flourishing and little wonder, too, that they managed to identify the prosperity of the country with their own.

Such prosperity could only be kept up, as Sir Thomas Gresham once remarked in a different connexion, 'by art and God's Providence'. While few Englishmen doubted the latter the merchant community felt that it was manifestly the business of His Majesty's Government to supply, or at least to assist, the former. It was considerations of this kind which encouraged them to play as large a part as they could in the world of politics. No one engaged in either the colonial or the older European trade could be indifferent to the foreign policy followed by the ministers of the Crown. Nor could they be untouched by the laws which governed economic relations between this country and her colonies. Political influence, if not vital, was highly desirable. It was because so many of their interests lay outside Britain that the merchants were forced to extend their activities to her internal affairs. Where public opinion might promote their interests they did their best to mould it, where Parliament could provide favourable legislation they did their best to secure it. It is for these reasons that the eighteenth-century merchants have a double importance: they provided much of the liquid capital with which further developments could be financed and, because of this wealth, they had some influence in shaping both domestic and foreign policy.

In the eighteenth century political influence meant parliamentary influence. Because merchants had business interests to protect which were often alien to the sympathies and aims of the country gentry it has become something of a commonplace to describe them as the allies of the great Whig party. Statements of this kind do less than justice to the complexity of the politics of Georgian England. As Professor Pares has reminded us: 'To talk of "whig" and "tory", or of "party", as if these terms meant the same thing throughout the eighteenth century is to imply a fallacy which is now exploded. The parties of 1760 were certainly not the same as those of 1714'. [1] After 1760 there were both 'opposition' whigs and 'government' whigs and even before the accession of George III it was the grouping within the Whig party which was important. Nor should it be forgotten that eighteenth-century governments were, in the main, composed of men who called themselves Whigs, though historians later may have described them as Tories, and that it was from 'government' that favours must be sought. Opposition to ministers was not, for most merchants and financiers, likely to pay dividends. To say, therefore, that in parliament the merchants tended to attach themselves to the Whigs, though substantially true, is to shed little light on their behaviour, once the Treaty of Utrecht had been signed. They were not likely to ally with the country gentry, and all the effective politicians were Whigs of some description.

Though to ascribe too much influence over foreign policy to the merchants would be a crude over-simplification of a mass of complex events, even a cursory examination of its course after the

[1] Richard Pares: *King George III and the Politicians* (1953), p. 71.

Restoration reveals a tenderness towards their wishes which can hardly be accidental. The first two Dutch wars were fought unashamedly for purely commercial reasons. The desire to cripple Dutch competition in the carrying trade and to seize from her vital trading stations, and, therefore, her trade in America and along the African coasts, was a motive strong enough to swing the country into war without the politicians thinking it necessary to put forward any other excuse for their aggressive policy. The Dutch proved tough antagonists, well able to protect their own property, and except for New Amsterdam, then but lightly valued, England got little for her fighting. In Charles II's reign, though the economic rivalry between the two countries continued, the merchants became aware of what they felt instinctively was a greater menace than even Dutch competition. This was the growing design shown by the Crown to reverse the decision of the Civil War. This policy, if successful, would have challenged the new control which, since their victory, the Commons had exercised over the government of the country. A muzzled parliament would deprive the merchants of one of their most formidable weapons. Moreover, a royal despotism, which relied on French help, as that of the Stuarts threatened to do, would have been even more detrimental to English trading interests. Dutch competition might be irritating but a Europe controlled by the France of Colbert would be much worse.

Already it had become a cardinal point in the policy of the merchants that no one power must dominate Europe lest they might be cut off from their markets. It was better to act with the United Provinces, better even to have Dutch William as their king, than to face that risk. In consequence the last of the Dutch wars was fought half-heartedly for royal and French interests and there was no punch of popular approval behind it. After the Revolution of 1689 the Dutch and English found themselves allies. In the war of the League of Augsburg the English fought ostensibly to secure French recognition of William's title and to enforce the withdrawal of Louis XIV's aid to the Stuarts, but behind it lay the desire to safeguard trade. Even then Englishmen feared Louis's designs on the Spanish inheritance. It was clear that Charles II of Spain would die without issue, and it was felt that if the French king were 'left at liberty to make himself master of Spain . . . by adding Cadiz to Toulon and Brest [he could] give laws to all the trading parts of Europe'.[1] This was the strongest link that joined the merchants of England to those of Holland, though time and again French diplomacy was able to play on the separate interests of each, showing how well the French diplomats realized the importance of economic and commercial considerations.

In the century after Ryswick the influence of the merchants on foreign policy became still more marked. It is clearly seen in the whole of the negotiations that preceded the outbreak of the war itself and in the shaping of the Treaty of Utrecht that brought it to a close. The war would never have been fought to keep Philip of Anjou from ascending the throne of Spain, humiliated as William felt over Louis's repudiation of the Partition Treaties, and distrustful as he was of his ambitions ; parliament would not have been willing to provide the necessary funds for war unless it had felt that English interests were involved. It was not until the merchants found their markets threatened by the use Louis was making of his new connexion with Spain that they swung public and parliamentary opinion into line behind the king. When merchants trading with Spain found their profits attacked by the monopoly given to a French company trading from St. Malo, when English woollen manufacturers found the fine wool of Spain being reserved for French looms, then they began to see how dangerous Louis's new sphere of influence might be. Then they were willing that England should fight. In his pamphlet *Two Great Questions Considered,* Defoe pressed the point of view of the merchants, showing how French domination endangered our commercial interests in the Mediterranean, the Baltic and the East and West Indies alike. The weight given to this argument is clearly seen in the Grand Alliance, signed in September 1701, which put forward, as one of the main objects of the war, the securing to England and to Holland not only the safety of their dominions but also that of the navigation and commerce of their subjects.

In the conduct of the war, and in particular in the negotiations between the English and their Austrian ally, the Archduke

---

[1] W. T. Morgan: 'Economic Aspects of the Negotiations at Ryswick', *Trans. Roy. Hist. Soc.*, 4th Series, Vol. XIV, p. 334.

Charles, the interests of the merchants appear to have been carefully considered. In return for help and loans that enabled him, though only temporarily, to secure the Spanish throne and the occupation of Madrid, Minorca, a most valuable base for our Mediterranean trade, was secured. We also obtained important privileges in the matter of trading with the Spanish colonies. There was little chivalry shown in these negotiations. The Archduke needed British naval and financial help, and, ally though he was, he was made to pay in solid and much coveted privileges. These concessions endured long after the temporary advantages for which he had bartered them had disappeared. Ironically, what had first been granted by an ally was, in the Treaty of Utrecht, confirmed by the Bourbon Philip V. It is significant that the gains secured by this treaty for Britain were all of value to our expanding commerce. Nor were they haphazard in selection: it is possible to see a very real and coherent plan behind them. They bear eloquent witness to the growing importance of the colonial market. Except for Gibraltar and Minorca, which secured our Mediterranean trade, our chief acquisitions lay in the New World. In the Far North, British rights to the territory of Hudson Bay, valuable because of the luxury furs it supplied, were recognized. Nova Scotia gave us a real foothold on the St. Lawrence, though the French still retained Cape Breton Island at its mouth and their right to their share in the valuable fishing grounds. They kept, too, Canada, though our possession of Newfoundland was no longer challenged. From France, therefore, valuable bases for future expansion had been acquired.

In the treaty with Spain we were not content with safeguarding our position in the Mediterranean with the possession of Minorca and Gibraltar. An attempt was made to secure for British merchants the long-coveted privileges of trade with the Spanish colonies. For thirty years the South Seas Company was to enjoy the privilege of supplying the Spanish colonies with 4,800 negroes per year, and when the annual fleet sailed from Seville one British ship of 500 tons was to accompany it. It was this grant that underlay the wild optimism of the South Seas Bubble, an optimism which the application of the commercial treaty between the two countries did little to justify. In fact, the trading treaties were not advantageous, and the privilege of the annual ship was largely illusory, since the fleet did not sail every year. In any case its burden was too small to have affected the volume of trade very considerably and the myth that its cargo was constantly replenished has been exploded by later research. The desire to benefit British trade was evident but the skill in commercial diplomacy was lacking and it is probable that the old-established mercantile houses trading with Spain before the war found more profit in the old system than they did in the new. Certainly after 1715 matters of trade were a constant source of irritation between the two countries and led to a further series of wars after 1739.[1]

It would be rash, however, to assume that the causes of this strain were completely economic. Spain in the years immediately after Utrecht had been a profoundly dissatisfied country, very discontented with the political resettlement of Europe which she had been forced to accept. Knowing the immense importance which English merchants attached to the Spanish trade she hoped to use this as a lever to force English ministers to back up Spanish pretensions. In her attitude to English trade therefore she blew now hot, now cold, sometimes doing everything she could to smooth out difficulties, sometimes indulging in endless procrastinations that nearly broke the hearts of the envoys negotiating with her. One constant cause of irritation between the two countries was the seizing and searching of British ships in Spanish colonial waters. For this the Spaniards often had some excuse. The merchants chiefly engaged in the smooth running of the legal trade with the Spanish colonies, conducted via the Mother Country, were substantial, well-established men. Of their activities there was little complaint. The trouble came from West-Indian merchants, who were always being tempted by their nearness to Spanish territory to indulge in contraband trade.

It was understandable that Spain should wish to stamp out such illicit transactions, but she lacked adequate means to do so. An efficient system of coastguards and naval craft would have cost more than she could afford. The expedient to which she was driven by financial stringency was to rely on the services of men who undertook to suppress smuggling on the basis of recompensing themselves from the seized cargoes. Such men, more than half pirates themselves, had every incentive not to be too scrupulous

[1] J. O. McLachlan: *Trade and Peace with Old Spain, 1667–1750* (1940), *passim.*

in the exercise of their right to search. Nor, even if they had been prepared to be meticulous, would the task have been easy. It was difficult to know whether vessels intercepted in those waters were really bound with contraband to a Spanish port. Ships were often driven off their course by an unfavourable wind, and it was not always possible to establish whether their presence was due to accident or design. So there can be little doubt that sometimes it was not the West Indian contraband runner but the respectable British merchantman that was stopped, searched roughly and on occasion unfairly seized. Controversy over the vexed question of responsibility and compensation for such incidents was perpetual between London and Madrid: the cases of some ships dragged on for years. In such circumstances it was easy for those men who disliked Walpole's long tenure of office to raise the cry that he was being too accommodating, that British trade was being sacrificed to his ignoble desire for peace. Hence the outbreak of the War of Jenkins's Ear.

With France even the attempt to secure favourable trading conditions by means of a commercial treaty broke down. The negotiations entered into at the end of the War of the Spanish Succession collapsed, largely due to British fear of French economic rivalry. The aim of the negotiations had been to secure a freer trade between the two countries and to remove the impossibly high duties and even prohibitions that years of economic and political rivalry had created. But behind the antagonism of the two countries vested interests had dug themselves in and now feared that a return to a more reasonable tariff might jeopardize their gains. In particular the Spitalfields industry, built up and protected by the prohibition of French silk, doubted its ability to stand the competition of French products if they were once more admitted. An increased consumption of French wines, always more popular than the heavier wine of Portugal, would, it was thought, affect our export of woollen goods, since a decline in our purchase of port would reduce the ability of the Portuguese to buy our cloth, so destroying the advantages gained by the Methuen treaty with that country. Although a freer exchange of goods might well have benefited the overall trade of both countries, those interests which felt themselves threatened by particular clauses were strong enough first to insist on the commercial clauses being regulated by a separate treaty and then to block such a treaty being signed at all. Consequently, French and English traders remained bitterly opposed to one another, refusing one another's goods and fighting for markets both in the Old World and the New, with the result that the enmity felt for Louis XIV's France was perpetuated and coloured all English foreign policy for the next century.

This antagonism to France was no doubt further strengthened by England's growing interests in the colonial and Indian trade. Here Spain with her old empire and France with her growing ambitions were Britain's main rivals. Portugal, jealous though she often was of England's influence, lacked both the vitality and the resources to expand further, and the United Provinces had in the East Indies and at the Cape as much as they could consolidate and exploit. Spain herself had now begun the long period of her decline. Though still far from negligible she could hope to do no more than cling to what she already held. She was not capable, as France was capable, of challenging Britain in new fields of expansion, or of dominating Europe and regimenting it against British trade. Therefore, the mainspring of our policy was to be found in the clash of our overseas interests with those of France. In particular we fought bitterly to monopolize the American continent and the Indian trade. When France allowed herself to be entangled in European politics and became involved in European campaigns, England seized the opportunity of further weakening her, partly by direct attack but chiefly by subsidizing allies against her. The wars in which England took a part in this century, though they might wear the appearance of being European struggles, were never really so; their object was always to weaken a rival who threatened essential trading interests overseas.

For more than twenty years, British foreign policy was to be chiefly expressed in terms of war for colonial domination. The situation in 1740 is well known. In America French expansion both north in Canada, and south, based on the great river system of the Mississippi, by its domination of the land that lay beyond the Alleghanies, was threatening to check the westward expansion of the British colonies. There was a very real danger that they might be hemmed in between the mountains and the sea, and to avert this clashes for the control of the Ohio were already taking place. In India the struggle was for trade rather than for territory. But to secure trade it was necessary to have political influence with the native rulers. In some ways both the French and the British East India companies were well situated to secure this since their armed forces, although small, were modern and well equipped compared with the unwieldy Indian levies armed with out-of-date weapons. The support of these European forces, therefore, was something that any native ruler, engaged in his own political schemes and private wars, was anxious to secure. But for English or French help a price had to be paid, not so much in cash as in trading rights and privileges. The extension of French influence meant the shutting of markets against English traders, and vice versa. Almost inevitably, therefore, both companies began to interfere in Indian politics. Insensibly trade rivalry led to fighting, and each company was inspired to increase its own army and to extend it own sphere of influence. Almost unavoidably the home governments became involved, and fighting on a serious scale was fed by regular reinforcements from Europe. Though to Newcastle and George II continental issues were more generally predominant it was the need to protect markets in American and India that reconciled most merchants and financiers to British participation in both the War of the Austrian Succession and the Seven Years War and it was as a spokesman for their interests that the elder Pitt won popularity.

The Peace of Aix-la-Chapelle was merely a breathing space while both sides accumulated fresh resources, but the Peace of Paris illustrates clearly the fundamental importance of the commercial interests that went to shape it. Nothing shows this better than the protracted consultations that went on as to the terms to be offered to France and to Spain. The vital issue in dispute was which of the colonial possessions should be handed back and which kept. It was recognized that either Canada or valuable West Indian islands like St. Lucia or Guadeloupe must be returned. The wealth of Canada was potential and perhaps hardly recognized; in the economic judgment of the day the West Indian islands were much the more desirable prize. But their retention came up against one of the strongest of the economic pressure groups to be found in London, the 'lobby', to use an American political term, of the West Indian planters. Sugar was the main product of the islands, and in the growing of sugar the French islands were superior to the British. Already their rivalry was keen and a contraband trade flourished between them and the New England colonies, though the home government, stimulated again by the planters, had tried to stop the trade by the prohibitive duty of Walpole's Molasses Act of 1733. If by annexation the French islands were brought within the British economic system, the British planters saw themselves being ruined by the competition that would follow. They were insistent, therefore, that the sugar islands should be returned and Canada kept. This was not because they valued the latter or thought its acquisition particularly in British interests, but because they were sure that the retention of the former would be highly detrimental to their own. In the Peace of Paris, in consequence, it was decided that France must cede all Canada and Cape Breton, though her valuable fishing rights off Newfoundland and, subject to the nine-mile limit, those in the Gulf of St. Lawrence, were to be restored to her. Pitt, in the earlier negotiations, would have denied her even these, but Bute was prepared both to concede them and to make them workable by handing back the little islands of St. Pierre and Miquelon to provide a base for the French fishermen. In the West Indies, where England and France had long pressed conflicting claims, the English were left in possession of Grenada, Dominica, St. Vincent and Tobago, but, for reasons which have already been suggested, Martinique, St. Lucia, Marie Galante and Guadeloupe were handed back.

Though this arrangement suited the interests of the West Indian planters its political and strategic wisdom was doubtful. As shrewd observers at the time prophesied, once the threat to the American colonies of the French in Canada had been removed they were much less dependent on the Mother Country for protection. Also the continued possession of excellent naval bases, like Martinique, gave France the chance to attack British sea communications should the propitious moment arrive, as it did in the American War of Independence. For the time, however, the merchants had obtained a very advantageous position. Nor were English gains confined to French territory. From Spain, Florida was obtained, while the long-disputed claim of the English to cut logwood in Honduras was at last conceded. Closely

3

connected with the position of the West Indies was that of the
African trading posts, because if the islands were to be adequately
developed, slave labour was a vital necessity. Here, though we
handed back Goree, we still kept the important base of Senegal.
In India, too, all the gain that Dupleix's brilliant conquests had
brought to the French company were wiped out and the situation
of 1749 was again restored. The year 1763 saw, therefore, the
widespread and apparently firm establishment of a great British
dominion from which it seemed that unending commercial resources could be obtained, so that English merchants might look
forward to a long era of prosperity and ever-increasing fortunes.

If the merchants were anxious to secure a practical backing for
their activities in the shape of a favourable foreign policy they
were equally anxious to mould public opinion in their favour.
This was not, of course, a coherent policy carried out by an
organized body. It was rather the result of numerous pamphlets
written to recommend particular objects in which writer after
writer strove to make it appear that some policy, likely to benefit
the particular merchant group whose interests he was upholding,
was also in the best interests of the nation. The two, however,
as Adam Smith observed, were not necessarily identical. 'The
interests of the dealers', he wrote, 'in any particular branch of
trade or manufactures, is always in some respects different from,
and even opposite to, that of the public'.[1] He therefore warned
his readers that, 'The proposal of any new law or regulation of
commerce which comes from this order, ought always to be
listened to with great precaution, and ought never to be adopted
till after having been long and carefully examined, not only with
the most scrupulous, but with the most suspicious attention'.
Viewed from this angle the development of that body of opinion
on economic matters that is loosely labelled Mercantilism is
interesting.

The origins of eighteenth-century mercantilism are probably
to be found in the economic nationalism of Elizabethan England,
which, as Mr. Fay has pointed out, is a different thing from
mercantilism.[2] To the sixteenth-century English statesmen there
were certain attributes necessary for any well-run and prosperous

[1] *Op. cit.*, Vol. I, p. 250.
[2] C. R. Fay: *English Economic History, mainly since 1700* (1948), p. 13.

country, and these were all qualities that emphasized its independence of surrounding states. It must be able to feed itself without recourse to foreign supply, and it must have not only a numerous population but one drawn from those walks of life that produced the best soldiers, the sturdy ploughman not the urban worker, so that the country could be well defended. Because England was an island, by every art the mercantile marine and the fishing industry must be encouraged to produce the necessary men and ships to supplement the navy in time of emergency. Munitions of war must, as far as possible, be manufactured at home, and the monopolies granted for the mining of copper and the making of brass, for the finding of saltpetre and the manufacture of gunpowder all testify to this belief. Above all, the country must be well supplied with bullion so that in time of need it should not lack the liquid capital that could be quickly mobilized to finance its defence. If these ends were to be obtained then the power of the state must be used and the national effort canalized in the necessary directions by the grant of monopolies to those who would produce the desired supplies and by the prohibition of those activities that threatened this programme at any point. Such would seem to have been the underlying assumptions of public policy in Elizabethan England.

To disentangle public interest, honestly conceived, and private interest followed under its guise, is peculiarly difficult at this time. Because of the assumption that the State must use its power for economic ends, the Court, as the effective centre of that power, was the distributing agent of economic privilege. There was nothing in the morality of the time to prevent those very men who were shaping public policy from benefiting in their private capacity as landlords, as investors, as industrialists, as merchants, from the policy which as ministers of the Crown they sponsored. At the same time it would not be true to portray men of the calibre of Cecil as being no more than material self-seekers, anxious to line their own pockets without regard to their responsibility to the country. Nor was Elizabeth I any man's fool, willing to see what she regarded as her estate despoiled for private interests. The real danger came not so much from the inception of economic policy as from its application. Here the incomplete control of the central government over local administration, the poverty of the Crown, the corruption of minor officials, all made it possible for the wealthy merchant to adjust official policy to his needs. At this time merchants, financiers and rising capitalists had little to fear and much to gain from a doctrine that magnified the economic functions of the state. Where its mercantile thought could be used to uphold their particular interests well and good: where it opposed them the machinery with which the government could enforce its policy was often sufficiently inefficient to be ignored.

In the seventeenth century, when both the interests of the merchant and the capitalist were growing, and the centralizing efficiency of the Crown was increasing, it became more difficult to ignore government policy. In particular, bitter quarrels arose between those men who enjoyed royal favour and those outside the privileged ring. The latter turned to the House of Commons in an attempt to secure some influence over economic policy. When, after the Civil War, parliament did succeed in increasing its control over the Crown the merchants shared the fruits of victory. By the eighteenth century the House of Commons afforded them a means not only of expressing their views but of enforcing them. As a result of their new position in the State, economic nationalism was slowly transformed into mercantilism as Adam Smith would have understood the term. It was no longer a question of business men adapting to their own needs a policy put forward by a centralizing and autocratic government. Instead, it was a policy sponsored by a government in which they were personally influential though by no means dominant. Mercantilism, therefore, came to embody the general views of the merchant community, a fact which helps to explain the many contradictions in its teachings. Though the interests of the merchants as a whole might seem to be homogenous when compared with another social class, for instance the country gentry, they were, after all, only the sum of many particular wills. Moreover a consensus of beliefs that receives general acceptance, so far as aims and objects go, for over two centuries, must suffer many modifications as circumstances alter.

As it has so often been observed, it is useless to look for any consistent and well integrated theory of mercantilism. All that can be found is a rough and ready standard by which the merchants suggested that the wellbeing of trade, and the general prosperity of the country could be measured, and a set of rules, infinitely contradictory in application, by which it was hoped these results could be achieved. In shaping these standards the particular circumstances of the East India Company had been of importance. Older theories had stressed the necessity of bullion and before the Restoration its export had been forbidden. But to carry on trade with India without silver was all but impossible, since the market there was indifferent to our staple products. From the propagandists of the East India Company came the theory of the balance of trade which was to figure so largely in the arguments of the merchants and the economists henceforth. The importance of bullion was not denied but the stress was shifted on to the means of obtaining it by exporting more goods than we imported, so that the balance would have to be paid in the precious metals. By this reasoning a moderate transference of silver to India was not only excused but justified, since it would be repaid by the import of Indian produce, which could be sold again in the markets of Europe at a substantial profit, so on balance making England a gainer by a considerable sum. By this argument the need of the East India Company to export silver was sanctioned. In addition the export trade, which was the concern of all overseas merchants, was shown to be a vital national interest. Such a doctrine was eminently fitted to the wellbeing of the merchant body.

Because of the stress placed on the supreme necessity of a flourishing export trade domestic policy was often subordinated to it, thus giving to the merchants an influence wider than they would otherwise have had. For example, labour was viewed largely from the angle of the export market. A growing population was desirable not because it would increase domestic demand for our commodities but because it would provide man-power to be used in the production of goods for export. Low wages were favoured for the same reason: the more cheaply we could produce the more we could sell abroad. Parliament was quite willing that a great proportion of the people should live not much above subsistence level, since it was argued that only by the compelling fear of hunger could the poor be forced to undertake the long hours and arduous work that the export market demanded. The eighteenth-century Poor Law was a natural corollary to this theory: it at once lessened the fear of disorder and prevented wages from being forced up. That this attitude towards these domestic problems dovetailed in with the interests of the merchants is clear, though it is difficult to know how far they were responsible for it.

Much of the process was unconscious, at least in its wider implications. Men are most apt to be convinced that whatever brings prosperity to the circles which they know must be in the general interest. Eighteenth-century merchants were no more machiavellian or hypocritical than other men. Nor were the theories they held peculiar to England. The belief that the prosperity of one country could only be secured at the expense of its neighbours was widely held. That being so it was natural that the authority of the State should be pressed into service to secure by every ingenious stratagem the increase of the nation's share of world trade. If low wages and long hours were thought necessary to achieve this desirable result, at least it could be argued with some plausibility that the livelihood of the poor was as dependent on the expansion of trade and its general prosperity as was the wealth of the commercial magnates. To expect the merchants to view their interests other than narrowly could hardly be looked for in the circumstances of the times, and to condemn the actions of the past by the social standards of the present is to distort the picture. It is enough to recognize how greatly, though often half unconsciously, the theories of the mercantilists were shaped by the needs of the merchants, and how these ideas in turn influenced, as we have seen, not only English trade but also foreign policy and internal administration alike.

The influence of the merchants in securing legislation favourable to their own interests is probably nowhere so clearly apparent as in the Navigation Acts and the Laws of Trade of the seventeenth and eighteenth centuries. By 1651 the device of attempting to build up naval strength by confining certain branches of trade to English ships had already a long history behind it. Even in the Middle Ages a series of scattered enactments had made tentative efforts of this kind. The idea, therefore, of Navigation Acts was something with which both mercantile and shipping circles were familiar. Their original object, to build up sea-power, certainly commended itself to the Elizabethans, interested as they were in the vital problems of self-defence against a great naval power like Spain. But England's economic position was not strong enough for such drastic measures in the sixteenth century. The most profitable branches of the trade to be confined to English shipping would have been those with Spain and with the Low Countries, and it was hardly likely that Spain would submit tamely to seeing its own subjects shut out of so lucrative a business. Consequently, an attempt in 1563 to impose by proclamation restrictions on non-English ships taking cargoes from this country to the Netherlands brought forth prompt reprisals, and Cecil found it necessary to abandon any serious schemes for developing our shipping by such measures. He turned instead to the establishment of national fish days to encourage the fishing industry, that 'nursery of seamen', through the hope of a steady market. By the middle of the seventeenth century, however, Spain was a declining power and much of her carrying trade had been captured by the Dutch, who were rapidly becoming England's chief economic rivals.

During the reigns of James I and Charles I the idea of regulating maritime trade was very much in the air and the fact that England now had colonies on the American mainland gave it a new twist, prophetic of the future. Thus colonial tobacco had to come to England, and, what was more, to come in English ships. But though the idea was popular in the Mother Country the legal position was often far from clear. Older statutes conflicted with more recent ones, while scattered proclamations made the position still more obscure. It was not surprising, therefore, that the Council of State and Council of Trade of the Commonwealth should attempt to provide legislation that would be at once clearer and more comprehensive. The result was the Navigation Act of 1651. It is likely, however, that the impetus that led to the passing of this measure came more from important pressure groups seeking legislation to protect their special interests than from Government initiative. The earliest promoters of the measure seem to have been shipowners. They were suffering severely from the competition of the Dutch fly-boats, which could carry larger cargoes and required smaller crews than the English-built ships designed for the twin purposes of trade and defence. To exclude the Dutch from at least some branches of the carrying trade was, therefore, likely to be of considerable benefit to the English shipper, and for this purpose the Navigation Acts promised to be a useful device.[1]

Although the original clamour for regulations to control the handling of English imports and exports came from the shipowners the demand appears to have been supported by the merchants. This at first sight may seem surprising, for the merchants can hardly be supposed to have welcomed the idea of either restriction or higher freights. They had, however, interests of their own to press against the Dutch, for which the difficulties of the shipowners provided useful cover. The Eastland Company and the Levant Company in particular were finding that their own monopolistic position was seriously threatened by the entrepôt trade which the Dutch had developed in commodities from the Baltic and the Far East. For though their charters gave them a monopoly against other English merchants within the area assigned to them this monopoly could be easily undermined by Dutch merchants acting as middlemen and exporting from Holland the commodities that the Eastland Company or the Levant Company imported into England direct from the country of origin.

That these companies wanted to prevent such dangerous competition is understandable but, in view of the bitterness with which monopolies were being attacked in the seventeenth century they could hardly avow the real grounds for their dislike of the Dutch entrepôt trade. Arguments for the strengthening of the navy, on the other hand, received a good deal of popular support even when the proposals themselves might cause some public inconvenience. It was, therefore, much better from the point of view of strategy and propaganda to show a lively concern over shipping and to leave in decent obscurity the monopoly profits which Dutch activities threatened to curtail. It is very probable that some such motive lay behind the apparently straightforward proviso that goods from a European port should come to this country either in ships of the country of origin, or of usual first shipment, or in English ships, since such a regulation would effectively prevent the importation of Levant and Baltic goods

---

[1] L. A. Harper: *The English Navigation Laws: A Seventeenth Century Experiment in Social Engineering* (1939), *passim.*

via Holland. The further provision that no goods from Asia, Africa, or America could be imported except in English ships aimed at preserving both the 'long haul', as it was called, for English shipping and at cutting out the Dutch trader.

Later the Act of 1651 was replaced by the more famous Navigation Act of 1660 which, despite many modifications, remained the basis of the system until its abolition in the Free Trade furore of the nineteenth century. This new Act was rendered inevitable by the refusal of the Restoration Government to be bound by the laws of its predecessor, but it has been suggested that in any case administrative difficulties would have made it necessary to replace the earlier Act by some more workable, if less simple and comprehensive, measure. In the new Act the provision that all European goods must come from the country of origin and in the ships of the country producing the goods disappeared and was replaced by a long list of enumerated commodities to which this restriction alone applied. Any goods not contained in these schedules could still be imported by anyone and from any place, though if they came in foreign bottoms alien duties would have to be paid. In this way a real measure of freedom was given to our trade with Europe, and in the 'sixties London imported only slightly fewer commodities from the free list than she did enumerated commodities.

Whether it had been the original intention of the legislators to increase the area of unregulated trade is not clear. Indeed, it seems likely that loose drafting and subsequent judicial interpretation were more responsible for this increased measure of freedom than deliberate design, for, though it suited many of the smaller merchants engaged in the European trade, it once again placed in danger the interests of the Eastland and Levant Companies. It is significant of the pressure which they were able to exercise that two years later, in 1662, the Act of Frauds conferred on them the protection they desired and forbade the importation of wines (other than Rhenish), spicery, grocery, tobacco, pitch, potashes, tar, salt, rozen deal boards, fir timber or olive oil, from either the Low Countries or Germany. Whether this provision was advantageous to English shipping or not has been much debated; that it was inserted in conformity with the wishes of a section of merchant community seems reasonably clear.

By the Restoration the attitude of the merchants towards the colonial trade was also hardening. Though the provisions of the 1651 Navigation Act applied to the colonies as well as to the Mother Country, it does not seem, in either intention or in origin, to have been a measure primarily directed to the securing of a monopoly trade with the infant colonies in America and the West Indies, but in the Act of 1660 and in subsequent amending and amplifying legislation the importance of the colonies in the economic life of England is clearly understood. By this time the sale to Europe of their tropical and semi-tropical produce, in particular, the sale of tobacco, of sugar, of rice and dyewoods, had become a very profitable business. In this trade the fortunes of many prominent mercantile houses were built up, and the whole transaction was exceedingly advantageous to those engaged in it.

To extract the full measure of profit it was necessary to establish a monopoly over the raw materials. If the industrious Dutch, content with lower profits and a quick turnover, were able to get a firm hold over the colonial trade, then for the English merchants re-export to the continental markets would be ruined. Already, by the middle of the seventeenth century it was apparent that the Dutch had realized the prizes to be won, though as yet the volume of the colonial trade was much less than it afterwards became. Their trading posts on the Hudson were exceedingly well placed to tap the resources of both the southern and the northern colonies, and as a result of our Civil War, followed not long after by the war with Spain, a large share of the carrying trade was in their hands. This, from the point of view of the English merchants, was disastrous, though it served the interests of the planters well enough by providing them with alternative markets. Mercantile opinion, however, did not recognize the interests of the planters, or even of any particular colony, as being the deciding factor in shaping imperial policy, and since the merchants had been directly responsible as a class for the fostering and financing of the early American colonies, or at least for the practical fulfilment of other men's dreams, they felt all the force of the argument that 'he who pays the piper calls the tune'.

Mercantile theories were very much in line with this assumption. In the sixteenth and early seventeenth centuries, men were oppressed by the spectacle of swarms of vagrants and masterless men seeking work and not finding it, and assumed that England was over-populated. As a consequence public opinion had been predisposed to welcome emigration as a solution for the social and economic maladjustment of a period of transition. By the Restoration this view had been abandoned. It was now held that a large population was necessary to make cheap goods for export. Colonies were no longer thought of as an outlet for surplus population but as a drain on man-power. For this loss, it was argued, England was entitled to some recompense, which was to take the shape of strengthening her own economic system; what she now wanted were raw materials and markets. An adequate flow of raw materials would make her independent of European supplies, for which she had at the moment to pay with her only staple commodities or much-grudged bullion, and would give her additional quantities of tropical goods to sell in European markets. Secondly, by providing for the needs of the colonists new markets would be secured for English exports.

In so far as colonies conformed to this programme they, too, like the various branches of the European trade, were ranked as good or bad. The West Indies were the most highly valued because of the sugar plantations, but the tobacco crop of Virginia and the rice of Georgia were very important. The New England colonies, on the other hand, were far from popular. They produced little that was of use to the Mother Country. They showed an independent tendency to manufacture their own woollen goods and other necessities. They much preferred to trade with the French colonies, buying molasses with which to make their rum, in exchange for barrel staves and salt fish and the other goods required by slave-worked plantations. Even when prohibitive duties were imposed by the Molasses Act of 1733 the traffic continued almost without abatement, as the means of enforcement were quite inadequate.

Another advantage that England hoped to get from New England was an alternative source of naval stores. It was felt that the virgin forests of the north ought to be able to produce the timber and the tar that, before, England had been forced to buy from the Baltic countries. That trade, from the viewpoint of mercantilism, was undesirable in that the balance of trade was

consistently against this country. Such a policy had two distinct
advantages. It would lessen our dependence on the northern
Crowns and so wipe out an unfavourable balance of trade. It
would also, it was hoped, divert New England energies into fields
profitable to the Mother Country, and lessen the danger of a rival
woollen manufacture being set up there. Consequently, every
encouragement was given, and the special ships that were built
for carrying the masts became the regular liners of the Atlantic.

Such policy was open to criticism. The long Atlantic crossing
made freights high, labour in America was costly, and the policy
known as that of the Broad Arrow, by which certain trees were
earmarked for naval use, was unpopular with the colonists. Indeed,
resentment over the prohibition of the sale of timber to either the
West Indies or Europe may be counted as one of the economic
grievances that led to the final breach with England. Nevertheless, by a mingling of the encouragement afforded by the provision of bounties on the export of naval stores to Britain and the
regulations which prevented the colonists from cutting and selling
suitable timber elsewhere, supplies of naval stores were obtained,
though the cost both in money and in friction was high. In addition to the wood sent to England for purely naval purposes,
much was sent for other needs, and this trade, though it only
totalled one-twentieth of the colonial trade, was the most valuable
contribution that the northern colonies made to the economic
life of the Empire, as conceived in terms of the old colonial
policy.[1] Much less popular with the home authorities was the
very active shipbuilding that the New Englanders developed,
preferring to build their own ships and participate in the advantages of the Navigation Acts directly rather than to be dependent
on British ships and shippers.

The southern and West Indian colonies fitted more easily into
the pattern of English economic needs because their energies
were largely directed towards the production of staple crops
which could not only be used for domestic consumption in this
country but also exported to Europe. Though there were exceptions the colonists were not allowed to send these crops directly to
continental ports; England was to be the entrepôt for colonial
products. Adam Smith calculated that Maryland and Virginia

----

[1] R. G. Albion: *Op. cit., passim.*

sent us annually ninety-six thousand hogsheads of tobacco of which this country used not more than fourteen thousand, the rest being re-exported at considerable profit. The handling of the sugar crop of the West Indies was another lucrative branch of the colonial trade. Nor was the marketing of colonial produce the British merchants' only source of profit. Equally valuable was the monopoly of supplying the colonial market with consumer goods conferred by the provision that the goods imported into the colonies must come *via* England. This double monopoly of both purchase and supply meant that British merchants controlled both ends of the trade. They could buy cheap and sell dear. Whether they took full advantage of their position or not, it is not surprising that they were popularly supposed to have done so. Certainly, the American planter, buying imported goods on the security of his growing crops and ultimately receiving a disappointing price for his tobacco, blamed them for many of his problems and the greed of the British merchant has often been held to be at least partly responsible for the loss of the colonies. American research has now refuted these grosser charges of exploitation; falling prices were not caused by the cupidity of the merchants so much as by the over-abundant supply of tobacco which could no longer be as profitably resold to European buyers.[1]

Even without gross exploitation the advantages of the colonial market were such that it is not surprising that so many eighteenth-century merchants were attracted to it. But though the high profits of this trade seemed to depend on the virtual monopoly conferred by the Navigation Acts this does not mean that these laws were the work of a set of men who deliberately sacrificed the real interests of their country to their private profit or that their ostensible aim, to increase British shipping, was nothing but skilful window-dressing. If it could be clearly shown that the Acts in question did little or nothing to increase our shipping then it could be argued that the parliaments who passed them and the merchants who supported them were either stupid or disingenuous. But of their effects it is difficult to speak with any certainty; by contemporaries and by historians alike they have been both strongly condemned and hotly defended. That a large body

[1] J. C. Miller: *Origins of the American Revolution* (1945), p. 19.

of merchants had an interest in the continuance of the system is clear; that this interest was prejudicial to the general wellbeing is less so.

In support of the view that the Navigation Acts were a costly failure it has been pointed out that though the tonnage of British and colonial shipping did increase after their enactment this increase was not necessarily due to the Navigation Acts, as the shipping of other European states was increasing in much the same proportion. Moreover, as a result of the Acts, English shipbuilding costs rose, putting English merchants and manufacturers at a serious disadvantage with regard to foreign competitors in all but the protected markets. In handling naval stores from the Baltic it is argued that the Dutch had been keen and able middlemen, content with a small profit and a quick turnover, and competition had helped to keep prices reasonable, but with the Navigation Acts they were no longer allowed to serve the English market with naval stores. The English, on the other hand, often lacked the special ships required for the timber trade, and were, therefore, forced to rely on the supplies brought by the Baltic ships, since the naval stores were among those enumerated commodities which had to be imported either in English ships or in the ships of the country producing the goods. Even where English ships could be provided, the Baltic merchants, knowing that the English merchants were dependent on them for supplies and could not buy elsewhere, put up prices against them. As a result the raw material rose in price and so started the vicious circle that meant that freights were higher in English ships, and, therefore, the price of British goods carried in them rose in proportion. Where we had a monopoly of the goods to be supplied this did not matter, but where we had no such advantage the difficulties of the British merchant were much increased. English manufacturers were hit, too. Whereas, in the case of nets and rope, we had before imported the raw material via Holland in Dutch ships and made the finished goods in this country, now the Dutch turned to working up the material themselves and selling us the manufactured goods as the produce of Holland. Thus, it is claimed that the Navigation Acts definitely lessened our share in the trade of Europe, while the advantages that they bestowed on our shipping were largely illusory, and the increases that did take place were due more to the growth in the volume of trade than to the fostering care of parliament.[1]

It is a formidable case and if true would lend colour to the argument that the merchants, whose influence in promoting the Acts was by no means negligible, were perfectly ready to sacrifice the European trade, which was of widespread benefit to the community as a whole, to the interests of building up a monopoly in the colonies under cover of the needs of the mercantile marine. The latest assessment of the evidence, however, tends to lean the other way. L. A. Harper, in a full and careful survey of the origin and working of the Navigation Acts, thinks that, though a price had to be paid for the Navigation Acts, at least they did increase shipping. With regard to the American trade there is very little controversy. It was strictly reserved for English and colonial shipping for all the commodities that were important, though exceptions, allowing transport of salt needed for the fisheries, or giving permission to ship rice direct to southern European ports, gave some flexibility to the system. Before 1650, when special provisions were made against the encroachment of foreign merchants by directing that no foreigners were to trade with the American colonies without licence from the Council of State or parliament, the Dutch had been active in this trade, which their possession of New Amsterdam certainly encouraged. Without the passing of the Navigation Acts, once the temporary political conditions of hostility between England and Holland and the aftermath of the Civil War had disappeared, it does seem very probable that the Dutch would most certainly have retained, and very likely increased, their share in this traffic, and that other nations would also have increased their proportion, since England was not the natural entrepôt for supplying continental markets or for obtaining their commodities in return.

But the real issue is not so much whether the trade with the American colonies increased as whether it did so at the expense of the trade with Europe to such an extent that what this country gained on the swings it more than lost upon the roundabouts. The evidence is complicated and not easy to weigh. It would certainly seem as if the proportion of British tonnage entering and

[1] 'The navigation policy reacted adversely upon the industry and commerce of the country'. E. Lipson: *The Economic History of England* (1931), Vol. III, p. 132.

leaving our ports after the system came into force was greater, even taking the general growth of trade into consideration, than it had been during the Commonwealth. The statement is not itself, however, conclusive. The fluctuations and difficulties of our trade and the predominance of the Dutch may have been due to wartime circumstances, and it is possible to argue that with the coming of more stable conditions British shipping would have gained the position that it did without the aid of special protection. But though it is possible to argue in this way it must be remembered that not all the conditions were favourable for the building up of a great mercantile marine. In particular, this country was severely handicapped by the shortage of the necessary shipbuilding materials. Timber, cordage, tar, all had to be procured from abroad, since by the seventeenth century our own forests were quite inadequate. Whether we bought through the Dutch or direct from the place of origin, we were, as far as this country was concerned, purchasing in a seller's market. In this case we were likely to find prices running against us. In such circumstances without the protection given by the provision that ships should be English owned and, except when specially licensed, English built, it seems improbable that a flourishing shipbuilding industry would have developed in this country. Mr. Harper also suggests that the insistence on English crews was necessary if ships were not to be short of trained seamen. If wages had not been protected from competition, and so made more attractive, the danger of being pressed into the navy in war-time, together with the general conditions of life at sea, might have made recruitment for the merchant navy very difficult. A certain price in operating costs, it is argued, had to be paid in order to be sure that in time of war Britain was short of neither ships nor men.

There were two main reasons for these. The Navigation Acts narrowed the area from which our shipbuilders could obtain their raw materials. Naval stores had to be brought directly from their place of origin. This gave Baltic exporters a tactical advantage: they knew that we must either buy from them or else rely on the even more expensive alternative colonial supply. Moreover, the rule that all these commodities must be shipped to this country either in vessels belonging to the producing country

The Custom House, London, 1792

Smugglers Attacked, 1793

Trade Card for the Liverpool Packet, 1705

The Funeral of Trade
(This cartoon is typical of the attacks made on Pitt's Free Trade
policy in 1785)

or in British ships placed our shipbuilders at a further disadvantage with regard to freight charges. Here the difficulty arose from the fact that England had few ships suitable for so specialized a trade. This meant depending on alien ships and these paid higher duties even when carrying cargoes in strict conformity with the Navigation Acts. This question of higher transport charges was intensified by the elimination of the Dutch from the trade, so that we had, in effect, to rely on Scandinavian tonnage. As a result of their monopoly, artificially created by ourselves against ourselves, the costs of carriage, it is argued, were higher than they need have been.

Supporters of the Navigation Acts have not denied these charges but they have contended that their effects have been much exaggerated. With regard to the charge that Baltic merchants demanded steeper prices because we had no alternative source of supply their answer is that to have bought *via* the Dutch instead of direct would have made very little difference. The basic strength of the exporting countries lay in the fact that they had a natural monopoly. As evidence that the Navigation Acts added little to shipbuilding costs on this score it is pointed out that the prices of naval stores from the Baltic had risen sharply before the passing of the Acts and that they had shown no startling increase afterwards. In dealing with transport charges the apologists are on less sure ground. That these were somewhat increased is not denied, but the popular plea that it was 'only a little one' is put forward with some confidence. Naval stores brought here in alien shipping would have been burdened by alien duties, whether they had been brought in Dutch or Scandinavian ships, but, it is contended, on these commodities the native shippers only paid a little less. In addition it is argued that though Dutch freight charges might have been a little lower than those we paid to the Baltic shipowners, yet had these attempted to push their monopoly profits of transport too far we could have either built or bought the necessary specialized ships and worked our trade ourselves.

Nevertheless, though they may have been magnified, it seems clear that some increase in the price of naval stores resulted from the Navigation Acts. Nor should it be forgotten that such increase as occurred was due to the selfish pressure of the Eastland merchants. British ships gained few additional cargoes because

4

timber and other naval stores were placed on the list of enumerated commodities. The merchants of the Eastland Company did however, obtain a most decided advantage in that English shipbuilders were forced to buy through them at prices not pared by Dutch competition. In this way they were able to establish a real monopoly in supplying the home market, for American competition, due to the high cost of the Atlantic crossing, was not economically serious. Had it not suited the Eastland merchants there seems little obvious reason why naval stores should have been included among the enumerated commodities. The ships used and the men employed in the trade were not English. It is difficult to see, therefore, how the provision that such commodities must come direct from the country of origin in the ships of either the producing country or in those belonging to Englishmen did help to increase our mercantile marine. Whatever, therefore, this provision added to the cost of ship-building in this country, however little this addition may have been, was added not to benefit English naval strength but merely in order to give monopoly profits to merchants engaged in this vital trade.

To say this is not, however, to imply that in every case purely selfish mercantile interests prevailed and that no benefits were conferred on English shipping by the Navigation Acts. In certain branches of our trade with Europe it seems at least likely that English shipowners did retain a greater share of the trade than they would have had without some measure of protection, since the scarcity of raw materials and the high wages of English seamen operated to make freight charges greater than those of some of our European competitors. Moreover, where a trade route was partially protected, as that between Russia and this country, ships that were sure of a profitable freight on the homeward run could offer artificially low, because subsidized, freights in the inter-port traffic that lay along their route. They could, therefore, contrive to act as third-party carriers between European ports in a way that would have been impossible if the low freights which they charged for this service had not been compensated for by the high monopoly rates which they were able to make on the protected part of the run. In post-war periods also, when the release of shipping by combatants competed bitterly with the increased trade that neutrals had built up, the fact that certain trades and certain enumerated commodities were the preserve of the English shipper helped to provide some cushion against the cut-throat competition for cargoes that tends to prevail at such times.

To make any kind of judgment as to what interests were best served by the Navigation Acts is clearly no easy matter. They were apparently neither a dead letter nor ineffective in stimulating an English-built and English-manned mercantile marine. It is, of course, always possible to argue that had trade been free from all such restrictions its volume would have increased. Such an approach implies that even if the Navigation Acts did increase English tonnage, the strength of our shipping was bought at the expense of our manufacturers and of the general consuming public, since our great competitors, the Dutch, could probably have carried our goods more cheaply and supplied us with what raw materials we required on more advantageous terms. But the basis of judgment cannot be purely economic, at least in any narrow sense. Vital political circumstances, the struggle for power and for colonies were factors which any eighteenth-century government had to take into most careful consideration.

It is true that the decision as to what commodities should be placed on the enumerated list was often made under the pressure of special groups of merchants. But because the choice was sometimes influenced and distorted in this way is not to say that the whole code is to be condemned as being against the interests of the State; that it served merely private interests. Suspicious as Adam Smith was of the activities of the merchants as a whole, and much as he would have modified the provisions concerning the enumerated commodities, he yet opposed the wholesale repeal of this legislation, holding that at times power was to be preferred to plenty, that a moderate supply of guns could be, in some circumstances, a better thing than unlimited supplies of butter. It was a system of which the merchants could and did take great advantage; it was not one which they had been able to create merely in order to serve their own interests, though their acuteness was demonstrated again and again by the way in which they intertwined private profit with what was then accepted as being for the general good.

By the closing years of the eighteenth century it is clear that a new critical spirit was abroad and that the basic assumptions of mercantilism, on which so much of the nation's commercial legislation and policy had hitherto been based, was being increasingly questioned by more and more people. The revolt was both physical and intellectual, and it is interesting to notice how closely the dates of the two are intertwined. Though economic discontent was not the only driving force behind the revolt of the American colonists it was a potent factor in it. Since the victories of 1763 their sense of independence had been greatly increased. This was partly due to the share they had taken in the struggle, and partly to the removal of the French menace from the mainland. At the same time their economic irritation, always just beneath the surface, had been augmented by the tighter control which Grenville had instituted over the administration of the laws of trade.

Walpole's Molasses Act with its prohibitive duties had been a dead letter as far as the flourishing trade between the colonists and the French West Indies had been concerned; Grenville's much more moderate proposals were intended to be enforced. Governors and naval officers were ordered to be active in the matter, and customs officials who had been leaving their work to deputies were hounded back to the personal performance of their duty. At the same time the trade laws were made more restrictive of colonial commercial liberty. Important additions were made to the enumerated commodities, which were now to include not only the old staple products, but coffee, pimento, coconuts, hides, whalefins, raw silk, potashes, colonial iron and lumber. As in addition certain drawbacks, which it had been the practice to repay when goods, originally imported into this country, were re-exported for colonial use, were no longer allowed, the cost of the goods exported from this country, already high because of monopoly profits, was still further increased to the colonial consumer. The practical disadvantages of the system, from the American point of view became, therefore, ever clearer at a time when questions of defence, questions of taxation, were already providing a prolific crop of grievances about which public opinion, not uninfluenced by the propaganda of interested persons, was becoming resentful.

If physical revolt came from the American colonists the most powerful intellectual attacks came from the British economists, and these attacks were concurrent with, and not subsequent to, the breakaway of the American colonies. Of them all, the assault of Adam Smith was probably the most penetrating, the most reasoned and the most devastating. In many ways he spoke for the interests of the new industrialized Britain that was coming into being. It was one of the characteristics of mercantilism that it underestimated the potentialities of the home market. So far the production of consumer goods for home use had been gravely hampered by the diversion of the available capital to the profitable colonial trade. Once the bait of monopoly profits had been destroyed then it was argued that both the home market and those afforded by our older customers in nearby countries could be more adequately developed. The profits of the colonial trade might be gratifyingly high to the small cliques that enjoyed them, but the return on the capital employed was slow, tying up for long periods resources that were urgently wanted in other directions. A quick turnover and a lower profit were necessary if home production was to be stimulated and if profitable employment was to be provided for the mass of the people. Small groups adversely affected by monopolies had always been vocal against them. Now, in view of our growing industrial potential, commercial monopolies were declared by Adam Smith and kindred writers, for in many ways he interpreted a trend, to be in the interests of the few rather than for the wellbeing of the nation as a whole. 'It cannot be very difficult', he wrote, 'to determine who have been the contrivers of the whole mercantile system, not the consumers, we may believe, whose interests have been entirely neglected; but the producers, whose interests have been so carefully attended to; and among this latter class our merchants and manufacturers have been far the principal architects'.[1]

By the end of the century the tide was setting strongly against the mercantilism of the past. The independence of the American colonies did not destroy the trading links between the two countries; custom and connexions were too strong for that, but it deprived the British merchants of their special privileges and probably led to the diversion of some capital to other spheres. Other monopolies still remained. In Canada and the West Indies the old system persisted, while in India the East India Company

[1] *Op. cit.*, Vol. II, p. 160.

still dominated the scene. But even before the Napoleonic Wars mercantilism was in retreat. Attacks on the Indian monopoly were fierce, the prosperity of the West Indies was declining, and at home the power of the growing industrialists was providing a serious challenge to the older mercantile houses that had built their fortunes on their monopoly trade in colonial produce. Soon a place would have to be found for their interests in the country's commercial policy, and as the flood of machine-made goods gradually rose higher and higher it engulfed the classic tenets of mercantilism. Although the merchants remained a powerful pressure group, by the nineteenth century they were forced to share their empire with the industrialists to whom, less than a century ago, they had been able, through their parliamentary influence, to dictate policy. Thus a great change in the social structure of the country was confirmed and the Age of Mercantilism, long a-dying, expired.

Chapter Two

THE SOCIAL STRUCTURE

It is impossible to understand eighteenth-century England, and equally impossible to estimate the effect of the economic developments which marked its closing decades without a fairly detailed knowledge of its social structure. Prominent though the merchants were in moulding the policy of this country in its relations, both economic and diplomatic, with the rest of the world, England was still basically agricultural. For the greater part of the people the tie with the land remained close: the landowner was still the most potent influence in shaping its social structure.

Misled by the sophistication of so much of eighteenth-century thought and literature and by the polished elegance of its ruling class, it is easy to forget how much of the medieval foundations of society still remained, hidden, it is true, by this superstructure, but still sustaining it. Towns no doubt were growing, but, with some few exceptions where trade provided the impetus, their growth had not that staggering quality that was to mark their progress in the nineteenth century. Most of them remained small, hardly more than glorified villages except in a constitutional and legal sense. Their relation to the countryside that surrounded them also remained virtually unchanged in that their chief function was still to provide a market for the adjacent rural areas. Their population rarely numbered more than a few thousands: the great majority of people still lived in the country.

It would be a mistake to think of this rural population as being purely agricultural. By the opening years of the eighteenth century the domestic system,[1] with its flexible organization, had scattered the possibilities of industrialization up and down the countryside. Probably by this time there were few localities where

---

[1] The term *domestic* or *outwork system* is generally used to describe the type of industrial organization in which the craftsman works in his own home and (usually) with his own tools. His relationship to the merchant who supplied him with the raw material and took his finished goods varied from one of almost complete economic subordination to one of comparative independence.

some people were not spinning or weaving for the clothier. Many it is true were only supplementing the produce of a small-holding or the enjoyment of common rights, but for others industry was their main source of livelihood. But, though craftsmen, they remained essentially country dwellers, congregated in small clothing villages or living in the scattered homesteads of the North but always in intimate contact with the rural life around them. The concentration of industry, with its savage demand for hands, and still more hands, combined with an increased shortage of land as the population grew, had not yet produced that divorce from the country, which was so fundamentally to alter the structure of society in the nineteenth century. In consequence it is not surprising that though labour services and serfdom had long disappeared the whole tone of rural society was still feudal. Power was still in the hands of the man who possessed land. The merchant and the financier, important as their part in the national economy was, had still in many ways to operate within the framework of a society that had been shaped by landowners for landowners. To this extent England was still medieval in its fundamental assumptions.

The medieval distribution of population was still apparent. This, too, is understandable; while agriculture remained the basic means of livelihood for the majority the density of population continued to be dictated by the fertility of the land. Hence the old corn-lands still supported the maximum number of people that the agricultural methods of the time allowed. In other less fertile areas people were encouraged to settle by the advantages offered for the breeding of sheep. Here the fact that the land itself afforded a living to comparatively few, as the demands of pastoral farming on labour were not heavy, was offset by early industrialization. It was the clothier with his capital, his organization and his contacts with wider markets who, from the fifteenth century on, encouraged the growth of the clothing villages in those areas already noted for their fine fleeces. As a result the population had thickened in districts like the Cotswolds, Wiltshire, East Anglia and the bleak valleys and moors of Yorkshire. Even this was no modern development. Much of it was medieval. Though, therefore, there had been increases, the population was still, in the main, distributed much as it had been when Henry VII came to the throne. Only in a few areas, often where coal was mined or could be easily obtained, or where the expansion of trade encouraged the growth of port facilities, had any very marked changes taken place by the beginning of the century.

It was certainly not easy to move from one part of the country to another. What purported to be roads linking towns and districts were often mere tracks indicating the way to go rather than making it practicable. The turnpike movement which, whatever its deficiencies, had by the end of the century made coach travel comparatively fast and comfortable, was still in its infancy. The business of improving rivers had hardly got much beyond paper projects and the canal era lay more than fifty years ahead. Goods still went by pack horse, by river or by sea and travellers on horseback or on foot. In consequence local life, local traditions and local loyalties were strong. This makes generalizations about the English social structure or the English way of life dangerous. What is true of Lancashire is not true of Middlesex, what is true of Devon may well be false for Essex. Villages could be cut off from the nearest town not for a few days by snow but for months by the impassability of winter roads or floods. A visit to London for most people seemed an impossible adventure, and social life, even for the gentry, centred round the county town, in so far as it was urban at all. In such circumstances great ignorance was possible and so was great clannishness which combined to produce an acceptance of existing social patterns and arrangements. The difficulty of transporting goods had the same conservative influence. People bought and used the products of local industries and supplied themselves from local markets and the innovating pressure of an expanding market on social habits came only slowly. Within a limited area movement and migration were common enough, but for the majority that area was not the nation. One of the great factors making for social change as the century went on was the ease and speed with which news, people and goods could be conveyed from place to place, bringing into closer contact town and country, the provinces and London.

In spite of the phenomenal growth of London and the increasing number of persons who earned their living by trade or industry, by the close of the seventeenth century urban development had done little to affect the general structure of society. Gregory King was being starkly realistic in his famous analysis of 1696[1] when he used the possession of land as the measure of a man's importance in society. It was his relationship to the land that gave a man his obvious and unchallenged place in the social hierarchy, for, though no longer the sole key to wealth, it was still its most unmistakable symbol and the channel through which political power flowed. Yet, even when he wrote, the possession of large estates was no longer the exclusive prerogative of the gentry and aristocracy. Because land was everywhere recognized as being the basis of social and political power it was eagerly coveted. Unlike some continental countries, there were no restrictions on its transfer between class and class, so that the first aim of the financial upstart was to purchase an estate. From the fifteenth century, merchants had been buying, some in a modest way, others on a big scale, as befitted their growing fortunes. Few of those families which dominated the social and political scene when King made his calculations had their roots in medieval England. Thus by the eighteenth century much of the land had passed into the hands of men who thoroughly understood, and were quite prepared to exploit, its social and economic possibilities. They had shaken themselves free of royal control by their victories of 1649 and 1688, and it was they who gave the tone to and dominated the society of the day.

The landowning class was, however, far from uniform either in its social or economic power. At its head stood the great aristocratic families who, whatever their sixteenth or seventeenth origins might have been, were now in possession of great estates. These families dominated the counties in which they lived. Next in the rural hierarchy came the substantial local worthies, baronets, knights and squires. Some might enjoy incomes of as much as £2,000 a year drawn from rents, but £1,000 was a more usual figure. The smaller squires with rentals ranging from £800 to £450 were less affluent. Under them in the rural hierarchy came the lesser freeholders. These men, if the term is to be used strictly and not as it often was, to describe any working farmer, whether he owned or merely rented his land, were the often publicized

---

[1] G. King: *The Natural and Political Observations upon the State and Condition of England, 1696, passim.* Ed. by G. Barnell. (Baltimore, 1936).

'yeomen of England'. They, too, were by no means of an equal economic status. Gregory King drew a dividing line between the freeholder with an income of some £84 a year and those whose incomes fell below £50. In those areas where the open fields remained, or where the nature of the soil favoured the small agricultural unit, farmers of this type were common. In the North they possessed tiny homesteads, often in the upland areas, to which were attached fairly large grazing rights over the fells. Where the soil was poor, such holdings were barely adequate, even with the severest toil, to maintain a family. The 'statesmen' of Westmorland, as this class was named in that county, found it difficult to wring some kind of bare living from the soil.

It is possible, however, that many of these small-scale landowners did not attempt to make a living by farming the few acres they owned, but followed some rural craft while, like their social superiors, they leased out their land. Evidence on this point is lacking for the early part of the century, but the Land Tax Assessments and the information supplied in connexion with parliamentary enclosures later suggest that there may have been many small freeholders who let their land rather than farm themselves. Not all King's 140,000 freeholders, therefore, were necessarily occupying owners. Like the greater landowners they, too, may have benefited by drawing rents, using the income so obtained to supplement other means of earning a living. To think of the lessor of land in eighteenth-century England as being always a gentleman or the owner of a big estate is, in many areas, an oversimplification.

Lower still in the social scale came the cottager who owned the cottage in which he lived, with perhaps a strip or two in the common fields, or some grazing rights on the waste. In a group of Suffolk villages, examined after the enclosure of the common fields had been completed, and in conjunction with a new Bill to enclose the waste, out of 205 peasants owning land 92 of them possessed three acres or less.[1] These men, too, though in a very small way and to a degree that gave them no power over the economic destinies of other men, were landowners with their own small stake in the country which might not be large enough

[1] V. M. Lavrovsky: 'Parliamentary Enclosures in the County of Suffolk (1797–1814)'. *Econ. Hist. Rev.*, Vol. VII, No. 2 (May 1937), p. 190.

to entitle their owners to vote in parliamentary elections. Yet, at least in these Suffolk parishes, even these insignificant land-owners often let their tiny properties.

Closely connected with the land, and getting their living from it, though not owning the land on which they worked, were the tenant farmers. These varied both in the size of their holdings and in the tenures by which they held them. The most considerable among them were the leaseholders who rented the older enclosed farms, some of which ran to three or four hundred acres, though others were as small as those of the poorest freeholder. Some-times these men were purely tenant farmers, owning no land of their own and renting from the local gentry or from small owners who did not wish to occupy their own holding. In other cases they were also landowners who supplemented their own freehold by leasing additional land. In yet other cases they were both leas-ing land to other tenants and renting land, whose location suited them better, for their own farming activities. The leaseholders, therefore, were drawn from very different elements in the rural community.

Intermingled with them, particularly in those counties in which there had been less redistribution and enclosure, were the copy-holders. With the newer landowner copyhold was not popular because of the restraints it put upon his power, both to regulate the terms on which the land was farmed, and also to regain con-trol of it speedily should the need arise. Nevertheless, even at the opening of the eighteenth century, land management remained in many districts remarkably conservative and tied to the traditions of the past, and the copyholder was still an important figure in rural England, though the century was to see serious inroads on his position, as well as upon that of the small occupying owner. Very often the copyholder, like the yeoman, was only a very small farmer. He used his cash crops to pay his rent and dues, but for the rest was content to live very plainly upon the produce of his holding.

By the eighteenth century, however, there were already many countrymen who had even less stake in the land than this. Some were the younger sons of small farmers working as cowmen, as carters, as ploughmen, for the larger farmers. In the North it was customary for such workers to live in and to accept both the security and the restraint of the yearly hiring, and such men, saving a large proportion of their wages, no doubt looked forward to the time when they would be able to lease a tiny holding, marry and pass into the ranks of the small farmer. But in many counties this kind of agricultural labour seems to have been supplied on a day-to-day basis by the small cottager who had himself a scrap of land, either owned or rented, and, where sufficient waste-land was available, supplemented by common rights. Generally his wife made her own contribution to the family income, since, even where other employment was not available, a few pence could always be earned by spinning, and often, in hard times or bad weather, the whole family followed some kind of by-employment. Even lower in the rural hierarchy came the squatters on the waste, the kind of wandering and half-vagrant poor against whom the Act of Settlements and Removals had been aimed, who somehow scraped a precarious livelihood from casual and seasonal agricultural work for wages, and from the opportunities to keep a beast or two and gather fuel, combined with a little spinning.

Other country dwellers, sometimes in combination with the ownership or renting of a little land, more often in conjunction with rights on the waste that allowed the keeping of a cow, earned a modest living as rural craftsmen, as thatchers, as shoemakers, above all as blacksmiths, a class so numerous and important that even as late as 1851 the census reveals them to have been nationally more numerous than the entire labour force employed in the important coal mines of Durham and Northumberland.[1] Then, too, in many rural districts there was to be found a small sprinkling of middle class and professional men, the vicar or a local clothier. But though rural society contained both non-landowners and landowners or land users of varied economic and legal standing, in most areas, other than in the wide and wild stretches of the North, this society was held together and dominated by the Big House. The influence exercised in this way by local landowners of substantial standing was not and never could be in any sense uniform. Much depended upon the structure of society within a given locality. Where there was the seat of a peer his influence tended to be dominant and to be exercised over a wider area than

[1] J. H. Clapham: *An Economic History of Great Britain* (1937), Vol. I, p. 169.

his own acres comprised, because of his relations with the local gentry. Here again much depended on the personality of its owner, some taking a prominent local lead while others were content to see lesser but more energetic neighbouring landowners sway local affairs. But in many districts it was the wealthy squire to whom unchallenged homage was paid. In part it was a tribute to his economic power; many rented land from him or received wages or enjoyed his patronage, many of the young people were employed as his servants. To oppose the lord of the manor was to court economic ostracism and to be a dangerous man to know.

To state the relationship between the local magnate and those people who lived within his sphere of influence solely in terms of economic domination is to over-simplify the situation. At least some of his power to interfere with those who were not his tenants was derived from the fact that, as a considerable land-owner, he was extremely likely to be also a justice of the peace. As such he would exercise wide but perfectly legal administrative as well as repressive powers in his own locality. It was not simply as a landowner but also as an agent of governmental authority that he was able to influence and direct the society around him. In addition to such specific powers he also owed something to tradition: that tradition that looked to the local gentry as the leaders of the countryside. Long habit had made it natural for rural communities to turn to the manor house for guidance in local affairs. Much depended on accidents of geography and personality. Villages that lay remote from the family seat, where estates were extensive or scattered, probably had little personal knowledge of, or contact with, their landowner. His authority was exercised through agents, and was more economic than social in its effects. In the North, with its great stretches of moorland and isolated valleys, the head of the ruling family was regarded more as a feudal chief, a symbol of local feeling, than as an ever-present and interfering personality. In these areas the outwardly rather servile attitude of people who have authority ever on their doorstep never developed ; here some of the more repellent aspects of the squirearchy were not found. Master and man were terms still interpreted in the spirit of the old Border tenure, that called for companions in arms rather than for mere manual workers. The attitude of the fell dweller was at once more critical and more loyal than that of the average South-country villager.

When, however, the village clustered round the gates of the Hall the squire was an ever-present reality. Then, indeed, he often tended to develop into the 'petty tyrant' of a small kingdom, interfering, controlling, punishing, often helping, but always dominant; the 'Squire Western' of Fielding's portrait. In such cases personality counted for much; it was easy for paternal government to degenerate into trivial tyrannies, and for personal spite or a love of power to express itself in ways that trenched seriously on the economic and social freedom of his dependents. Such was the rule of the squire at his worst, but even at its best it left long persistent marks on the social life of much of rural England, though often it had a lighter and more charming side, as a report from the *Oxford Journal* for 27 September 1766 shows.

> On Monday last James Pye Esq., of Farringdon in the County of Berks, and his new-married Lady, arrived at the Crown and Thistle in Abingdon, on their way to the Family Seat, and gave a publick Breakfast to some Hundreds of the Gentlemen, Farmers and Persons of his Neighbourhood who, on this joyful occasion, had accompanied or given them the Meeting. Upon their Arrival at Abingdon the whole Cavalcade were so condescending as to go quite round the Market House, preceded by Musick, with colours displayed, before they alighted at the Inn, and likewise used the Same Ceremony at their leaving the Town during all which the Bells rang incessantly. Money and Liquor were likewise given to the Populace at Abingdon; and upon their Arrival at Farringdon, Illuminations, Ringing of Bells, etc., etc., and an open Festival demonstrated a Revival of Old English Hospitality.[1]

To stress the importance of a man's relationship to land is not, however, to suggest that the interests of the landowners as a whole were homogeneous or to imply that they were limited to the activities of the agriculturalist. It is necessary to distinguish between the class that based its economic power on the possession of land, and the merchants and financiers who, though they owned estates which they managed with due regard for the profits to be drawn from them, nevertheless really relied for

---

[1] J. Townshend: 'News of a Country Town'. Being extracts from *Jackson's Oxford Journal* relating to Abingdon (1914), p. 57.

their economic strength on their command of liquid capital, which
they employed in trading and financial enterprises. The social
relation between the two groups could at times be very close;
men such as Sir Robert Walpole often represented land on the
paternal side, and trade and the City on the maternal, for intermarriage between the landed gentry and the merchant interests
was common. Grosley, commenting on this, expressed the
opinion that

> The mixture and confusion, as it were, which results from hence,
> between the nobility and the mercantile part of the nation, is an
> inexhaustible source of wealth to the state, the nobility having
> acquired an accession of wealth by marriage, the tradesmen make up
> for their loss by their eager endeavours to make a fortune, and the
> gentry conspire to the same end by their efforts to raise such an
> estate as shall procure a peerage for themselves or their children.[1]

Yet, however much they might mingle, might look alike, might
talk alike, might dress alike, particularly when the second generation inherited an estate that had been acquired through the profits
of successful trade, so long as the family fortune was dependent
on commercial rather than agricultural enterprises, the interests
of the true landowner and the merchant possessing estates could
at times diverge sharply, though to a considerable extent the
possession of land camouflaged the gulf between them to the eye
of the casual observer.

Even the pure landowner was not necessarily concerned with
agricultural interests. Land produced not only cattle and crops
and wool, it was also the source of raw materials vital for industry,
such as iron ores, copper, tin and lead, and the ultimate supplier
of all fuel, both wood, charcoal and coal. In the sixteenth century,
when the importance of coal had first been realized in this country,
families who had been fortunate enough to possess coal-bearing
land had engaged eagerly in the business of promoting mining
and sinking shafts. By the eighteenth century, however, much of
this hopeful enthusiasm had long waned as the financial hazards
of deep mining had been painfully driven home by the spectacle
of ruined fortunes and mortgaged estates. Though some families
continued to play an active and profitable part in the working of
the deposits on their estates, the majority were content to lease

[1] P. J. Grosley: *A Tour to London*. Trans. T. Nugent (1772), Vol. II, p. 270.

A Portrait Group by Daniel Gardner, 1775

A Group of Englishmen in Rome, attributed to Reynolds

The Morning Visit
A dean soliciting a bishopric from a statesman, 1773

London Merchants at the Royal Exchange, 1788

their mines to others, and to be satisfied with the reward in the way of royalties that the possession of coal-bearing land conferred on them, without risking their own capital in producing and marketing the coal. Yet even these men, dependent as they were for an important part of their revenue on royalties and leases and wayleaves, could not be completely indifferent to the prosperity of the industries that used their products. But though a section of the landed gentry and aristocracy were, for this reason, to some extent connected with and dependent upon the wellbeing of the extractive industries, and though the real interests of the man who was primarily a landowner might often clash with those of a man who, though busily engaged in building up an estate, nevertheless still mainly depended on the profits obtained in trade, yet between them they dominated the society of eighteenth-century England. Capital sunk in industry was growing in importance, but at the opening of the century it could offer little or no challenge to the combined power of land and commerce.

Yet, though the social structure of the country was still so closely related to the possession of land, which still made the foundation on which all else rested, even by the close of the seventeenth century there was a growing body of people, as Gregory King recognized, who had little or no connexion with the land, though some of them might hold wealth in the shape of urban property or in stocks of goods or of clothes or furniture or cash. Many merchants had no liquid capital that they could spare from their business for the purchase of an estate; many a younger son who followed the law, or who held a commission in the army or navy, had no land of his own. The connexion, too, of the clergy with the land was more generally through the offices that they held in the Church than through their own personal and inherited wealth, while the unbeneficed clergy lacked even this. As administration became more complicated, as standing armies and navies in regular commission grew, as lawyers multiplied and a growing population and rising standard of life began to demand more schoolmasters and doctors, more writers and architects, so professional men, who owed their standing in society to their specialized skill and learning, increased in number, thus creating a new social group unconnected, except by family accident, with the land.

5

The steady growth of industry operated in the same way. Clothiers and linen drapers were not poor men, they had considerable sums of money locked up in their stocks of raw material, but for the most part such wealth as they had was not invested in land. Nor was there necessarily any connexion between the host of craftsmen employed in the textile industry and the land, though those who lived scattered throughout the rural areas often had some such connexion, even if it were only the possession of common rights or of some smallholding. But for the town artisan the link had long been broken and he was already forming part of the urban proletariat. In the towns, too, shopkeepers were congregating, ready to serve the needs alike of the manufacturers and of the professional man. It is the existence of these people which breaks the homogeneous picture of England as a society of landowners and land users, and suggests that on the old stage, and mingling with the older types, new actors are claiming an increasing share of the limelight.

These new actors are not infrequently described as 'the rising Middle Class'. By now it has become something of a commonplace to assert that any period of transition in English history is characterized by a 'rising middle class' and to attribute to its activities much of the subsequent changes. In itself the statement is no doubt valid enough, if over-simplified. It is, however, really very little more than a statement of the obvious. As soon as society began to differentiate itself at all, so that various income groups and cultural groups emerged, there must always have been 'a middle class'. What concerns the historian is not their existence but their composition. This varies from period to period. As a preliminary to understanding eighteenth-century England it is necessary to study in some detail what is meant by the term at this time and to know whom it includes. Only then is it possible to assess the nature and extent of the changes brought about by later economic developments.

Perhaps for England no completely satisfactory answer can be given because the concept of class in this country is social and economic, not legal. In the eyes of the Law, by the eighteenth century all men were equal, save for that privilege, of doubtful benefit, which allowed a member of the House of Lords to be tried for certain offences by his peers. Even the slave setting foot

in this country, said Lord Mansfield in his famous judgment of
1772, was automatically freed. Habeas Corpus applied to all. So
did the terrors of the sponging-house and the debtors' prison. It
is true that for many people this vaunted equality was of no practical importance. To quote the well-known wisecrack: 'though all
men were equal some were more equal than others'. In an age
that rejoiced in legal subtleties and quibbles the poor man who
could afford neither skilled counsel nor fees was at a grave disadvantage. Litigation was not for him. Once in the clutches of the
Law the same inequalities persisted. Basic conditions were
scandalous, but for the man who could satisfy the rapacity of his
jailer they were much ameliorated. To be without money was a
graver handicap than to be low-born. The hardships which the
poor suffered were the fruit of economic circumstance, not of
the Law, and that all Englishmen were, at least in legal theory,
equal was a matter for national pride. It was a fact that impressed
foreigners, used to the more rigid class systems of the Continent.
Madam Roland, for example, observed with some approval that
the laws were not made for the benefit only of those who rode
in chariots.

Denied legal definition the historian is left with the more
elusive classifications based on economic, on cultural, on religious
differences. Yet the issue is important for a correct understanding
of the eighteenth century because, though the law made no distinction between the gently born and the rest, society was less
catholic in its acceptance. Gentility was no empty concept. The
right to bear arms was guarded by the College of Heralds and
still meant something, though doubtless pedigrees could be manufactured at a price. Nor was the designation 'gentleman' one of
empty form accorded to any male as a common courtesy by an
equalitarian age. On many an eighteenth-century tomb the word
'gentleman' was inscribed to denote the place which the deceased
had filled in the world he had now left. One of the first questions
that must be asked when attempting to define the term 'Middle
Classes' as used in Hanoverian England is whether the gentry are
to be included or whether they are to be regarded as a separate
layer in the social strata. Certainly the line between them was, in
individual cases, often blurred, for eighteenth-century society,
though less fluid than our own, was far from static. The majority

no doubt lived and died in that station in which they had been born, but the number of those who, in the course of their lives, passed up or down the social ladder was not negligible.

In this connexion the professional class was important. Since the sixteenth century, and even more noticeably in the seventeenth, it had been growing in both numbers and status and now constituted a kind of hyphen between the gentry and those men whose money had been made in industry and trade. There was nothing derogatory in a gentleman following one of the professions. Members of the Inns of Court, of the higher ranks of medicine, of the clergy, officers of both services, were often younger sons who had to make their way in the world. But though the gentry, and even cadets of noble houses might be prominent among the more successful professional men, they had no monopoly. Education, ability, luck could all advance the man of humble birth. To the social aspirant the professions were what Holy Orders had been in the Middle Ages, the ladder by which a poor boy could attain to wider opportunities and responsibilities if his inclinations and abilities led that way.

A lawyer might well be a scion of a noble house, prominent in society and politics, and earning a large income at the Bar. He might equally well be a small-town attorney, consulted in the capacity of their man of business by the local gentry, but most definitely not counted as one of themselves. In such cases the distinction was clear. The first man belonged to the ruling class, the second to the middle. But the pushing young attorney from the country town by adroit handling of a patron, by ability and lucky investment, might come to be accepted in the society of his betters, and by his death have passed into a stratum socially superior to his own. Though Thomas Parker's origin was not so undistinguished as Hutton implied in his *History of Derby*, since his mother was a co-heiress of Robert Venables of Wincham, Cheshire, his father was only an attorney. Yet he, by the practice of the Law, was raised to the peerage as Viscount Parker of Ewelme in 1716 and became Earl of Macclesfield in 1721. The army, the navy, the Church, all afforded similar opportunities which make it difficult to say where the line between the two classes should be drawn.

The practice of medicine made the same distinction between

the physician and the apothecary. The rights of the former were rigorously safeguarded by the Royal College of Physicians, founded by Henry VIII. Only graduates of Oxford, Cambridge or Trinity College, Dublin, were elected as fellows, the assumption being that a physician must have had a liberal education as a foundation for his medical studies. This meant that only a man who had received the customary education of a gentleman was deemed fit to be a physician. In so far as their fees were high and their services chiefly in request by patients of ample means, there was some justification for thinking that the dignity of the profession could be fittingly upheld only by persons whose birth and breeding protected them from being treated as superior tradesmen.

Because of the paucity of their numbers, which meant that they were mainly to be found only in London and the bigger towns, and because, too, of the size of their fees, their services were often beyond the reach of all but the well-to-do. In many cases this may not have been a serious deprivation, for the medical expertness of the fellows of the Royal College of Physicians was not always as high as their social standing. In the eighteenth century the leading medical schools were to be found in Edinburgh and Leyden. It was to these universities that the Quakers and other non-Anglicans, shut out from the English universities by the Test Act, went, and it was here that some of the leading figures in the world of medicine studied. Yet the most that the College of Physicians would concede, despite the continual struggles of those who were excluded, was to confer a licence to practice in London on those men who had qualified themselves for a medical career in other ways. In medicine as in the Law the line was decisively drawn. Though there were some personal exceptions in the case of celebrated practitioners, the fellow of the Royal College of Physicians was a gentleman, the licenciate occupied an intermediate position and the apothecary was regarded as a mere tradesman.

If it is not easy to place the members of the professions in their correct grouping the merchants, too, present difficulties of their own. Here the decisive factor is largely economic. If a merchant of humble origin prospers and buys an estate where does he belong? Is he now a landed gentleman? Has his purchase removed him from the ranks of the middle class merchant? This was something of a problem even in the sixteenth century. Cecil, jotting down notes, as was his wont, for a conservative reconstruction of society, recognized that degrees of wealth must also command degrees of social respect. Though the scheme never materialized he was contemplating putting a statutory limitation on the amount of land a merchant might buy. 'No merchant', he wrote, 'to purchase above £50 a year of inheritance, except aldermen and sheriffs of London who', he added significantly, 'because they approach to the degree of knighthood, may purchase to the value of £200'.[1] By the eighteenth century substantial success as a merchant was attended by social promotion. Defoe wrote satirically of:

> Innumerable City-Knights we know,
> From Blewecoat-Hospital and Bridwell flow.
> Draymen and Porters fill the City Chair;
> And Footboys Magisterial Purple wear.
> Fate has but very little Distinction set
> Betwixt the Counter and the Coronet.[2]

The distinction was somewhat wider than Defoe implies, and the origins of most merchants more respectable. Often, like the Braunts or the Pinneys, they came of yeoman stock, and the journey to gentility had taken more than one generation. William Braunt's father had come from Devon to be apprenticed in London. He was a member of the Vintners' Company and a citizen before he bought a country estate near Upminster, where he died. William in his turn having been both a director of the East India Company and one of the managers of the Sun Fire Office, also retired to a country estate in Essex.[3] It was a common occurrence, and the Home Counties were dotted with the small estates of merchants where their families could live in the cleaner air of the country, taking the advice of John Armstrong, who, as both doctor and poet wrote,

> Ye who amid the feverish world would wear
> A body free of pain, of cares a mind,
> Fly the rank city, shun its turbid air,
> Breathe not the chaos of eternal smoke

---

[1] R. H. Tawney and E. E. Power: *Tudor Economic Documents* (1924), Vol. I, p. 326.
[2] *The Collections of the Writings of the Author of the True Born Englishman* (1705), p. 19.
[3] L. Sutherland: *A London Merchant, 1695–1774* (1933), *passim*.

And volatile corruption, from the dead,
The Dying, Sic'ning, and the living world
Exhal'd, to sully Heavens transparent dome
With dim mortality.[1]

and themselves helping to establish the tradition of the English week-end.

Nor was the social progress of the successful merchant a phenomenon of London and the Home Counties alone. The Pinneys, also of Devon stock, became, through the personal misfortunes and enterprise of Azariah Pinney, the owners of a West Indian fortune, and it is interesting to notice how, in each generation the urge to return to England and acquire property manifested itself. In 1778 John Pinney wrote, 'my greatest pride is to be considered as a private country gentleman, therefore I am resolved to content myself with a little and shall avoid even the name of a West Indian'.[2] As 'this little' eventually consisted of a commodious house in Bristol, an estate at Somerton Erleigh, and some £70,000 lent out on mortgage, he may be considered to have obtained his modest ambition. In the North-east of England the same process was taking place. Here Newcastle merchants and businessmen who had made money in coal were busy buying estates. By the end of the century only a handful of the older gentry survived, their place had been taken by men who did not owe their fortunes to the land, so that it could be said: 'In the North the rent-roll is not the true index of economic power. Thanks to coal, there was always a greater degree of fusion of landed and merchant interests in these parts than elsewhere'.[3]

Successful bankers, too, moved in good society, having above all men its golden key. Men like John Coutts went everywhere. It is true that he had some good blood among his ancestry: his people had been well-established merchants in Edinburgh, but Scottish blood was no passport to acceptance in England, and further, Coutts had committed the indiscretion of marrying the servant maid who had helped to bring up his brothers' children. Despite her origin, Mrs. Coutts was accepted everywhere; in

---

[1] J. Armstrong: *The Art of Preserving Health*, 2nd Edition (1745), p. 19.
[2] R. Pares: *A West India Fortune* (1950), p. 141.
[3] E. Hughes: *North Country Life in the Eighteenth Century* (1952), p. xix.

Paris the British ambassador graced her receptions, as did Prince Henry of Prussia, and all Coutts's daughters married well. He was admittedly a man of outstanding reputation and of great financial power. The aristocracy needed his loans too badly to affront him: social barriers were not built to exclude men of his calibre. The small banker in a growing town was in a different position. In Liverpool the earliest seem to have been linen drapers. In the Directory of 1774 William Clarke was described as 'banker and linen draper', but by 1781 he had concentrated on banking, had bought land at Everton and built a large house on it.[1] William Roscoe, later to be so active in Liverpool's economic and cultural life, had been apprenticed to an attorney and came into banking as a result of his services being called in when the affairs of Wm. Clarke and Co. were in difficulties; but he, too, was connected with linen in that he married a linen-draper's daughter. He, also, by 1793 was buying land and had started to build.

Instances such as these illustrate how fluid English society was. All that can really be said is that the distinction between the gentry and the middle class was not one wholly of birth, nor of wealth nor of manners and deportment, but a mixture of them all. No hard-and-fast line can be drawn. Foreign observers found the position confusing; they were conscious that there was a distinction between the gentleman and the rest and that the English were well aware of it. Yet they were puzzled by the fact that so many ways of earning a living were open to, and followed by, both the gentleman and the non-gentleman and that both were equally concerned with the pursuit of wealth. As Grosley commented,

> The Gentry do not consider themselves as beings that have nothing in common with the good men. They look upon the wealth that has raised them to that distinction, as the only means of supporting it: through gratitude as well as necessity, they continue to act as merchants, husbandmen, insurers, lawyers, physicians, etc., and in bringing up their children to these professions. In their opinion, rich and industrious gentlemen are as important and respectable, as those who loiter away their time in sloth and indigence.[2]

[1] J. Hughes: *Liverpool Banks and Bankers* (1906), pp. 56, 60.
[2] P. J. Grosley: *Op. cit.*, p. 270.

Nevertheless, the barrier was there, and the historian is forced to ask how much wealth must a man of humble birth acquire, what standard of social behaviour must he reach before he ranked among the gentry? Or to what depths of poverty and economic impotence must a gentleman-born sink before forfeiting his social status? It is this fluidity which makes eighteenth-century English society so difficult to analyse, since both individuals and families were endlessly changing their position on the social ladder, and since the criteria both of wealth and of gentility must be used to measure it. To contemporaries the problem was less perplexing. Either one was 'in society' or one was not, and the social climber was well aware of the invisible line to be crossed. In doubtful cases the deciding factors were more likely to be religious or cultural than purely economic.

Jane Austen's novels bring out very clearly the nuances of those ranges of society where these mingle and overlap. When it came to a question of matrimony it was clearly a matter of importance which side of the social fence the persons concerned found themselves. Indeed, much of the plot of *Pride and Prejudice* turns on this very point. Elizabeth Bennet counted herself as a gentleman's daughter but her mother's people fell into a more dubious category. One aunt was married to a local attorney, while her uncle, Mr. Gardiner, described as a 'gentlemanlike man', was engaged in some line of business in the City. In consequence the Gardiners lived in a quarter of London too unfashionable for it to be probable that the Bingleys would meet them accidentally. And though Elizabeth's affection and respect for her uncle and aunt were undoubted she was obviously conscious that in the eyes of Mr. Darcy they would not rank as gentlefolk, and therefore noted, with some considerable satisfaction, his surprise that persons so courteous and well-bred in their bearing could derive their livelihood from trade.

It is because the subtle nuances of class are so unconsciously indicated that novels like *Pride and Prejudice* illuminate the social structure of their age. The England of which Jane Austen wrote was even less touched by the shadow of the Industrial Revolution than it was by the Napoleonic Wars, and mirrored the peaceful backwater of small town and countryside. Here is the representative of the old landed gentry in the person of Mr. Darcy, conscious at once of his social obligations and his own position; here, too, are the Bingleys, more conscious of the fact that their father had been a member of a respectable family in the north of England than that his fortune had been made in trade, and anxious, by the purchase of an estate, to establish definitely their own social position. Here, too, is Sir William Lucas, who, having made his money in business, was so overwhelmed by the honour of his knighthood, bestowed as a reward for a loyal address presented to the King during his mayoralty, that he carefully devoted the rest of his life to being a gentleman! All these people met one another socially, they attended the same public assemblies, dined at one another's houses, wore similar clothes, and yet the social distinctions remained, and remembering them the fissure between the gentleman and the man of equal, perhaps even superior, wealth who could make no such claim, still remains as something that the historian must recognize also.

If the gentry, whether landed or not, are excluded, the problem of defining the middle classes is made easier, though difficulties still remain because the term is apt to retain a slightly urban tinge, and to suggest a lack of ancient roots. Where, for instance, should the yeoman be placed? Neither in his own, nor in anybody else's eyes did he rank as a gentleman, nor in most cases did he wish to be so counted. He had his own place in society and was proud of it. Here, perhaps, the eighteenth century nomenclature, 'the middling sort' is more accurate than the modern term, since among 'the middling sort' a place can be found for yeoman and townsman alike, provided they were neither gentle by birth nor yet dependent only upon their manual skill for their livelihood. In the rural areas the prosperous yeoman, the substantial miller, the enterprising clothier, the successful innkeeper, might well be counted among their number, but their greatest strength was probably, even at the opening of the eighteenth century, to be found in the towns. They could not yet have been described, as Brougham was to describe them in 1831, as comprising 'the wealth and intelligence of the country, the glory of the British name'.[1] Their power came not from following professions that might in favourable instances be considered as not derogatory

[1] R. Lewis and A. Maude: *The Middle Class* (1952), p. 16.

to a gentleman, but from their solid control of the growing internal economic life of the country. While the great merchant capitalist concentrated on foreign markets and on the fortunes to be made in overseas trade, they devoted their attention to internal trade, to the increasing scope to be found in applying new methods to industry, and to the business of distributing and retailing the new flow of goods to a growing population.

To assess the social weight of a class made up of such heterogeneous elements is not easy. The basis of its power was economic, and this had not yet been transmuted into other forms. In shaping the organization of production and the flow of the internal distribution of goods it was very powerful. Socially its influence was still restricted. Probably the gulf between the industrial wing of the middle class and the mass of the gentry was further increased by religious differences. Many of the leading figures in the new world of industry were Quakers. Some were Methodists, though Wesley's main appeal had been to the labouring poor rather than to their employers, others were Baptists or Presbyterians. Though Dissent was no longer illegal, it was far from being socially acceptable. Moreover, it carried with it certain practical disadvantages. These two factors combined to produce a steady drift of the ambitious to the Established Church. As Voltaire wrote: 'This reason (which carries mathematical evidence with it) has converted such numbers of dissenters of all persuasions, that not a twentieth part of the nation is out of the pale of the establish'd church'.[1] Those who remained outside were apt to be persons of little economic importance or people who put their conscience before their social ambitions.

To accept the badge of the Dissenter was a severe test of character in a world where its social inferiority was recognized. Elizabeth Fry had a long struggle between her inclinations, her temperament and her conscience before she could bring herself to be a 'plain Quaker'. Among the more prosperous of the Friends their religious peculiarities had become much blurred as they moved into the social orbit of their economic equals: to become a 'plain Quaker' was to nail one's colours to the mast. It involved wearing the Quaker dress, using the Quaker speech and giving

[1] Voltaire: *Letters Concerning the English Nation* (1733), p. 35.

up dancing, music, cards and theatres. As she wrote in her Journal:

> If I could make a rule never to give way to vanity, excitement or flirting, I do not think I should object to dancing, but it always leads me into some one of these faults; indeed I never remember dancing without feeling one, if not a little of all these, and sometimes a great deal.[1]

After much thought she concluded:

> I still continue in belief that I shall turn plain. . . . I find it almost impossible to keep up to the principles of the Friends without altering my dress and speech. . . . They appear to me a sort of protector to the principles of Christianity in the present state of the world.[2]

It was a conflict which many well-to-do Quakers had to face, and by the end of the century those Friends most eminent in the business and financial world were more and more marrying out of the Society and adopting the manners of the world around them. William Savery's account of the Hoares' establishment at Hampstead Heath describes the grounds and gardens as being 'in high stile much beyond the Symplicity of a frd', and his sons and daughters as 'quite in high life and gay in their Appearance', summing up his impressions with the words: 'Here seemed to be almost Everything this world Could wish and an open Reception for Frds; but more conformity to the Simplicity and ways of truth Would have made it still pleasanter to me'.[3] But though, later, snobbery and wealth were to bridge this gulf, as they had already bridged so many, when on the one side there was the desire to cross and on the other a welcome for the solid claims of wealth, by the middle of the century only a few uncertain planks had been thrown across, and the pattern of the social life of the majority of the middle class was still markedly different from that of the gentry.

Equally pronounced were the differences that marked off the middle class from the mass of the population. The picture implied in Gregory King's survey of late seventeenth-century England is a grim one. To him the greater proportion of people seemed to

---

[1] J. Whitney: *Elizabeth Fry* (1937), p. 77.
[2] *Ibid.*, p. 77.   [3] *Ibid.*, p. 62.

fall below the poverty line. They were 'the labouring poor' possessing no property and dependent on the minority for the right to work and, therefore, to eat. Like the middle class, however, they too were very far from being a homogeneous body. They fell into as many, if not more, subdivisions as the classes above them, and what is true of one section is very far from applying to another. Just as it is difficult to draw a clear line between the upper middle class and the gentry, so it is difficult to draw it between the lower ranks of the middle class and the most prosperous section of the class beneath them. In neither case is it a purely economic line. Many a prosperous artisan was quite as comfortably placed with regard to his financial resources as the clerk who regarded himself as socially his superior. Here the question was one rather of manners and social habits than of income. The position of the small but independent craftsman who manufactured the goods that he sold, often without the help of even one journeyman, was another marginal case. Perhaps the widest and most general description of this great class, for which no satisfactory label has been found, would be to say that they comprised all those who, without employing the labour of others, themselves worked with their hands, whether as skilled craftsmen or as simple labourers. Both their economic strength and their contribution to society as a class depended on their manual skill or physical strength.

Not all these people, either in town or country, were wage-earners in the sense that the nineteenth century would have used the term. Indeed, if domestic workers working at home for a putter-out are regarded as independent craftsmen rather than as wage-earners it is probable that the majority of them cannot be so described, though, due to the mesh of indebtedness in which such workers were usually entangled by their employers, such independence was largely illusory. Nor was it necessary for a man to fall definitely or exclusively into one category or the other. For instance, a great many labourers in husbandry were not employed regularly by the farmers for whom they worked. Many of them combined paid labour of this kind with either the cultivation of a scrap of land of their own or supplemented their earnings by a frugal use of the waste, in order to keep a little livestock, a few hens or geese, a pig, possibly a cow or a sheep or two of their own. Probably still more combined agricultural work, when it was to be had, with some by-employment, on which they worked on piece-rates in the home. On the other hand, particularly in the towns, the wage-earner, working on his employer's premises for a regular wage, was common enough by the middle of the century. It is clear, therefore, that the economic structure of the working class was far from uniform. Some of its members, both in town and country, were completely dependent on the wage paid to them by their employers, others were partly wage-earners and partly dependent on a smallholding, or the use of the waste, or on some form of domestic industry. Others again were, at least nominally, independent, though in reality very much under the control of the entrepreneur, who owned and gave out the materials on which they were working. Thus, alike in the country districts and in the towns, considerable variations were to be found.

Nowhere were these variations more marked than in London, which stood in a class by itself. The concentration of population there, its clustering industries and its problems of transport and feeding, meant that all types of employment were available. Within its confines were to be found a working population of almost infinite variety. Craftsmen of every type congregated there: the builders and joiners and kindred trades that were needed for the building and keeping in repair of its ever-increasing houses, the tailors working for every rank of society, from the Court with its elaborate dress to the humble requirements of the petty shopkeeper, were all to be found in London. Thus, whether they were required to supply the immediate and day-to-day wants of the people of London, or whether they were employed on the production of those commodities for which it acted as a centre of distribution, either abroad or to the Home Counties, the number of skilled labourers in and around the City and its fast-growing suburbs was considerable. In addition, employment of a less skilled kind was afforded by this concentration of people and of markets in the London area. The London porters alone made up a considerable army, while many of the subsidiary industries were making extensive demands for untrained labour to fetch and carry, to stoke furnaces and to perform the repetitive tasks of industries such as the making of bricks and the refining of sugar.

Below these again was the accumulation of casual labourers, the feckless, the unlucky, the drifters and the sickly ; men, women and children who picked up a precarious and often disreputable living from the multitudinous activities of a great town. Even by the reign of Elizabeth, writers were commenting on the magnet that London, with its hope of employment or of adventure and easy pickings, was exerting on the masterless men of England. Some of these, no doubt, prospered : many probably sank to the extremes of poverty.

Another activity which provided one more strand in the fabric of working-class London was the great growth of the retail trade. The shopkeeper had become a prominent figure even by the end of the sixteenth century, and within the ranks of this trade were to be found both men of substance and very small retailers. Though the prosperous shopman, whose premises were well situated, may be regarded as belonging to the middle class, and provided an increasingly important element in that group, in the poorer parts of the town dingy shops handling an odd assortment of wares, doubtful pie-shops and cook-shops, catering for the poor, sprang up rapidly. This gave employment not profitable enough to raise their owners to the ranks of the middle class, but sufficient to add the small shopkeeper as yet another class to the varied pattern of working London. Below these small shop-keepers must be classed the hawkers who paraded the streets of London crying their wares and providing for the needs of many of her poorer citizens, and whose 'cries' in retrospect provided so picturesque an element in her street life, and in practice added so much to its clamour.

Though London emphasized the variety to be found in the social structure of the urban working class, and though no other town could rival it in this respect, big ports like Bristol which had attracted subsidiary industries and were engaged in the double business of both supplying the needs of their hinterlands and ex-ploiting their resources had something of the same richness of structure. Most towns were less diverse. The proximity of a market and the type of that market dictated both the variety of work that was available and the local wage level. Clearly specializa-tion depended on the degree of industrialization that was possible. In the small market town, the centre of a rural area, the small shopkeeper, the craftsman who met local needs, provided the upper ranks of the working population, while the unskilled labourer and the porter, though to be found in a less proportion than in the bigger towns and ports where building was in progress and cargoes had to be handled, made up the lower.

Even the smaller towns which catered chiefly for local demand offered a fair choice of occupation to the craftsman. In Bedfordshire, a predominantly agricultural county, the indentures of apprenticeships in the first decades of the eighteenth century are surprisingly varied. They included apothecaries, bakers, bankers, barber-surgeons, blacksmiths, bricklayers, carpenters, chandlers, clockmakers, clothiers, collar-makers, coopers, cordwainers, curriers, cutlers, farriers, fell-mongers, gardeners, gingerbread makers, glaziers, glovers, grocers, hair-buyers, hatters, hempdressers, inn-holders, jersey combers, joiners, lace makers, linen drapers, locksmiths, maltsters, mantua makers, masons, mercers, merchant tailors, painters, stainers, peruke makers, pipe makers, saddlers, shoemakers, stone-cutters, tailors, tallow chandlers, tanners, tilers, victuallers, weavers, wheelwrights, whitesmiths, wool combers, wool staplers, wool winders, and woollen drapers.[1] To enter some of these occupations a premium of between £40 and £50 was required, and they had to be considered as middle class avocations, but many of them were open to the sons and daughters of the craftsman and artisan. We find a blacksmith giving £8 with his son when he apprenticed him to a glover, or a husbandman giving £7 10*s. od.* to place his son with a shoemaker. Nor must the very considerable demand for domestic servants be forgotten. In London, in the provincial towns and throughout the rural areas there were, as one saucy maid told Defoe, more places than parish churches, and a large number of the working class, both men and women, were absorbed in this way. Those employed in respectable families were drawn from the families of craftsmen, of artisans and of husbandmen, others, maids-of-all-work and drudges, came from the ranks of the labourers and the very poor. It is a fairly reasonable assumption that the great mass of female apprentices, where the name but no other details of the mistress are given, were in actual fact placed

---

[1] Mrs. Hilary Jenkinson: 'A List of Bedfordshire Apprentices, 1711-20'. *Bedford Historical Record Society*, Vol. IX.

The Attorney, 1799

The Steward, 1799

Harvest Home, 1813

The Cottage Girl, 1807

A Farmer and his Wife, 1787

out to domestic service under colour of being bound out as apprentices: indeed, 'apprenticed to housewifery' was a common term.

No description of eighteenth-century social structure would be complete without some reference to the casual poor and the pauper. They were a section of the population of which contemporary opinion was most certainly very conscious and more than a little resentful. Defoe declared roundly that in his day no man need be poor merely for want of wages, and that what was wanted was to see that the poor worked rather than to give them alms. Yet the existence of a poor rate in every parish, and of workhouses and poorhouses in many, was testimony enough to the fact that there was a class of the poor and destitute below that of the unskilled labourer. In the absence of statistics it is difficult to say how numerous it was, but at least it was large enough to produce exasperation and alarm. Its composition is rather clearer than its numbers. Many of the rural poor, whether employed as agricultural labourers or scratching a bare living from the waste plus a little by-employment, were never far from the poverty line. Sickness, or even too large a family of small children, or the inevitable feebleness of old age, was each sufficient to push an individual or a whole family over it and into the pauper class. Many, indeed, of the rural workers belonged to it intermittently all through their working life. In town and country alike single women without a skilled trade were often depressed into the ranks of paupers, since as a spinner, or in other poorly paid trades, it was only possible by the most unremitting toil to earn a bare subsistence. Even more helpless were the orphan or deserted children, the victims of both a high death-rate which made the number of parentless children surprisingly large, and of an economic and social instability that made desertion a surprisingly common practice. Since for most poorly paid workers there was neither the opportunity nor the tradition of saving for old age, they, too, when past employment, had no resource except the parish. This was true of sickness as well as of old age.

Not all paupers came into the category of hard cases. What eighteenth-century opinion was chiefly concerned with was the 'undeserving poor'. Doubtless, here, the contemporary writer was over-lavish with this term of abuse. Many of those described

6

as work-shy or improvident were often persons of less than normal ability or dexterity or strength, the unemployables or only partially employable of any society, of whom that of the eighteenth century had its full share. Yet, even so, it seems evident that the vagrants that swarmed on the roads and the beggars that haunted the London streets, the world of prostitutes and pimps, of thieves and fences, that Gay has portrayed in *The Beggar's Opera*, between them provided a muddy squalid sediment that comprised the dregs of eighteenth-century society, and that cannot be omitted from any attempt to describe its structure. Into its depths the bankrupt aristocrat, the broken tradesman, the drunken artisan, the poverty-driven labourer, could all sink and be sucked down.

Such was the structure of eighteenth-century society before the developments of that era of technical inventions known as the Industrial Revolution had been sufficiently pronounced to modify and change it. Outwardly at least the position of the great landowners and the landed interest generally was still dominant, though a careful examination reveals how strong was the influence of the merchants and financiers in shaping both domestic and foreign policy. On the surface, though the aggregate of industrial capital was already large, the political and social power of the manufacturers, in the early nineteenth century sense of the term, was extremely limited. Individual groups might press for special and favouring legislation, but in public affairs as a whole, where wider issues were involved, the industrialist had little voice. Nor had the concentration of industry as yet urbanized and solidified the interests of the labouring poor. The mob in London might on occasions make its views unpleasantly clear to the politicians of the day when they appeared in public, while in the provinces shortage of corn or of other commodities essential to the poor family might cause a sudden riot, but organized labour as a whole had no voice, nor did it, indeed, even exist, though here and there little bodies of craftsmen, like the journeyman tailors of London, might organize to fight for better wages or shorter hours, only to be quelled by special parliamentary legislation directed against this embryonic shape of things to come. Between the middle of the century and the end of the Napoleonic Wars significant changes were to take place under the twin pressure of war and increasing industrialization. Until then the old dominance of landowner and merchant continued, and, since they were still paying the piper by their contributions to the national revenue in the form of the land tax and customs dues, they were still, to a very large extent, calling the social and political tunes that were best suited to the measures they proposed to tread.

Chapter Three

CONSTITUTIONAL ARRANGEMENTS

ENGLISH constitutional arrangements mirrored very accurately the structure of eighteenth-century society. Like it, they too were based on the unquestioned assumptions of a class system in which the most effective power lay in the hands of the landowner and the merchant. Control over the central government and, therefore, over the broad outlines of policy, both domestic and foreign, was, for all practical purposes, confined to these two sets of men, though in local affairs, and more particularly in that local business which was considered to be tedious and burdensome, there was some place for the middle class. For the rest, to be propertyless was to be without political rights.

At the time when the central government had evolved, the power of the landed classes was not merely dominant, it could better be described as monopolistic. All political power as a consequence was by tradition dependent on the possession of land. As Defoe wrote, ''Tis in the power of the Gentry of England to reform the whole Kingdom without either Laws Proclamations or Informers; and without their Concurrence, all the Laws Proclamations and Declarations in the world will have no Effect; the Vigour of the Laws consists in their Executive Power'.[1] Between them the Crown and the landowners controlled all aspects of government, local and central. It is true that over the centuries the balance between these elements altered, as first the Crown, by building up a class of professional administrators, filched power from the feudal lords, and as in turn the new landed families of the sixteenth and seventeenth centuries shook themselves free from the bureaucratic control of the prerogative courts and seized the initiative in the Houses of Parliament.

[1] D. Defoe: *The Poor Man's Plea Concerning the Reformation of Manners* (1703), p. 129.

But whether Crown or the aristocracy and gentry predominated, land and the power to exploit it remained the basis of political authority.

This is strikingly illustrated by the changing role of parliament. In the later Middle Ages it had been used primarily as an instrument in the struggle for political control, fought out so bitterly by the two great cliques of noble houses of Lancaster and York over the almost prostrate body of the Crown. The victory of the Tudors transferred to them the control of this instrument. Parliament, and particularly the House of Commons, became a weapon in their hands to use against the rival authority of the Church. By the reign of Elizabeth profound changes in its temper and its point of view had already begun. It was coming more and more to represent the interests of the new Tudor gentry and aristocracy. In the main, during the sixteenth century, the interests of this class, as opposed to the old feudal nobility with its fondness for the economic and legal arrangements of the past, and those of the Crown remained closely linked: the conflict between them, though potentially important, remained inarticulate. Even so, 'The House of Commons reached maturity in Elizabeth's reign. The instrument was tempered with which the Crown was to be resisted and conquered'.[1] By the time the unlucky Stuarts had succeeded to the throne the situation was changing rapidly and the new gentry were increasingly ready to challenge the control that the Crown exercised in particular through the prerogative courts. They especially resented the various restrictions, some of them due to the legal provisions of feudalism, and some of them due to the official policy of preventing enclosure for pasture and so of maintaining the peasantry in their traditional place in society, which combined to prevent them from making the most profitable use of their estates.

By 1660 it appeared that the gentry had won an almost complete victory. The prerogative courts had gone and were not restored, the old feudal tenures were abolished, and the dependence of the King upon parliament made him much less able to pursue a policy against their wishes. Beneath the surface, however, the position was not, from the point of view of the landed classes, so satisfactory. The King still had dangerous resources as

[1] J. E. Neale: *The Elizabethan House of Commons* (1948), p. 320.

Charles II showed when, repudiating Danby's policy of co-operation with the Church of England and the country gentry, he was able to maintain the succession of the Duke of York, against all the manufactured fury of the Popish Plot, to contrive the political ruin of his opponents, and, for the last four years of his life, to dispense with parliament altogether. Clearly the victory of 1660 had been incomplete and the danger of a counter-attack by James II, aided by the autocratic power of Louis XIV, was very real. Such a victory might once again have placed the landed families in the bureaucratic leading strings of the Crown, and this was not to be endured. The events of 1688, though they led to the overthrow of James II and the substitution of William and Mary, were not so much revolutionary as a determined and concerted operation on the part of the great landed houses to make secure the political control which they had already seized. In this they were successful, and parliament became primarily the instrument through which the landed proprietors expressed and exercised their political power.

The earlier composition of the parliament made this easy. Since the Reformation the ecclesiastical element had been confined to the bishops, appointed, it is true, by the Crown, but drawn very largely from the aristocratic and gentle families of the realm. Moreover, the Church had always been a great landowner, and, when so much of their income came from the estates of their bishoprics, the bishops, as a whole, could hardly be distinguished from the propertied aristocracy amongst whom they sat. The peers owed, as they had always owed, their position to their close connexion with the land, and, therefore, in the House of Lords there was no conflicting interest represented to challenge the monopolistic claims of the landlord. In the House of Commons, too, land was the basis of power. Since 1430 the county franchise had been confined to the forty-shilling holder, but the borough franchise, as is well known, was wider and more varied. Even so, in most boroughs it was connected in some way with the possession of property. Sometimes it was attached to certain tenements, sometimes to those burgesses who paid scot and lot, and who, therefore, were responsible for the financial stability of the town, sometimes it was confined to the members of the corporation. Only in a few cases was the right to vote conferred on all the householders who had a hearth on which to boil their pot, the so-called 'potwalloper' franchise.

Few of these franchises could be described as democratic and most of them were very limited indeed. In the parliament of 1761, analysed by Professor Namier, only twenty-two of the boroughs had an electorate of over a thousand, another twenty-two varied between five hundred and a thousand, while a further eleven had about five hundred. The electorate in many of the boroughs, described significantly enough as 'close' or 'rotten' or 'pocket', was smaller still. None in Cornwall had more than a couple of hundred; of thirty in Surrey and Sussex only two had more. In Wiltshire, there were none with more than three hundred voters; five of the eight Cinque Ports had less than forty.[1] It must be remembered that at this time the majority of towns were still small, but even so the disproportion between those burgesses who possessed the right to vote and the general population, which did not, was very striking. Though there were individual exceptions, due to local idiosyncracies, the franchise to all real intent was confined to the propertied class, who might be expected to return a House of Commons that would interpret the national wellbeing in terms of land. To make their victory doubly sure, however, the parliament of Anne's reign laid down the provision that no man should be eligible for election as a county member unless he were in possession of property valued at £300 per annum; for the boroughs the qualification was £200. Thus electors and elected were both drawn only from those who possessed a stake in the country. Land was the sole legal basis of political power. It is true that these provisions were not always observed with much strictness. Promising candidates were put up for election possessing far less than the statutory requirement of land, the letter of the law being covered by fictitious bargains and conveyances. Nevertheless, it is reasonable to suppose that such candidates, supported as they usually were by aristocratic patrons, were hardly likely to attack the landed interest or to attempt to alter the structure of society.

During the sixteenth century, the power of the Crown to control parliament had been considerable. In the Lords the bishops were royal nominees, chosen for their political reliability even

[1] L. B. Namier: *The Structure of Politics at the Accession of George III* (1929), Vol. I, pp. 100–2.

more than for their spiritual pre-eminence. The peers were men who either looked to the Crown for protection in a changing world or who owed to the Crown their advancement, and were inspired by a lively sense of favours to come. Over the Commons the royal power, though often indirect and exercised by the Speaker and by the Privy Councillors in the House, 'those near the Chair', was considerable. True, the Crown rarely interfered directly and by the method of direct command in the selection of members, but its wishes were frequently made known and only infrequently disregarded. By the eighteenth century the position had changed completely. Not only had the Crown lost its power to interfere in elections but it had become increasingly dependent on the support of a majority in the Commons to carry on its business. The direct means by which it could create this support was very limited. In the parliament of 1761 the government had only thirty-two seats more or less under its control, together with three not very reliable ones that had been pawned to it by Thomas Pitt.[1] Consequently, the real method of creating a parliamentary majority was by a series of bargains with the landed families who controlled the nomination of candidates. The real struggle took place not over election, but over nomination. Once this had been secured it was quite usual, particularly in the counties, for the nominated candidate to be returned unopposed.

In the counties a kind of gentleman's agreement dictated the distribution of influence. Here, generally, the Government had no direct pull, for, even in a county like Hampshire, Portsmouth and the Gosport Docks could be used to influence only some one-tenth of the electorate.[2] The real choice lay, therefore, with the landed proprietors of the county. In the South-west and the West, consequently, the matter was usually settled in accordance with the wishes of the county families. In the North and in the East the aristocratic houses played a greater part, but even so they confined their activities to the choice of one of the members, the other, by mutual arrangement, being left to the informal caucus of the leading gentry. Thus, for the most part, the county members were the representatives of the country gentry. This was reflected

---

[1] L. B. Namier: *The Structure of Politics at the Accession of George III* (1929), Vol. I, p. 174.

[2] *Ibid.*, Vol. I, pp. 85–92.

in the returns of 1761, where out of eighty members returned, only sixteen were the sons of peers, while sixty-two of them represented the leading county families.

Many of the boroughs, with their restricted franchise, offered even greater opportunities for political manipulation. In those few where the franchise was in any sense popular, elections were, as a rule, keenly fought. At a time when the use of bribery was very inadequately restricted, and when many devices of doubtful probity but of financial profit to the electors were the order of the day, an election undoubtedly brought money to the borough. It brought also the excitement of a fight and the thrill of a show; free beer and free speeches were not to be despised in breaking up the drabness of routine life. In consequence, contests were encouraged and most lustily fought. The result, however, was generally to add yet another landowner to the House of Commons. Despite the obvious advantage of the merchant or financier, who might have been expected to understand and represent the interests of the bigger towns, voters apparently preferred a local lord or a notable figure in public life. For example, Westminster in 1761 returned Lord Pulteney and General Cornwallis. Of the twenty-two boroughs with an electorate of between a thousand and five hundred none could be classed as close or pocket boroughs, though many of them were under the influence of the local nobility and gentry. Of the two members returned by Yarmouth between 1722 and 1784 one was always a Townshend and one a Walpole. From 1754 the members returned by Bedford were chosen as a result of an arrangement by which the Duke nominated the one and the Corporation the other.[1]

Boroughs with a smaller electorate rarely went to the polls; of the eleven with about five hundred voters only three did so in 1754 and none in 1761. The real choice centred round the right to nominate. Small constituencies were still more under the influence of their local patron. The ownership of even a comparatively safe pocket borough was, even so, no sinecure. In most cases the nursing was expensive and could be tricky. Parliamentary patronage was valuable and to neglect to keep up your influence was to risk someone else poaching and undermining your position. Consequently, it was not usual for a man or a family to

[1] *Ibid.*, pp. 129, 128, 151, 181.

control many seats. In 1761 fifty-one peers between them had either the right to nominate, or the controlling influence over, one hundred and one seats, but of these only the Duke of Newcastle, who was considered a notorious borough-monger, controlled as many as seven. Again, although fifty-five commoners between them nominated to or controlled ninety-one seats, only five had influence in more than one borough. Such an analysis shows how very great was the influence exercised by the landed class over the choice of representatives to send to Westminster.

That the landed proprietors had so great an influence over the choice of members did not, however, mean that only landowners, in any but the technical sense required by the qualifying acts, were returned. Borough owners who belonged to great families with political traditions to maintain were always on the look-out for likely protégés. Many a great parliamentarian of the eighteenth century owed his start as a young man to the patronage of some borough-monger. Without this device Burke might never have been elected, nor Sheridan, nor Canning. It was a system that had at least the advantage of recruiting for the service of the House young men of promise. Even so its benefits were almost inevitably limited to young men of gentle birth for, except in a few cases, they alone had the necessary social contacts to bring themselves to the notice of the patron with parliamentary influence.[1] A few literary men like Burke and Sheridan overcame this obstacle, but for most it was an insurmountable one to political life. Land and family connexions were not, however, the only avenue to political life for the wealthy. There were always some boroughs to be bought at a price that ranged from £1,500 to £2,000, though it has been calculated that even to sell at these figures did not repay the trouble and expense of nursing them.

Such seats might be bought by the social climber, anxious to give political respectability to a fortune made in trade. Occasionally they might be purchased by a so-called 'Nabob' whose money had been made in India by means they were not eager to reveal, and for whom the cloak of parliamentary privilege might be

---

[1] *Vide* Professor Pares's comment on the Whig Opposition: 'Though it opened its doors to such talent as might be necessary, it was an aristocratic clique; nobody without a profound respect for birth could have thought Portland or Rockingham fit for the Treasury'. *George III and the Politicians*, p. 59.

extremely useful. Many men, too, by means that fell short of actual purchase, managed to get themselves nominated for a seat. Boroughs where the freemen or the corporation were in control of the franchise often preferred business men or merchants to represent them, since they were likely to further the economic interests of the town. Nor should it be forgotten that many of the new landed gentry were only camouflaged merchants, who had purchased estates while still drawing most of their income from and putting their real energies into trade.

For such men a seat in the House was doubly useful. To have an adequate body of merchants able to explain, defend and press their interests when national policy was being shaped was extremely useful. A parliament composed only of landowners would hardly have evolved the complicated system of the Navigation Acts or led the country into wars of expansion to secure markets and access to raw materials. Secondly, and in a more personal way, a seat in the House was often a very good investment. In this connexion it is surely significant that in 1761, of the fifty merchants and bankers who were returned, thirty-seven had extensive commercial or financial dealings with the government.[1] War contracts, always very profitable, went as a rule to those men who had parliamentary influence. The money to be paid in this way was limited only by the watchfulness of the genuine landed gentry, who argued that excessive expenditure would have to be paid for by an increase in the Land Tax. The active and practising landowners were also further diluted by those men who had sought a seat for the purpose of advancing their professional career. At a time when promotion in the Army and Navy went by political favour there were sixty-four army officers in the parliament of 1761, while all the prominent admirals, such as Boscawen, Hawke, Rodney, Keppel and Cornwallis, had secured seats. Ambitious lawyers, too, found that membership of the House was one of the soundest ways of securing business, reputation and advancement.

Thus, though the landowner was the basis of the parliamentary system, and though he had more influence than any other class in determining who should sit, the eighteenth-century House of Commons was diluted by merchants and financiers, by soldiers,

[1] L. B. Namier: *Op. cit.*, p. 61.

sailors and lawyers. Dr. Johnson by no means approved a too-wide recruitment of members, and doubtless had a considerable body of opinion behind him when he observed that 'the statutes against bribery were intended to prevent upstarts with money from getting into Parliament'. He then added the remark that 'if he were a gentleman of landed property, he would turn out all his tenants who did not vote for the candidate whom he supported'. When this drew from his listener the comment, 'Would not that, Sir, be checking the freedom of election?', Johnson replied stoutly, 'Sir, the law does not mean that the privilege of voting should be independent of old family interest; of the permanent property of the country'.[1] Yet this very fact, that it was a cross-section of the ruling classes made the Commons a very able chamber. Within the limits of its vision it was an intelligent, patriotic and often genuinely critical assembly. The parliamentary debates of the period reached a very high level of both oratory and good sense. Certainly it was very far from being a rubber-stamp assembly; the government always had to listen to the feeling of the House, and often had to yield to it. It could not, however, be described as a democratic body. Just as the property-owner dominated society, so he dominated the great institution of parliament. Public opinion had only the right to beat its unorganized waves against the Palace at Westminster.

The comparatively small number of persons who were able to control the composition of the House of Commons were also able to gain a disproportionate influence in both the direction of policy and the control of administration. The choice of ministers still lay nominally with the Crown and the personal likes and dislikes of the monarch could still play an important part in their selection. Indeed, it was all but impossible for a man to attain and keep high political office in the teeth of royal opposition, as Charles James Fox was to discover to his cost. Nevertheless, experience showed that it had been since 1688 increasingly hard for any ministry to maintain itself for long without a backing in the House of Commons. At a time when the party system was more full of sound and fury than of patient organization it was completely ineffective as a basis for organizing government majorities, since party

---

[1] J. Boswell: *The Life of Samuel Johnson, LL.D.* Edited by A. Glover, 1901. Vol. II, p. 127.

funds, the party ticket and party whips were alike non-existent. As Danby had realized, and as subsequent ministers found, majorities for government policy could most smoothly be created and maintained by an organized system of official corruption.

The great landowners were particularly well placed to take advantage of the government's need of organized support. Through it they were able to exercise influence not only in parliament, but in the control of the administration, in the Church and in the universities. Because the government rarely bought votes by the crude method of money bribes, and possessed comparatively few seats whose members it could nominate, it was forced to barter its right to fill offices, to appoint to church patronage, to grant army and navy contracts, in return for parliamentary support. To nurse a borough was an expensive business, and the right to nominate to a safe seat was a marketable commodity. The borough-monger, therefore, if he agreed that his nominee should support the ministerial policy in the House, expected some return on his outlay. This took the form of appointments for his friends and relations according to their several necessities, a deanery for one, a job in the Customs for another, a court sinecure for a third, a profitable contract for a fourth. Much of the most tricky political manœuvring of the period took the form of adjusting the competing claims of borough-mongers, all pressing the cause of their own clients. In this scramble for patronage there was no slur, rather, indeed, the reverse; not to obtain the favours for which you asked was regarded as a mark of being of little consequence, with the result that even men who had no real need, pecuniary or otherwise, to clamour for the largesse of the government, were forced to do so in order to keep up their political credit.

Such a system was bound to have wide repercussions. It meant that the administrative machine was often clogged and choked by unnecessary and unwise appointments. Sinecures could not be abolished since they were a necessary part of the system. Duplication, too, was almost unavoidable. In office after office one man received the title and the emoluments while a deputy appointed because he was cheap did the work. The profits of office in this way became almost the preserves of a narrow class while the administration of the country was handed over to men who had little incentive to build up a tradition of disinterested public

service. The influence of this system on the higher ranks of the
ministers of the Crown was equally strong if differently expressed.
Men had often to be appointed to great offices of state, not because of their ability to discharge them, but because of their connexions with the more prominent borough-mongers. The great
Duke of Newcastle was probably less a figure of fun than many
accounts would suggest, but the fact remains that his value to
Pitt lay in his ability to manage parliamentary patronage and to
organize support for the government, rather than in his grasp of
the more important questions of foreign policy and imperial expansion. Thus any eighteenth-century cabinet had to be constructed with a nice eye to this balance if it was to function successfully. If the borough-mongers gave, as undoubtedly the more
politically enlightened ones did, young men of promise to the
country, they also ensured the continuance of the system that
made men like Newcastle necessary in English public life.

Though the structure of parliament and the organization of
political life placed so much power in the hands of the landed
classes, the merchants, who had already attained a position of importance in the economic life of the country, and who, through
the purchase of estates, had penetrated into the ranks of the gentry,
had made a place for themselves also in the sphere of government. Compared with that of the landowners it was a modest
place: no merchant would have expected to hold high political
office. Despite this the advantages of a seat in the House were
considerable from the point of view of the individual, while the
existence of favourable parliamentary lobbies was invaluable to
the interests concerned. That merchants often had very serious
interests to defend against unconsidered, or ill-informed, official
action, the following episode, in itself of limited importance,
illustrates. Colonial indebtedness to British merchants was a constant source of friction and difficulty between the American colonies and the home government. In 1749 a Colonial Act, 'Concerning
Executions and for the Relief of Insolvent Debtors', declared that
executions for debt should be levied in current Virginian money
plus twenty-five per cent. to cover the differences in exchange
rates.   Apparently the Act had been confirmed by the King in
Council before the British merchants engaged in the Virginian
trade had quite realized what was happening. When they did they

pointed out in no uncertain terms that English mercantile interests had been most ungenerously handled, as for the last years the
gap between the Virginian currency and the English exchange
rates had been at least thirty-three per cent. and was likely to grow
to forty per cent. John Hanbury, a leading London merchant and
a member of the Ohio Company, presented a memorial to the
Board of Trade in November 1751 on behalf of the Merchant
Adventurers of Bristol. They were informed that nothing could
be done as, on the advice of the Lords Commissioners, the Act
had been confirmed. This answer caused considerable dissatisfaction and the pressure they were able to organize led by 1754 to the
Council sending formal instructions to the Governor to secure a
re-enactment of the law deleting the objectionable clause.[1]

The powerful interests of the City of London, with its ability
to float loans, was usually very well represented. Through the
recommendations of the nobility, who were often indebted to
him, or of the gentry with whom he had intermarried, the rich
and powerful London merchant frequently secured election. Probably his indirect influence was even greater than that conferred on
him by his vote, for his wealth enabled him to put pressure on the
government and helped him to create favourable lobbies within
the House. It was a commonplace of the politics of the eighteenth
century that the West Indian planters and the sugar interests, with
which they were connected, would fight tooth and nail, and generally successfully, for or against any project in which their profit
was involved. Another pressure group was composed of persons
representing the interests of the East India Company.[2] Several of
its directors were usually to be found among the M.P.'s, partly to
protect, speak for, and explain its policy, since the fact that
periodically the charter of the Company came up for parliamentary renewal made it particularly vulnerable to government pressure, and partly because, as prominent merchants, a seat in the
House was valuable as a method of securing government contracts. Apart from members who were directors, there were
others who held large blocks of East Indian stock and who

[1] L. H. Gipson: *The British Empire before the American Revolution* (1936-49),
Vol. VII, *passim*.
[2] For a full account of the interaction of the politics of the East India Company
with those of the nation, see L. S. Sutherland: *The East India Company in Eighteenth
Century Politics* (1952).

were, therefore, likely to be active in promoting the interests of the East India Company, should those in any way seem to be threatened.

Though not heavily represented in the House, the Company could muster a good deal of support outside, since the ramifications of its commercial and financial links with the City were considerable. The East India Shipping Interest with capital invested in the great ships that carried the traffic between this country and India, might with confidence be regarded as subsidiary allies. They brought in their train a host of ship-chandlers, warehousemen and shipbuilders. Factors at Blackwell Hall, who handled cloth that the Company exported, merchants who depended on its licences to export bullion and coral and bring back diamonds and other precious stones, bankers and brokers whose customer it was for the bullion needed to feed the Eastern trade, were all likely to be susceptible to its pressure if political support were required. Thus these widespread connexions, the directors' 'Household troops' as they were nicknamed, could all be mobilized either to bring pressure to bear on an obstinate government or to reward a complaisant one by helping to swing elections, both parliamentary and civic, in a direction favourable to the government of the day. Nor was this the only reward the Company was prepared to offer to a government sympathetic to its needs. As the century progressed the patronage that the Company could dispense grew with its growing territories, and to ministers of the Crown, ever on the lookout for lucrative offices with which to meet the claims that the borough owner made upon them, a director of the East India Company was worth cultivating, if only for this reason.

But important as the goodwill of such groups was, the real control of the central government lay with the landed interest. No government, whether it called itself Whig or Tory, dare openly disregard it, though it is true that the county members, who represented with great permanence and solidity the country gentry, were not always very quick to see the implications of a line of policy, so that frequently the more nimble-witted merchants ran rings round them. Essentially the outlook of the country member was limited, and his political education sketchy; in consequence when issues arose that concerned overseas markets

Old Palace Yard, Westminster, 1796

The Two Patriotic Duchesses on
their Canvass, 1784

A modern fine Gentleman bribing
the Electors of a Borough to make
him their Representative, 1780

Clerical Prosperity—or Riding with the Wind! 1807

Clerical Adversity—or Riding against the Wind! 1807

and involved changes in foreign policy, he frequently found himself out of his depth. Lord Pembroke writing to the Marquis of Carmarthen in 1780 on the desirability of increasing the number of county members felt it incumbent on him to add 'though I should be sorry that the House of Commons should consist only of County Members, because, vue le bois dont la plupart de ces Messieurs sont faits, I do not think business could go on at all without some other help'.[1] Comments such as this help to explain why, though landowners preferred peace, eighteenth-century England embarked on a series of wars that continually enlarged the sphere of her trade and brought great fortunes to her merchants. Circumstance and the stage of the economic development of Europe no doubt helped this expansion. It is probable that overseas possessions were the by-product rather than the planned objective of the merchants' activities. Even so, without their strenuous participation in the affairs of government it is hardly likely that a parliament of landowners would have furthered the colonization of America or founded a great economic bridgehead in India.

Sheridan, discussing with Boswell the haphazard character of English education, told him, 'My plan would be that young people should be perfectly qualified to be good citizens in the first place, and that there should be particular opportunities of instruction for every particular way of life. There is one rank for which there is no plan of education, and that is country gentleman. Surely, this is of great importance: that the landed interest should be well instructed.'[2] When Arthur Young was asked by the wool-growers of Suffolk to oppose a bill brought forward in 1788 to prohibit the export of wool, he recorded in his *Autobiography* that 'The opposition certainly would have been successful if Mr. Pitt had not found what so many ministers have experienced before—that the trading interest at large is a hundred times more active than the landed interest; for very few counties exerted themselves on this occasion'.[3] Nevertheless, instructed or not, when the county members did make a stand few ministers would dare a frontal attack. Throughout the period every ruling clique

---

[1] *Pembroke Papers, 1780–1794.* Edited by Lord Herbert (1950), p. 62.
[2] J. Boswell: *London Journal.* Edited by F. A. Pottle (1950), p. 153.
[3] A. Young: *Autobiography.* Edited by M. Betham-Edwards (1898), p. 166.

of ministers tried its utmost to keep the Land Tax down to a reasonable limit. In the same way bounties on the export of corn when home prices were low were designed to keep the country gentlemen happy and uncritical while the merchants were able to direct foreign policy into more adventurous channels.

Such was the system by which national policy was shaped and applied and national burdens apportioned. It was a system which had its roots in the traditions of the past and in a social soil in which the landowner was the predominant element. Though by the eighteenth century the influence of the mere landowner had been to a considerable degree modified by the more cosmopolitan interests of the merchant and the banker, yet even these men acknowledged the importance of land by buying as much of it as possible. It was not until the closing decades of the century that a few people began to challenge this age-old dominance by asking for a wider and more popular control of the affairs of the nation. But until it had been not only challenged but successfully challenged, the control of the great landowners and the merchants and financiers could hardly be shaken. While George III remained king the system of central government continued to mirror the basic structure of society, though by his death dimly apprehended changes in that society were beginning to foreshadow changes in political control. Nothing concrete, however, had been achieved except the few economical reforms of Burke and his friends.

In the sphere of local government the landowner still seemed without a possible rival in those areas where his interests were involved. The day-to-day administrative and judicial affairs of the boroughs were not a matter of any moment to him and could be left to middle-class men, but in rural England the real authority fell to him. Indeed, in some respects it would be true to say that the reward of the successful revolution of 1688 was to put the gentry in control of its own local affairs. This result was achieved by capturing the machinery of local government and adapting it to the needs of the country gentry. Previously the control of the Crown had been very real. The Tudors, in their determination to eliminate the rivalry and opposition of the great feudal nobles, had overhauled and modernized, in conformity with the new needs of society, the local government of the country. For this purpose they had concentrated upon two instruments of control, the justice of the peace and the local unit of the parish, which they took over from the Church and secularized for administrative purposes.

During the sixteenth century the justice played an important part in carrying out royal policy. He was selected from the most solid, dependable and influential of the local gentry, from those men, that is, who were thoroughly well acquainted with local conditions, and who were as anxious as the Crown to lop off the overshadowing branches of the feudal nobility so that they, in their turn, might have economic and political space in which to grow. Their interests were, roughly speaking, those of the Crown; they wanted order in which to develop their estates, a secure market for their produce in the neighbouring towns, and later they were often attached to the Tudor dynasty by the pickings from the dissolved monasteries, which had enabled them to build up the basis of new and more ample fortunes. At the same time, they were no apparent danger to the Throne, for their potential threat, which they developed in the seventeenth century, was not evident until late in the reign of Elizabeth. In any case, the Tudors must have been confident that the prerogative court of Star Chamber, and, if necessary, the even more flexible powers of the Council Chamber, would be more than sufficient to keep the justices in line with the Crown. Consequently, the justices, while keeping, and even having their judicial functions enlarged, were widely used by the Tudors for administrative work of every kind. Justices were empowered to watch for religious and political dissatisfaction, to check up on Roman Catholic recusants, to scrutinize the strangers who landed in out-of-the-way places on the coasts. They were given the task of supervising the carrying out of the hundred and one regulations by which the Tudors hoped to keep up the standard of English goods, whether it was by the prevention of excessive stretching through the use of tenters in the clothing industry, or by the minute directions given to the tanner for the curing of his hides. When vagrancy became a heavy burden on the economic and social life of the country it was to the justice that the Crown turned, for his help in stamping it out. When it was decided to regulate wages in 1563 the justice in Quarter Sessions was entrusted with the business of working out the appropriate scales. When it at last became apparent that some system of poor relief would have to be applied it was again to the justices that the Crown looked for a supervisory instrument. Thus it became the tradition that within the limits of the county, the local gentry should, according to their very extensive commissions, which Elizabeth I had revised in 1590, take the real responsibility for carrying out the policy of the Crown.

Before 1640, however, it was the policy of the Crown rather than the policy of their class which they were driven to enforce. The Justices of Assize when on circuit were ordered to keep a close watch on local conditions, and to report not only on the general efficiency of the county, but on the performances of individual justices. The slack or the politically unreliable, as, earlier, pro-Catholic and, later, men of Puritan leanings were felt to be, were admonished and could be called before Star Chamber or the Council when it was felt that an example must be made. Even so, rifts between the policy of the Crown and the interests of the country landowners were apparent enough as early as the sixteenth century, while by the seventeenth they were growing rapidly wider. The Tudor monarchy had been the protector of the peasantry. It looked to them to provide the corn and the manpower which the country needed for self-sufficiency in time of war; it realized the value of the small tax-payer; it disliked violent changes in the structure of society. Hence, in its official policy, it tried to prevent the substitution of landless labourers for cultivating copyholders. On this issue government policy and the interests of the landowner, anxious to improve his estates and his income by enclosure and sheep rearing, clashed. In consequence governmental intentions were very imperfectly implemented, for the justices, to whom so much of its execution had to be entrusted, were the people most adversely affected by it.

Faced by their non-co-operation the Crown was relatively powerless. It could admonish and punish individual justices guilty of slackness or disobedience; it could not punish or indict a class, especially a class upon whose political support it was so very dependent. This difference of opinion on agrarian problems provides one of the best-known illustrations of the weakness that the Tudors experienced when their conception of the national interest and that of the justices diverged. But there were others.

For example, not all the persistence of the central government was able to enforce the restrictions it desired on the use of tentering frames in the Northern clothing industry when faced by the opposition of local justices, themselves familiar with the business of a clothier. Yet, despite occasional clashes, the combination of main interests, together with the authority of the Crown and the efficiency of Star Chamber, were sufficient to keep local government in the leading strings of the central authority. The Tudors, therefore, never hesitated to pile fresh responsibilities upon their justices whenever the need to do so arose. Consequently, as the functions of government were steadily expanding, the sphere of activities of the justices grew with them almost automatically. By the eighteenth century the tradition had long been established that if anything wanted doing in the counties the justices of the peace were the obvious people to entrust with the task.

By the eighteenth century, however, the relationship between the local government, as exercised by the justices, and the central government, entrusted in the main to Whig ministers who were as dependent on the House of Commons as on the Crown, was very different from that which had prevailed in Tudor days. Then, the policy to be followed had been decided upon, or at least adopted, by the Privy Council, and the justices were expected to conform, whether their own private interests were adversely affected or not. It is true that in such cases the Privy Council found their real co-operation difficult to secure, but the principle at least was recognized and accepted. The Civil War had, however, destroyed this relationship for ever. Though the monarchy was restored in 1660 Star Chamber disappeared and the Privy Council was shorn of those powers that had made it the bogy of the unreliable justice. Local government continued to function, in many cases as vigorously as ever, but it was no longer functioning under a tight central control. Parliament passed the necessary legislation that gave to the justices their legal framework; there was no means of seeing that the law was carried out. Nor did the central government possess the necessary machinery. Local government was in a sense operating in a vacuum. If the justices were prepared to act in conformity with the law, then the law would be observed; if they were slack, negligent, or frankly obstructionist then very little could be done about it. Obviously this gave to the country gentry, who made up the main body of the justices of the peace, both great power and great latitude.

This power was further strengthened by being combined with economic predominance. Often the justice was administrator, judge and landlord. One function amply supplemented the others. Previously the Crown had been able to exercise some kind of check on the landlords as a class: now the powers of the Crown were actually exercised to buttress those of the landed gentry. The predominance of the squire, who was also the justice, over the society of his locality requires little more explanation once this fact has been understood. Also, by the eighteenth century the average justice was no longer hampered by the passing of legislation which he did not approve, since parliament was composed of landowners like himself. It is true that the other elements in it might frequently commit him to an expensive foreign policy, which he did not understand, but in the matter of local government he was something of an expert; here he was able to make his opinion and wishes felt. Most of the county members were also justices of the peace, while many of the peers were lords lieutenant of their counties and, as such, heads of the Commission for the Peace. In a sphere in which they were so closely concerned, both as justices and as landowners, their voice in parliament was paramount, particularly as their views were unlikely, in local matters, to cut across the wider programmes of the merchants and the politicians, since both believed in a conservative social policy based on low wages and an ample reservoir of cheap labour. In the rural districts, therefore, and these still predominated, it was hardly possible that local government could be anything but the expression of a class interest, tempered in most places by a tradition of respect for the law and by a recognition on the part of many of the landowners of their responsibility to the tenants, always provided that these showed themselves equally unquestioning of the 'status quo'.

In the towns the position was rather different. These were, for the most part, still small; they were enclaves of trade and business rather than of industry, embedded in the rural areas. Here the merchant and the professional man were in the ascendant. Here, therefore, was a sphere of government more appropriate to the middle sort. Though the machinery of town government differed considerably, not only between municipal and manorial boroughs, but even between the chartered boroughs themselves, the well-to-do burgess holding either manorial or municipal office was in effective control of administration. Generally the right to share in the government was confined to a very small group. The freedom of the town was a very jealously preserved privilege, not to be lightly shared with every unskilled labourer who might settle there to earn his living. It carried with it the right to practise a trade, the right to share in the profits of whatever town lands there might be and, where the common fields still existed, the right to turn out cattle on to them.

In many towns even the freemen exercised little direct control over the actual government. That was vested in the Corporation, and, particularly after the purging of the town charters by Charles II in his last drive for absolutism, many of them were co-opting, exclusive bodies. They were also frequently extremely corrupt. The temptation to be so was obviously great. Often the boroughs were wealthy, as the value of their common-lands rose with the extension of building and as the bequests of dead citizens accumulated in their hands. There was little tradition of public service and honesty to restrain them; as one man remarked, 'What is an office if a man profit not therein?' Public opinion had no weapons that were effective, and little enough knowledge of what was going on, and the system of co-option, or even of election by a small knot of freemen, made it difficult to eradicate corruption once it had crept in. In most of the boroughs, therefore, the tendency was to administer the affairs of the place in close conformity with the interests of the small ruling clique.

The corporate towns gave to the middle-class man of moderate means not only an opportunity of sharing in the administration of his community but some chance of administering justice, like his betters. It had long been accepted that the needs of the town and country were very different, and that the country gentleman, through the bulwark of Quarter Sessions, was likely to be little conversant with the needs and practice of urban traders. Hence, towns seeking incorporation strove to include in their charters as wide powers as possible over the administration of justice. Though such rights were one of the marks of a municipal borough there was no uniformity. Some boroughs were, judicially speaking, little enclaves within the jurisdiction of the shire, with power to exclude even the county justices. Others had more limited rights of jurisdiction. In the Borough Court of Quarter Sessions they could try misdemeanours and some felonies only. Others again could exercise jurisdiction only within the borough concurrently with the county justices, or could hold Petty or Special Sessions only. But though the opportunity was there it was not always possible to find a sufficient supply of able men who were willing to assume the arduous duties of a justice. The conception of public service for its own sake and without reward was not common amongst the business community; busy men were seldom willing to serve unless some personal advantage seemed likely to accrue to them. There were exceptions, no doubt, honest and conscientious men, with respect for their neighbours and for the law they were to administer, who would do their best to see that justice was done, but there were not nearly enough of them, particularly in the bigger towns. In the smaller boroughs, where the dignity of the office counted for something, and a man's performance of his duty was known to his neighbours, it was easier to find the right type to serve. He might well be self-opinionated and pompous, yet, nevertheless, moderately competent and honest.

In the big towns there was not this restraint, and here, particularly in the metropolitan area of Middlesex, were to be found the 'justices of mean degree'. In these busy congested districts, where no gentleman would serve unless he were animated by a passion for efficiency and service, such as inspired the Fielding brothers,[1] and yet where the need for a justice to be readily available was great, there was little alternative to the appointment of men of less social standing. How such men got on to the Commission is something of a mystery, nor is it easy to trace the channels through which their names were submitted to the Lord Chancellor. Informed public opinion was disconcerted by such appointments, and occasionally considerable agitation to get rid of the 'justices of mean degree' appeared. At the beginning of the century the Lords were discussing a bill sent up from the Commons which

---

[1] Both brothers received a government pension for their services, but their predecessor Thomas De Veil in addition to a pension as the unofficial Court Justice made a considerable income by exploiting the opportunities of his position.

would have imposed a heavy property qualification to remedy the state of affairs by which 'of late diverse persons of small estate and mean education have been deputed and assigned to be justices of peace in the said counties and shires whereof great inconvenience may arise'.[1]

In 1723 the agitation was revived and the *Gentleman's Magazine* took the matter up in its columns, and in 1744 a property qualification of £100 was in fact imposed. But such qualifications could easily be avoided, or secured by cottage property, let out at rack rents, an investment likely to appeal to those tradesmen who were anxious, for pecuniary reasons, to get their names on the Commission for the Peace. There would, perhaps, have been less objection to the lower social status of the justice if the fact that he possessed no private means had not meant that he was forced to exact as much as he could by way of fees from the performance of his judicial duties. Even this might have been considered comparatively unobjectionable if the temptation to create business had not been almost irresistible. Not content with attracting business and exploiting it when it came, the trading justice was rarely above taking bribes and selling justice. He knew well enough how to take a handsome rake-off from the prostitution and vice of a great city.

In the hands of such a man justice was a farce, and the reputation of the County of Middlesex Bench suffered in consequence. Quarter Sessions, which the trading justices rarely troubled to attend, made strenuous efforts to control these abuses, of which it was well aware. Occasionally its complaints were successful and some justice, whose conduct was more than usually outrageous, was removed from the Commission. But while there was no alternative, one scoundrel so removed was almost inevitably replaced by another justice of the same calibre so that the Middlesex trading justice became a by-word. In the May of 1780 Burke, admittedly driven on by political fury at their action in calling out the military as a safeguard against Whig mob demonstrations, described them as 'reptiles' and declared that they were 'the scum of the earth, carpenters, brickmakers and shoemakers; some of whom were notoriously men of such infamous characters that they were unworthy of any employ whatsoever and others so

[1] House of Lords Manuscripts, Vol. IV (New Series), p. 301.

ignorant that they could scarcely write their own names'.[1] Despite such protests the power of the Middlesex justices to charge fees was not taken from them until 1792. Then half a dozen stipendary magistrates in receipt of a salary were appointed in their place. Even this much-needed reform was to some extent vitiated by the fact that the earlier appointments were themselves far from free from the prevailing jobbery; only gradually did it become the practice to appoint 'blameless barristers' as stipendiary magistrates.

Nowhere else does the trading justice appear to have been such a menace, but the difficulty of providing justice for the new and unincorporated industrial towns was a real problem. Birmingham, for instance, had to rely on the justices of the county, none of whom lived near the town. This was not only inconvenient, it was sometimes dangerous, for when disturbances broke out there was no magistrate at hand to read the Riot Act and dispel the mob. In such places the burden on the nearest justice might be heavy, yet the Middlesex trading justice was a warning of what might well happen where, through a shortage of men of independent means, the Commission was diluted with justices of 'mean degree'. Remembering this, it is easy to understand the Merionethshire justices, who, even as late as 1835, nearly went on strike rather than accept as a colleague a man who had once been a grocer and was still a Methodist, and to accept, though with some reservations, the defence of their attitude as being inspired by 'the dictates of genuine patriotism',[2] on the ground that 'the spirit of aristocracy in the County magistracy is the salt which alone saves the whole mass from inevitable corruption'. For into the hands of the justices, whatever their defects, was entrusted the main responsibility for running the country, and to them the lesser officials looked for authority, backing and guidance.

Yet, powerful though the justices were, it would be a mistake to consider them all-powerful. In spite of the lack of control and direction by the central government since the interregnum, and in spite, too, of a complaisant parliament, there were checks which

---

[1] *A Parliamentary History of England,* Vol. XXI, p. 592.
[2] S. and B. Webb: *Statutory Authorities for Special Purposes* (1922), p. 374.

provided some limits to their authority. The Law gave them ample powers; nevertheless they still remained the servants of the Law, unable to do in their own person and on their own authority more than the Law allowed. It is true that the ignorance and the fear of the rural parishioner, combined with an obstinate and ignorant self-importance on the part of the justice, might lead in practice to some over-stepping of the Law, nevertheless the tradition of its supremacy still remained. Nor should it be supposed that the English villager was made of spineless and malleable material. The bitter fights of the sixteenth century, when copyholders pursued their lord from court to court rather than give up rights which they believed to be theirs, illustrate the toughness of their attitude. It is true that the losing battle which the peasantry had fought for two hundred years could not be without effect, yet to suppose that the squire and the merchant had it all their own way would be rash. Moreover, the justice could rely upon little paid help. He had his clerk to whom he could turn for advice, and Quarter Sessions, as a body, could look for a legal lead to the Clerk of the Peace who was, in theory at least, versed in the law. But for the carrying out of his decisions the justice relied upon the unpaid parish officials, the churchwardens, the overseers and the constables. This check probably gave little protection to the mass of the labouring poor but it did mean that the middling sort were actively, if somewhat unwillingly, associated with the gentry and the squirearchy in the running of local affairs. There was a point past which their wishes and prejudices would hardly be disregarded though just where this point was reached, in a community where government was largely a matter of personal relations, depended on the strength of the various characters concerned.

The parish officers were nearly as much the rulers of their little world as the justices were of the county. By the eighteenth century the parish had long been part of the very warp and weft of rural England. It had been the unit of ecclesiastical administration for centuries before Henry VIII realized its usefulness in the civil sphere and adapted it to secular needs. Long before the justices were functioning, the people of the countryside had been accustomed to think of themselves as members of a parish. They had looked for guidance to their priest and to the churchwardens, who were responsible for preserving the fabric of the church and superintending the secular side of its activities. When the Church came under the Royal Supremacy, Henry appropriated not only the monastery lands but also many of the Church's institutions. In particular he found the parish a most useful unit for local administration: its officers supplied just what the justices lacked, minor servants to carry out their orders. Perhaps the most useful of these was the parish constable. Originally the parish constable had not been one of the medieval ecclesiastical officers; he had been a manorial official attached to the court, doing his year of unpaid office as the servant of the lord in particular and the community in general. Sometimes he had been attached to the old Hundred Court. As these courts decayed or disappeared the constable became attached instead to the Tudor parish, becoming the 'maid-of-all-work' of the justices, just as they in turn have been described as the 'maids-of-all-work' of the Crown.

As the needs of local life became greater, and as the necessity to produce some rough and ready uniformity in matters of social policy became more pressing, other officers were added by Act of Parliament to the parish. With the great increase in trade in the sixteenth century the old highways were no longer able to stand the strain of the new traffic, particularly in those districts where the increase had been marked. The old machinery, therefore, for keeping the roads in repair was no longer adequate; indeed, with the dissolution of the monasteries much of it had disappeared, for the tending of roads and bridges had in the past frequently been regarded as a pious work. Some new device, therefore, was necessary to see that the responsibility was securely placed upon someone's shoulders. In this dilemma the Crown turned to the parish. The Act of 1555 declared the parishes to be responsible for the roads which ran through them, and for a statutory period of four days, later increased to six, the parishioners were to turn out with their carts and horses and help with their labour to repair the local highways. The responsibility for organizing the work rested upon the churchwardens, but the oversight was entrusted to a new official, the Surveyor of the Highways, who again was to be backed up and controlled by the local justices. Parishes which failed to keep their roads in a proper state of repair, though the words should be interpreted very laxly, could be indicted at Quarter Sessions before the justices and fined the amount necessary to do so.

Later in the century the problem of providing some sustenance for the poor, whether aged, infant, sick or unemployed, loomed large; the government, both for political reasons, and to preserve social stability, was forced to frame some kind of a policy towards the relief of the poor. Here again the responsibility was placed on the parish. A pauper's parish was declared to be the community that must, by the payment of a poor rate, relieve his necessity. The business, even at its simplest, called for some organization and some application. It was not felt that the churchwarden, who already had duties enough attached to his unpaid office, could shoulder the new burden alone. Consequently, the office of Overseer of the Poor was created. At a time when local offices were unpaid and the Crown could call upon whom it would for the service of the community, there was little objection, from the royal point of view, to creating new ones as they were required. In this case the justices, either resident in the parish or in adjacent parishes, were empowered to appoint four parishioners to act for a year at a time and to deal with this troublesome business. In practice, however, the strict letter of the law was rarely complied with, the parishes elected or bullied or chose by rota suitable persons to be overseers, and the justices confirmed the choice that had already been made. In the working of the Poor Law, however, the connexion between the justices and the overseers remained very close.

The work of the parish officials, whether churchwarden or overseer or constable, was certainly no sinecure. It could be arduous, exacting and unpleasant, but it was vitally important to the running of the country. It was here that the middling sort made their contribution to government, for the churchwardens in rural parishes were drawn from the local worthies, substantial farmers, inn-keepers, millers, while the overseers, whose office had slightly less dignity and more tiresome duties attached to it, came from a social layer just slightly below that of the church-warden: smaller farmer, small trader, the skilled artisan. Below them still ranked the constable, a bothersome, unpopular position that no one wanted to fill, and which was, therefore, assigned to those members of the community whose place in the social structure left them with little opportunity of protesting. Consequently, it was those men of little standing who were forced to accept its onerous duties. Here again, therefore, the social pattern of the rural community was pretty accurately mirrored. The small farmer, the prosperous rural artisan, who had a stake in the community, was also forced to shoulder part of the responsibility for running it, but he chose those offices which gave him some standing with his neighbours. Yet even the labourer had his part to play. It may be true that it was a privilege with which he would gladly have dispensed, yet it did mean, at least within the more sparsely populated rural parishes, that every able-bodied man above the standing of a pauper, might be called upon to assume some responsibility for the concerns of the community of which he was a part.

From the justice at the top to the parish constable at the bottom the framework of eighteenth-century local government mirrored the society in which it functioned. It was well adapted to meet the needs of a country that was still largely rural and where the majority of towns, as well as most country parishes, were communities small enough for their affairs to be managed on a very personal basis. Later, as population grew, and, above all, as the industrial towns increased with horrifying rapidity, there was a new need for trained and impersonal administrators and for a more detached and scientific attitude. In London the need was already apparent, and this was true also of some of the greater towns, but for rural England the pattern of government in parish and county was a surprisingly accurate reflection of the society of the day, a society in which the landowner played a dominant part, but in which the middling sort, and even the craftsman, had a recognized and even respectable role to play.

In eighteenth-century England it is not, perhaps, unreasonable to regard the established Church as a department of the State responsible for the administration of ecclesiastical business. At a time when government majorities had to be organized and controlled largely through the adroit use of patronage in order to gain and maintain support in the House of Lords, the bishops had to be chosen for political rather than spiritual reasons. Though it was no longer usual for them to be appointed to high secular office, their political power was still considerable, and it was

understood that it should be used to support the King's ministers.[1]
Their first and most obvious obligation was to attend punctili-
ously to their duties as members of the House of Lords while
parliament was sitting. This was far from being an empty gesture
of loyalty. Though the Lords during the eighteenth century
averaged about two hundred and twenty, it was rare to find more
than one hundred and twenty to one hundred and forty-five
attending. Consequently, the ecclesiastical vote of twenty-six was
not to be despised by party managers. On critical occasions the
bishops would be pressed to attend and give to the government
the support of their votes. On more than one occasion this solid
block of favourable votes helped the government to escape from
a very ugly situation.

Even when no crisis was impending, ministers liked to have
the bishops at hand. Where possible, the government looked to
them not merely for a colourless vote, but for active individual
support. As leaders of the Church their opinion on the questions
of the day, might be expected to carry some weight, and what
vocal aid the bishops could furnish was not only gratefully received but firmly solicited. This kind of assistance was varied; to
support the policy of the government by speeches in the House of
Lords might be desired but was forthcoming less than might have
been expected, many of the bishops being very indifferent speakers
on secular subjects and in a secular assembly. Newton of Bristol
explained his almost invariable silence by declaring that bishops
came too late to political life to become familiar with its conventions of debate, and that since the suppression of Convocation
they had little previous experience of handling such questions.
Though they were often silent voters in the Lords the government felt that it could at least depend on them to give in their
sermons a general support to the ministry of the day and see that
the clergy under their authority did the same. This was an important service and one that had been exacted by the Crown ever
since the Reformation, since so much of public opinion was
shaped by the oratory of the Church, at a time when other instruments of propaganda were less flexible and powerful. However,
by the eighteenth century the written word was becoming the
marked rival of the sermon, and the political pamphlet was coming

[1] N. Sykes: *Church and State in England in the Eighteenth Century* (1934), *passim*.

into its own. In these circumstances a bishop with a ready pen might hope to find favour with the ministers of the day, while the candidate for episcopal office was even more eager to oblige.

The bishops were not merely educated political henchmen, they were also great territorial magnates. In this role the aid which they could afford to the government was great. The bishop's palace could usually be relied upon to provide a centre of government influence. The tradition of hospitality, which was so great a financial burden in those sees where revenues were small, meant that all persons of mark within the diocese sooner or later came into contact with either the bishop or his servants. Probably few men had as good a knowledge of the currents of local feeling and the amount of support which the Crown might secure for any given policy as had the bishop. The information came from so many sources, since he was not limited by his own observations but could draw upon that of his clergy. Dangerous political dissatisfaction was certainly much rarer in the eighteenth century than it had been when Elizabeth I was queen, when the Bishop of Durham was still the great bulwark of order in the North, but the support which the Pretender got in 1715 and again in the '45 showed that it was far from non-existent. Carlisle and Chester, as well as the archbishopric of York, were all districts where devotion to the House of Hanover was very slight and where the government was very glad to have a dependable servant.

Nevertheless, in spite of frequent apprehensions, actual rebellion or even disaffection was not common, and the duty which the government looked to the bishops to perform was usually the more prosaic one of strengthening the parliamentary interest of those borough-mongers who were known to be their supporters. Candidates who were recognized as having the support of the ministers of the day could look without much hesitation for help from the bishop and such services as he could give were far from being considered as in any way derogatory to the dignity and authority of the episcopal bench. Whether the bishops were regarded as voters, as speakers, as propagandists, as sources of local information and control, or as useful instruments of the party managers, the connexion between them and the ministers was most intimate and their part in the smooth running of the political machinery an important one.

A Bond and Judgment, 1779

The Bosky Magistrate, 1796

The Wollaston Family
by Hogarth

The strength of the government's position in dealing with the bishops is easy to see. The inequalities of the revenues of the various dioceses were a very powerful weapon in the hands of the party managers. These, in England and Wales, as on the Continent, differed very considerably. Some were rich prizes for which an ambitious and extravagant man might well contend, others were more a source of embarrassment than of opulence, to be valued only as a stepping-stone to better things. Canterbury headed the list with revenues that were estimated at £7,000 a year, next came Durham with £6,000, Winchester with £5,000, and York with £4,500, and the additional dignity of the title of archbishop. At the other end, Bristol could only provide its bishop with £450, Oxford with £500, and Llandaff with £550. Yet the expenses of the poorer bishops could never be scaled down to their meagre resources. On them, as on their wealthier colleagues, the burden of hospitality fell heavily. This was one of the strongest traditions of the English Church. Its benefits were both spiritual and temporal, for the close contact which the bishop maintained with the people of his diocese made him a force in the political as well as the religious life of his flock. This obligation was not only personally exhausting; financially it was a serious drain. The duty of attending the sessions of parliament was also an expensive one. Travelling was never cheap and residence in London meant keeping up two large establishments. With such liabilities the poorer bishops could never have remained solvent without either private means or the attachment to their sees of various other pieces of preferment, held *in commendam* to supplement their endowment. For such additional resources they were dependent on the favour of the ministers of the day.

If a bishop hoped for translation to a richer see, and few men were given one of the prizes at first, he had to work for his promotion. He was expected to be useful, to give the most assiduous and unqualified support to the ministers of the Crown, both by his vote in the Lords, by his pen and by the unstinting use of his personal influence on both the clergy and the laity of his diocese. The more attractive sees came only to those men whom the government felt to be reliable; even the slightest coquetting with the Opposition was sufficient to ruin all hope of promotion. Bishop Secker was left, first at Bristol, then at Oxford, both of them almost punitive sees if held for a long tenure, for sixteen years because in March 1738–9 and again in 1741 he had voted against the government. Bishop Hoadley, on the other hand, who showed no such dangerous tendency to private independence, moved between 1721 and 1734 from Bangor to Hereford, then to Sarum, and finally was translated to the rich see of Winchester. Such examples of promotion following obsequious support of the ministers and being denied to those who were considered politically unsound could very well be multiplied. Compliance was the only road to tread. Independent men were seldom raised to the Bench except by some political accident as when Shelbourne got Watson appointed to Llandaff, because the latter's convictions drove him into literary support of Shelbourne's policy towards the American war. His subsequent career showed how seldom translation came without political subservience. As he observed himself, 'I could not bring myself to vote as a minister bade me, on all occasions; and I perceived that, such was the temper of the times, or such was the temper of the man, nothing less than that would secure his attention'.[1] When writing to the Duke of Norfolk in 1787 with reference to a vacancy at Carlisle he acknowledged that 'if I had wished for it ever so much, the determination I have formed, of conducting myself independently in parliament, would have been little likely to have promoted my pretensions'.[2] With such power, and even more, such openly recognized power, in the hands of the managers, it is clear that except for their purely spiritual duties the bishops were under very real political control, and had to shape their policy strictly in accordance with the needs and desires of the government of the day. Wherever the demand for change, for the reshaping of political or social life, might arise, it clearly could not come from the episcopal bench. The leaders of the Church could, with every show of reason, be regarded as ranking with the supporters of the *status quo*.

Nor did the interest which the ministers of the Crown took in ecclesiastical appointments cease with the bishops since the government could dispose of a great deal of other Church patronage. The cathedrals, with their many offices which did not require the cure of souls or protracted residence, provided many prizes in the

---

[1] *Anecdotes in the Life of R. Watson, Bishop of Llandaff* (1818), p. 303.
[2] *Ibid.* p. 305.

ecclesiastical lottery. The Crown had the right to nominate to many of these prebends, the Lord Chancellor nominated to others, so that between them their patronage was considerable. Some of these offices, notably the prebends at Windsor, were nearly as well endowed as the poorer bishoprics, and had incomparably fewer expenses attached to them. The revenues of the prebends at Windsor were £450, equal to those of Bristol, while the residentiaryships at St. Paul's were worth £800, which is more than the poorer bishops were getting. Naturally the competition for these plums was keen. It was generally recognized that such appointments would be filled for political purposes, not so much for what the clerics involved could do, for their sphere of political usefulness was much more limited than that of the bishops, but to oblige their relations or patrons, who themselves possessed parliamentary influence that was important to the ministry. Ecclesiastical patronage of this sort was, therefore, pretty consistently used in order to ensure the smooth working of the parliamentary machine. Not unexpectedly the cathedral clergy contributed little to the services of the cathedral, whatever their political usefulness. As a consequence, by the end of the eighteenth century, reformers were demanding that the revenues attached to the cathedrals should be reorganized, and that church patronage should cease to be regarded as a mere pawn in the political game.

While, however, the Church continued to be regarded as almost a department of the government, and while that government was dominated by the well-born and the landowner, it is hardly surprising that the social structure, which it mirrored so accurately, should be faithfully reflected in the Church also. If Dr. Johnson's opinion that 'No man can now be made a bishop for his learning and piety, his only chance of promotion is his being connected with some one who has parliamentary interest'[1] is somewhat sweeping, it does at least receive considerable confirmation from a perusal of the list of eighteenth-century bishops. Thus, Lord North's brother was in turn Bishop of Lichfield, Worcester and Winchester; Chancellor Hardwicke's son went first to St. David's, then to Gloucester and finally to Ely; from George III the Earl of Albemarle secured Exeter for his second son. These appointments are typical and need not be further

[1] N. Sykes: *Op. cit.*, p. 165.

elaborated. Indeed, it was freely admitted that certain bishoprics were all but reserved for 'men of family and fashion'. In this way the Church maintained its age-long tradition of providing for the younger sons of the nobility.

It had been equally the tradition of the Church to provide a career open to talent, and the social origins of many a medieval bishop had been lowly enough. To some extent the tradition still continued and some sees were considered 'bishoprics of business for men of ability and learning'. But though a poor man, via a scholarship to Oxford or Cambridge, might eventually reach prominence in the Church, even here the taint of secular and parliamentary interest remained, since he was hardly likely to be successful, whatever his learning and spiritual calibre, if he had not managed to attract the attention of some patron who could supply what he lacked in this direction. For the scholar the most secure path for ecclesiastical advancement lay in obtaining a tutor-ship to a noble family or in acting as tutor to a nobleman in resi-dence at one of the universities. The office of chaplain offered another opening, though as the number of chaplains was great and of bishoprics few, only a small proportion could be preferred in this way. Moreover, it may be doubted whether the qualities required by the successful chaplain were precisely those that would appeal to a man of strict zeal and piety. Dodsley's opinion, and it was shared by many contemporaries, was far otherwise when he wrote:

> When Dukes or noble Lords a Chaplain hire,
> They first of his Capacities enquire.
> If stoutly qualified to drink and smoke,
> If not too nice to bear an impious Joke,
> If tame enough to be the common Jest,
> This is a Chaplain to his Lordship's Taste.[1]

Indeed, it may well be a matter of some surprise that, recruited as they were, the eighteenth-century bench of bishops contained so many able and respectable men. It is not surprising, therefore, that though the universities could provide a means by which the poor boy might blossom into a scholar, generally the bishops were at least of gentle birth. Often, indeed, they were drawn from the younger sons, or from the cadets, of some noble family.

[1] R. Dodsley: *The Art of Preaching* (1738).

Much the same considerations governed the choice of the cathedral and beneficed clergy. Here, too, integrity and scholarship were not in themselves a sufficient recommendation for promotion. The prizes of the profession were rarely apportioned for purely spiritual reasons. The right to present to livings enjoyed by the private patron made this almost inevitable. Where a living was well endowed it was normally reserved for a son or nephew, or at least for a friend, of the patron. Such livings were regarded as the almost automatic provision for the younger son. Walpole, it will be remembered, had been intended for the Church and the family living if the death of his elder brother had not deflected his activities to the House of Commons. Where the living was in the gift of the bishop different considerations intervened it is true, but these, too, were often of a secular nature. The need to oblige the ministers of the day, if a bishop desired translation to a richer see, the need to conciliate the local gentry, the need to provide for his own ecclesiastical retainers, all tended to limit and to influence his choice. Only the poorer and less desirable livings were left for the rank and file of the clergy. Beneath them to remain a curate, little esteemed and underpaid, was the permanent fate of many.

In such circumstances applicants for holy orders fell into two main classes; those who had, or thought they had, sufficient influence to secure a good living or a desirable cathedral office, and those to whom even the poor country parish and the curate's scanty emolument represented either the call of conscience or a step up on the social ladder. It was for the latter, perhaps, something of a snare that the universities made provision for the poorer aspirants to holy orders who came up from the old grammar schools. The lot of most of the poor scholars so raised was an ill-endowed country living for the fortunate, a series of curacies for the rest. The supply turned out by the universities seems consistently to have exceeded the demand. Thus, the less pushing, or less able, were left to eke out a living, as a hedge-priest, that was not far removed from vagrancy. One letter received by a curate of long standing contained the advice, 'if you expect preferment you must bustle and try to peep after it, as most of the profession do in these days',[1] and even to secure a very mediocre benefice it was necessary to follow this advice.

[1] Quoted N. Sykes: *Op. cit.,* p. 205.

Nor was it always easy, even when a man had a patron, to secure an adequate living. Presentations were valuable, and even if a man did not require the benefice for his own kinsmen, he was apt to have many friends all seeking, for one reason or another, ecclesiastical preferment. Thus, William Drake had considerable difficulty in securing a presentation for a friend of his, the Rev. Thomas Pritchard. He was suitably qualified, being a Brasenose man, and had possibly acted as tutor in the Drake family, for he seems to have been living at Shardeloes. His attempt to secure the nearby vicarage at Penn from Assheton Curzon in 1768 was fruitless, and in 1771 he was using his influence with the Lord Chancellor, the Hon. Henry Bathurst, and after made application to Richard Lowndes. Finally he did secure the living of Winslow and Granborough after having, as he wrote, 'been long endeavouring to get something for Mr. Pritchard that he could call his own while he is able to enjoy it'.[1]

When, even with the help of a friendly patron, the difficulties in the way of securing a presentation were so great it is not surprising that many men served as curates for years and that the unlucky ones never obtained a living at all. The eighteenth-century curate is a well-known figure of fiction, but the novelist does not seem to have exaggerated his plight. If he were too poor to afford an episcopal licence he was in a very vulnerable position, not unlike that of the casual labourer. Often he found himself dismissed from his curacy upon very short notice and thrown on a market where supply was greater than demand. This was reflected in the lowness of the salary which he night hope to obtain —some £30 or £35 a year, together with certain fees was considered an adequate stipend. If the vicar in need of additional assistance was resident and, therefore, able to celebrate the required quarterly administration of the Sacrament he was often content to engage a curate merely in deacon's orders and to pay him accordingly. For this reason many curates, who despaired of ever obtaining a benefice, neglected to take full orders because of the expense this involved. Such men, without full professional standing or security, fulfilled all the qualifications for a clerical proletariat. They were wage-earners of uncertain tenure. Compe-

---

[1] G. Eland: *The Shardeloes Papers of the Seventeenth and Eighteenth Centuries* (1947), p. 308.

tition forced down their remuneration, living conditions were too often difficult, marriage a still greater drag on their slender resources while their children, if they survived infancy, seemed condemned to poverty. For daughters the position of a waiting-woman, such as Mrs. Slipshod, was as much as they could expect. Not all curates were quite so badly placed. In some localities they were able to alleviate their position by serving two neighbouring curacies or by teaching school, but, at best, a curate's was a hand to mouth, and socially inferior, position. Clerical and secular society, therefore, were alike dominated by the acceptance of privilege and by the distinctions that marked off one class of men from their fellows, though in the ecclesiastical as in the lay world the cry of the reformer was being raised within the Church while the whole Wesley movement, with its vast religious and social repercussions, had already broken away from the Established Church.

Such was the structure of government at the opening of the eighteenth century, and such, with very minor attempts at curtailing the amount of patronage available for the creation of government majorities, it remained at its close. It was not democratic, and few people would have desired to make it so, but it had at least the virtue of representing the social and economic structure of the country as it was. A man's relation to land was still a fact of major importance, and outwardly at least the direction of policy and the control of administration remained in the hands of the landowners. Even traders and financiers, important as their activities were in increasing the wealth of the country, paid land the homage of buying it, and voted or sat in parliament as landowners. Yet the fact that so many of the Members had interests which were wider than those of the country gentleman (in the parliament of 1761 there were one hundred and eighty-two, or almost a third of the House, who were members of the professions, or were merchants) meant that those forces which were turning the United Kingdom into an empire were well represented. If the bulk of the House were landowners there was a very notable tail of army and navy officers, civil servants, diplomats, lawyers and merchants, which, on occasions, was quite capable of 'wagging the dog', and this, too, was in line with economic realities, and reflected the social structure of the ruling elements. The fact that in the same parliament only forty members of the Lower House had 'no pretence to arms'[1] represents, too, pretty accurately the subordinate social and economic position of the middle class. Important though they were in the industrial development of the country, they accepted the leadership of the landowners in national affairs, and even, outside the limits of their borough charters, in local ones. Not until the closing years of the century, when the taxation due to the American War pressed hardly on their economic interests did they evince much concern in parliamentary matters. Even then in movements such as the Yorkshire Association it was clearly the more politically minded gentry who took the lead.[2] Only when prospective legislation clearly threatened some concrete industrial or commercial interest did they bestir themselves with any real alacrity. In Church and State alike they were content with modest rewards, and were satisfied, or at least resigned, to leave the plums to their betters. As we have been reminded, 'The distribution of political power between classes was hardly an issue in politics before 1815'.[3] Yet neither the middle class nor the great mass of the labouring poor could be completely ignored. Though politically their rights might be limited, or even non-existent, legally all were citizens, sharing in, if not controlling or directing, a common heritage, and where those rights were touched even the poorest would riot, though they be hanged for it. If, as has so often been said, the government of the eighteenth century was an oligarchy, then at least it was an oligarchy tempered by commonsense and by the recognition that social and even political rigidity past a point is a sign of weakness and not of strength.

[1] L. B. Namier: *England in the Age of the American Revolution* (1930), p. 253.
[2] *Vide* H. Butterfield: *George III, Lord North and the People* (1950).
[3] R. Pares: *George III and the Politicians*, p. 3.

Chapter Four

THE NOBILITY, THE GENTRY AND THE MIDDLING SORT

WHAT advantages and disadvantages could a society so constituted offer to its individual members? Such questions are always easier to ask than answer since they imply some recognition of the need of a standard by which those advantages and disadvantages can be assessed. The demands that men make on any society are not static. What had seemed good to the medieval Englishman would not have seemed good to his eighteenth-century descendant, nor are the criteria of that period necessarily valid to the citizen of to-day. However objectively historians set out to study their material, subjective judgments tend to creep in and they are tempted to use contemporary standards as a measuring rod for past conditions. Yet such judgments are both unhistorical and unfair. Nobody who fails to realize, or realizing deplores, the fact that eighteenth-century England accepted, as morally right, a society based on class distinction, can hope to understand it. Classes might well be fluid, their components might vary, individuals and families might pass up or down the social ladder, but the general framework of the class structure not only remained but was accepted as right and proper, as something without which no community could organize itself or live in harmony. It was a matter on which Dr. Johnson expressed himself forcibly, declaring to Boswell:

Sir, I would no more deprive a nobleman of his respect than of his money. I consider myself as acting a part in the great system, and do to others as I would have them do to me. Sir, I would behave to a nobleman as I would expect he should behave to me were I a nobleman and he Sam Johnson. Sir, there is one Mrs. Macauley in this town, a great republican. I came to her one day and said I was quite a convert to her republican system, and thought mankind all upon a footing; and I begged that her footman might be allowed to dine with me. She has never liked me since.

For the opinions which he held he advanced solid arguments.

Suppose [he asked] a shoemaker should claim equality with Dr. Robertson, as he does with a lord. How would the Doctor stare. 'But Sir,' says the shoemaker, 'I do a great service to society. 'Tis true I am paid for doing it. But so are you, Sir; and I am sorry to say it, better paid than me for doing something not so necessary, for mankind could do better without your history than without my shoes'. And so it would go on, were there no fixed, invariable external rules of distinction of rank, which create no jealousy, as they are allowed to be accidental.[1]

By common consent the aristocracy were regarded as the leaders of English society, giving that word its widest meaning. They were, in a very real sense, the 'Ruling Few'. Nevertheless, except for the peers themselves, there is no very clear line to mark them off from the rest of the gentry. The cadet of a noble house might often be able to command influence to a degree and in a way that was beyond the reach of a private gentleman, but the same way of life, within the limits of his economic resources, was open to both. For this reason the aristocracy and the gentry can be treated as falling within the same social category for the purpose of assessing the benefits and limitations which their place in the social hierarchy of Georgian England conferred upon them.

Their education, whether obtained at a public school or through the medium of a private tutor, was designed, if such a word can be used to describe what had grown so haphazardly, to fit them for leisure and for politics. During the eighteenth century the public schools, intended in the first place for the sons of tradesmen and artisans, were attracting more and more boys from the upper classes. In consequence the character of these schools was changing, though much of their traditional purpose, to train clerics and poor men's sons for the university, remained. The result was that within their walls there was at once a blurring of, and yet emphasis on, class distinction. By the eighteenth century they were taking poor boys on the foundation and paying pupils in boarding-houses run for profit. At Harrow a master's salary was £26 13s. 4d., which, by eighteenth-century standards, was less than many a poor vicar or curate got. In such circumstances the inducement to take paying pupils must have been considerable.

[1] J. Boswell: *London Journal*, p. 320.

When his adopted aunt, Mrs. Thomas Garrard, sent young James Powell to Harrow in 1775 his boarding fees were £7 for the half year, but books and teaching fees brought the sum up to £12 8s. 7d. In all his education for seven and a half years amounted to £206 17s. 8d., or, if clothes and other kindred expenses are added, £367 10s. 2d., which was no inconsiderable sum at that time.[1] At Eton and Westminster, which in the first half of the eighteenth century were the two leading public schools, with Winchester running third, the same thing was happening. When Henry Ellison went to Eton his 'dame', Mrs. Mary Young, the widow of a former master, informed his uncle that he could only have half a bed unless special terms were arranged, that he must bring eight or nine shirts if he changed his linen twice a week, and that he should also have a silver porringer and cup and spoon, a knife and fork, half a dozen plates, a chamber pot, a bason and a candlestick. In the way of linen she required a pair of sheets, a dozen napkins, and a dozen towels. His school bills for the half year came to just over £26.[2] At Sedbergh, where there were no 'dames' the Cotesworth boys in 1716 lodged with a landlady in the town.

In such schools the two social streams were for a time running side by side. There were still plenty of poor boys at the public schools: when 'barber' Davies was Head of Eton, the ranks of the Collegers were largely recruited from the sons of Eton and Windsor tradesmen. Even so the privileges of rank were preserved, crystallizing at Eton into the famous division between the Collegers, who were on the foundation, and the fee-paying Oppidans. The former lodged in the notorious Long Chamber, where in conditions of 'dirt, discomfort, riots and rats', seventy ill-disciplined boys were locked up from eight in the evening until next morning. For the Oppidan, life was more comfortable; like Ellison he lodged with a 'dame' and often had the advantage of being supervised by a private tutor. Nor was it only a matter of comfort. Canning, in spite of his ability and restricted means, fought hard to avoid being placed on the foundation, influenced, as he declared quite frankly, by 'the great difference of behaviour and respect paid to the one situation in preference to the other', since he found that in his experience 'A Colleger, among the boys

[1] G. Eland: *Op. cit.,* p. 76.   [2] E. Hughes: *Op. cit.,* p. 361.

even, is not looked upon in near so respectable a light as an Oppidan'.[1] By the end of the century the leading schools were thus beginning to cater more and more for the sons of gentlemen. In 1800 the Governors of Harrow declared that whatever 'the intentions of the founder might have been, the school is not now adapted generally for persons of low condition, but better suited to those of a higher class',[2] a circumstance due possibly to the effective headship of a series of old Etonians, Sumner, Heath and Drury, who from 1760 were making Harrow one of the leading public schools.

From the point of view of the type of education offered there was little to choose between the more fashionable public school and the small grammar school; both concentrated severely on classical learning, which, indeed, by the terms of their charters, they were obliged to do. To read the classical authors and be able not only to construe but to turn out a Latin prose or a Latin ode was, in the jargon of the day, school 'business'. To this the main teaching hours were devoted, though on holidays and in leisure time, which, at the public schools, where the boys were boarded, was ample, other subsidiary subjects such as history, geography and mathematics might be studied. More often than not, however, such subjects were taught by the private tutors, who accompanied their young charges to Eton or Winchester or Harrow, and not by the overworked regular masters. Whether a boy learnt much outside the regular curriculum was, therefore, dependent on individual circumstances, and extraneous to the regular educational training of the day. Indeed, whether the lazy or stupid boy learnt much at all is doubtful. The opportunity was there for those who wished to take it. Cowper in the course of his school career at Westminster read the whole of the Odyssey and the Iliad. Young Cotesworth, writing to his father from Sedbergh, told him: 'As to leaving off my School-Authors at College I hope I shall be very well qualified to do it by Christmas for I have already read through most of Latin Vergil, and with moderate study I shall goe through Horace before Christmas. Terence I have at my finger Ends, so that after I have finished Horace and Vergil I shall

---

[1] J. Raven: 'Some Letters of George Canning', *Anglo-Saxon Review* Vo II p. 49 (December 1899).
[2] J. W. Adamson: *English Education, 1789–1902* (1930), p. 63.

have got all that I can at Sedbergh'.[1] Where, however, a boy had
neither the bent for classical studies nor the desire to apply himself it was easy for him to escape with little solid furniture in his
mind, and to acquire no more than those tags of Latin quotations
that gave the superficial appearance of a cultivated man.

Such education was in no sense utilitarian, except possibly for
the politician, for whom Edgeworth thought

> a knowledge and a taste for classical literature is peculiarly orna-
> mental and useful, indeed indispensably necessary to every Briton,
> who aspires to distinction in public life, for in this country a states-
> man must be an orator. It is by eloquence, that he must bring him-
> self into notice; by eloquence, that he must preserve this power, and
> accomplish by his influence in the senate whatever designs he may
> form for his own advantage or the good of the country.[2]

But, though not utilitarian, such a training was eminently suitable
for developing the critical faculties and literary appreciation of
the man of leisure. Even so, there were disadvantages. There was
some danger of the overworked masters turning out dilettantes
rather than sound scholars. Conditions were hard, discipline both
savage and lax, because schools were understaffed; food and
living conditions were often deplorable. As a result, disorder,
bullying and uproar were common, and riots on a large scale no
unusual event.

In view of these conditions, both educational and material, it
is perhaps not surprising that parents who could afford it often
preferred to keep their sons at home and to employ the services
of a tutor to supervise their education. The question of public
school versus private tutor was much debated among the edu-
cationalists of the day. John Locke declared:

> How anyone's being put into a mixed herd of unruly boys, and
> then learning to wrangle at trap, or rook or span farthing, fits him
> for civil conversation or business I do not see. And what qualities
> are ordinarily to be got from such a troop of play fellows as
> schools usually assemble together, from parents of all kinds, that a
> father should so much covet it, is hard to devine. I am sure that
> he who is able to be at charge of a tutor at home, may there give

---

[1] E. Hughes: *Op. cit.,* p. 359.
[2] R. L. Edgeworth: *Essays on Professional Education* (1808), p. 372.

his son a more genteel carriage, more manly thoughts, and a sense of what is worthy and becoming, with a greater proficiency in learning into the bargain, and ripen him sooner into a man, than any school can.[1]

Cowper, recalling his own school days at Westminster, in his poem *Tirocinium* echoed much the same sentiments:

> Would you your son should be a sot or dunce
> Lascivious, headstrong, or all these at once;
> That in good time the stripling's finished taste,
> For loose expense and fashionable waste
> Should prove your ruin and his own at last;
> Train him in public with a mob of boys.

Philip Thicknesse, whose schoolboy misery led him into truancy which ended in an expulsion most welcome to him, would have endorsed this view heartily. So, apparently, would Lord Chesterfield, who in 1750, a year after Cowper had left Westminster, admitted in a letter to his son, 'You have hitherto I must confess, had very few opportunities of keeping polite society. Westminster School is, undoubtedly, the seat of illiberal manners and brutal behaviour'.[2] Possibly things improved. Later, all William Drake's sons went there, William junior and Thomas in 1750 and Charles, the youngest, not leaving until 1774, without either visible contamination of their characters or ruin of their careers.

By the close of the century conditions had become more tolerable at most schools. As Vicesimus Knox, himself head master of Tonbridge, pointed out in 1781, there were public schools and public schools, and that when he recommended them he must be understood to mean 'places of education where the intention of the founder is not quite forgotten'. For his preference for a public school education he had some cogent arguments to put forward.

> After all the confinement and trouble of a domestic education [he pointed out] it is probable that the boy will at last be sent to the University. There he will find the greater part of his associates to consist of young men who have been educated at schools; and if they have any vices he will now be in much greater danger of moral

---

[1] *The Educational Writings of John Locke.* Edited by J. W. Adamson (1922), p. 52.
[2] *Lord Chesterfield's Letters to his Son.* Edited by C. Strachey (1932), Vol. II, p. 23.

infection, and will suffer much worse consequences from it, than if he had not been secluded from boys at a boyish age.[1]

Edgeworth, too, favoured the public school as against the private tutor, as a means of correcting the sense of self-importance that the son of a country gentleman, might well derive from being the big fish in a little pond. 'For this reason', he wrote, 'they should be sent to public schools, at a distance from their friends and connexions, where, mixing with strangers and equals, they will be forced to seek distinction by other merits than merely those of bearing a certain name, or being heir to a certain number of acres'.[2] For one reason or another, therefore, the public schools, too, had their convinced supporters, and by the end of the century a school like Eton had much to offer to a boy of ability and character. There is no doubt Canning enjoyed his time there and benefitted from it, both in the narrower field of scholarship and in the opportunities it gave him of making friends and trying out his social and literary gifts.

Many parents, however, continued to employ a private tutor, positions, particularly in well-connected families, eagerly sought by poor scholars, since they were a recognized stepping-stone to the gift of a living and advancement in the Church. Among the Shardeloes papers are details of the education of little Montagu Garrard Drake that must have been typical of the education of many small boys. His tutor, Philip Ayres, was a minor poet of some distinction, whose patron was Sir William Drake, young Montagu's grandfather; but though he supervised he did not do all the necessary teaching. Entries appear with some regularity recording payments made to special masters, such as 'To Mr. Ivers, the writing master, paid a Guinea for entrance, and Two and thirty shillings & sixpence for Six week's teaching Master to write . . . £2. 14. 0'. Five months' dancing, imparted by Mr. Harry Hazard cost £10 15*s.* 9*d.*, and a month's lessons on the harpsichord thirty shillings. He also learned to paint 'flowers etc.' At the age of thirteen and a half, somewhat early, doubtless due to the excellence of the education so provided, he was entered at St. John's College, Oxford.[3]

[1] Vicesimus Knox: *Liberal Education* (1781), p. 35.
[2] R. L. Edgeworth: *Op. cit.,* p. 254.
[3] G. Eland: *Op. cit.,* pp. 70–3.

This was normally the next stage in the education of a gentleman. Perhaps even more than the public school, and certainly more than the small grammar school, the universities were the preserves of the aristocracy and gentry. Though many of the scholars were drawn from the smaller grammar schools, university scholarships being eagerly sought after by tradesmen's and husbandmen's sons who had academic or clerical ambitions, the great mass of the middle classes were not interested in university education for their sons. At neither university during the eighteenth century was the number of students large. At least a few terms' residence were, however, considered necessary to complete the education of a gentleman. Here, after the lack of privacy and disorder of a public school, life must have been very pleasant. Though there were ample opportunities for study, chiefly in the form of leisure, books and congenial friends, there was no pressure to attend lectures and no bogey of an examination to face. Though Cambridge did offer a mathematical Tripos from 1747 it was not until 1800 that Oxford revised its examination system and made some real demands on candidates for degrees. Throughout the eighteenth century the older system of disputations still persisted and, excellent as a test of mental agility and scholarship as these were when seriously used for this purpose, by now they had long degenerated into a farce. Intending candidates could learn by rote a string of syllogisms and, going through the empty forms of the disputations, could make sure of obtaining a degree with little inconvenience to themselves beyond that of residence, while a nobleman could normally obtain an honorary degree after a few terms' attendance.

At the universities class distinctions and privileges were as marked as those between the Collegers and Oppidans at Eton. In addition to the scholars on the foundation, who were usually the product of the grammar schools, each college had its complement of fee-paying students graded according to rank as Noblemen, and, at Cambridge, Fellow Commoners and Pensioners, and, at Oxford, Gentlemen Commoners and Commoners. Noblemen, Fellow Commoners and Gentlemen Commoners were distinguished by special privileges; they were allowed to dine at the High Table, and were admitted to the Common Room or Combination Room, while their very dress marked them off from the

The South Front of Strawberry Hill, 1793

The Library at Sledmere, 1794

William Kent by
Bartholomew Dandridge

The 3rd Earl of Burlington
by George Knapton, 1743

ordinary undergraduate; their gowns were trimmed with gold and silver lace and their velvet covered caps adorned with gold and silver tassels or 'tufts' while on Commencement Sunday, according to Gunning, the noblemen of Cambridge appeared even more resplendent. 'Their robes', he said, 'which are now uniformly purple, at that time were of various colours, according to the tastes of their wearers, purple, white, green and rose-colour were to be seen at the same time'.[1] Such men rarely came up with the intention of doing any serious reading, though individuals such as Charles James Fox and George Canning seized the opportunity to widen and deepen their knowledge of the classics already begun at school. For many, however, just released from school, the temptation to join 'the Smarts' or 'the Loungers' must have been considerable. Such men were adept in passing the time in the frivolous fashion portrayed in the following verses:

> I rise about nine, get to breakfast by ten,
> Blow a tune on my flute, or perhaps make a pen.
> Read a Play till eleven, or cock my laced hat,
> Then step to my Neighbours 'till Dinner to chat.
> Dinner over to Town, or to James' I go
> The news of the Town, so impatient to know.

No doubt it was this type of time-wasting life that made Vicesimus Knox, when discussing the educational problems of his day write:

> I consider the sending a son thither at present, without particular precautions, as a most dangerous measure; a measure which may probably make a shipwreck of his learning, his morals, his health, his character, and his fortune, if he has one.[2]

The precautions which he recommended were little likely to endear him to a young man of spirit:

> Whenever the circumstances of the parent will admit, a private tutor of character must be engaged. A compensation must be made him sufficient to induce him to inspect his pupil not only in the hours of study, but also of amusement; I would [he advised] give particular directions that the pupil should never take a walk or a ride, but in the company of the private tutor or of those whom he may approve.[3]

---

[1] H. Gunning: *Reminiscences of the University, Town and County of Cambridge from the year 1780* (1855), p. 26.
[2] Knox: *Op. cit.*, p. 324. [3] *Ibid.*, p. 327.

In addition to this constant supervision the tutor was also to have complete control of his charge's finances. With these safeguards he was prepared to concede that 'no place is better calculated for studious youth than these venerable seats of the Muses'.[1] Even so he was insistent that boys should not be sent up to the university too young, declaring, 'It is really cruel to let a boy of fifteen be precipitated into drunkenness and debauchery'.[2] Despite Knox's view many Fellow Commoners and Gentlemen Commoners, having survived the roughness and dissoluteness of their public school, survived also the dangers and perils of the more emancipated life of the university, and as men made a considerable contribution to the public life of their day.

Nevertheless, many did not, and if one is to judge by the acid outpourings of satirical writers and poets the wastage involved in the process was considerable. Thus James Miller in his satire *On Politeness* published in 1738, wrote:

> To Eaton sent, o'er every Form you leapt,
> No studious Eves, no toilsome Mattins kept,
> Thence Christ's Quadrangle took you for its own ;
> Had Alma Mater e'er so true a Son!
> Half seven Years spent in Billiards, Cards and Tippling,
> And growing every day a lovelier stripling;
> With half a College Education got,
> Half Clown, half Prig, half Pedant and half Sot;
> Having done all that ought to be undone,
> Finish'd those Studies which were ne'er began;
> To foreign Climes my Lord must take his Flight.

Because to have undertaken the Grand Tour was an advantage which only the wealthy could afford, it was in a very special sense the hallmark of an aristocratic education. Usually the young man, accompanied by a tutor who might be a valuable guide and a man of character and learning (Adam Smith thought it no diminution of his reputation to accompany the young Duke of Buccleuch), or a mere panderer to his pleasures, visited in a leisurely way at least France and Italy. In the first case it might well be a most valuable experience, though, since not all travelling tutors were Adam Smiths, it was usually used for rather limited purposes which were largely social and cultural. The connexions between 'good

---

[1] Knox: *Op. cit.*, p. 329.   [2] *Ibid.*, p. 325.

society' in England and on the Continent was very close, and the English visitor in France or Italy was received into the homes of his social equals and given every chance of becoming thoroughly familiar with the social stratum in those countries that most resembled his own.[1] And though he possibly failed to understand much else about the country he was visiting, he did at least bring back from France some ideas on polite society, and from Italy some appreciation of painting and sculpture, though of its depth and integrity in many cases Pope expressed strong doubts, writing in his *Moral Essays*:

> 'Tis strange, the Miser should his Cares employ
> To gain those Riches he can ne'er enjoy.
> Is it less strange, the Prodigal should waste
> His wealth, to purchase what he ne'er can taste?
> Not for himself he sees, or hears, or eats;
> Artists must chuse his Pictures, Music, Meats.
> He buys for Topham, Drawings and Designs,
> For Pembroke, Statues, dirty Gods, and Coins;
> Rare Monkish Manuscripts for Mead and Butterflies for Sloane.

Such then was the educational equipment that Georgian England provided for the sons of the gentry and the nobly born. Satirists might write bitterly of the Grand Tour, and pillory the finished product of the educational process, as one who

> Just broke from school, pert, impudent, and raw
> Expert in Latin, more expert in Taw,[2]
> His honour posts o'er Italy and France,
> Measures St. Peter's dome, and learns to dance.
> Thence having quick thro' various countries flown,
> Glean'd all their follies, and expos'd his own,
> He back returns, a thing so strange all o'er,
> As never ages past produc'd before;
> A monster of such complicated worth,
> As no one single clime could e'er bring forth.
> Half atheist, papist, gamester, bubble, rook,
> Half fiddler, coach man, dancer, groom and cook.[3]

[1] For Boswell's experiences, see *Boswell on the Grand Tour*. Edited by A. F. Pottle (1953).
[2] A game of marbles.
[3] The works of Soame Jenyns. Edited by C. N. Cole, Esq. (1790) Vol. I, p. 65. The poem quoted was written in 1746.

Even so, though seriously deficient in some respects, according
to modern ideas, despite the satirists, it was not a totally inadequate training for a man of leisure and affairs. English society
produced among its upper ranks too many men of ability, character and taste for the conventional pattern of its education to be
condemned out of hand. Yet that there was often very real
grounds for such satires as those quoted above was the opinion
of a man as capable of judging his contemporaries as Lord
Chesterfield. In 1749 he wrote,

> they come home, the unimproved illiberal and ungentlemanlike
> creatures, that one daily sees them, that is in the park and the streets,
> for one never meets them in good company; where they have
> neither the manners to present themselves, nor the merit to be re-
> ceived. But with the manners of footmen and grooms, they assume
> their dress too, for you must have observed them in the streets here,
> in dirty blue frocks, with oaken sticks in their hands, and their hair
> greasy and unpowdered, tucked up under their hats of an enormous
> size. Thus finished and adorned by their travels, they become the
> disturbers of play houses; they break the windows, and commonly
> the landlords, of the taverns where they drink: and are at once the
> support, the terror, and the victims of the bawdy-houses they
> frequent. These poor mistakened people think they shine and so they
> do indeed, but it is as putrifaction shines, in the dark.[1]

But though the Grand Tour gave the foolish ample opportunity
to give rein to their folly, the more level-headed traveller must
have found it a stimulating and broadening experience.

In what ways and to what varied uses could the education so
acquired be later put? To a large degree the satisfaction that any
society, however it may be organized, can afford to the individuals that compose it lies in the opportunities that it offers, and
the outlets that it provides, for their energies and ambitions. The
finest education that the theorists could devise to bring out the
latent capacities of men could lead to nothing but the bitterest
frustration if afterwards the capacities so developed were left
without employment. This was certainly not the case in eighteenth-
century England. A gentleman's education might be somewhat
one-sided and inadequate, but the opportunities for self-expres-
sion and achievement given to those who had undergone it were
considerable.

[1] Lord Chesterfield: *Op. cit.,* Vol. I, p. 330.

To the aristocrat and man of means perhaps no society has ever offered more. Unlike their contemporaries in France or Italy, the limitations on their activities were extraordinarily small. There was little, if anything, that a gentleman could not do. He could make money or be idle, spend his days in strenuous activity or laze them away, observe the conventions of his class or flout them, and still be accepted in the society of his equals. In consequence the eighteenth-century gentleman was a man of many parts. Men like Lord Chesterfield might set the standard of manners but there was plenty of solid understanding behind that elegant façade. As he wrote to his over-instructed son, 'Idleness is only the refuge of weak minds, and the holiday of fools'.[1] Not that he was adverse to recreation; in his view, 'Business by no means forbids pleasures; on the contrary, they reciprocally season each other; and I will venture to affirm, that no man enjoys either in perfection, that does not join both. They whet the desire for each other'.[2] The pleasures available to a man of fashion were both considerable and varied; quite sufficient to absorb the entire energies of the stupid and the frankly vicious. To the man of frivolous mind life in London meant routs at the great houses of the hostesses of the day, meant high play and drinking at Whites', meant quizzing the fair ladies who promenaded in the park, meant Ranelagh or Vauxhall, and meant, too, the more disreputable amusements of the Town. Notwithstanding these distractions it was also the background to very different activities; the average man of means justified his position as a member of the ruling class by assuming the responsibilities that went with it.[3]

Birth and wealth gave the entry not only to the world of pleasure, but to the equally engrossing world of politics. Not only the hereditary peers in the Lords, but elder sons and cadet branches in the Commons contributed a decisive element in parliament. It was but rarely that the ministers of the Crown were chosen outside a narrow circle of families. Men without connexions faced formidable barriers to political advancement to which their abilities seem to have entitled them. A comment of

---

[1] Lord Chesterfield: *Op. cit.*, Vol. I, p. 345.   [2] *Ibid.*, Vol. II, p. 333.

[3] *Vide* Professor Pares's comment, 'It is a pity that historians should so seldom have recognized the fact that men were in politics not only for party and for profit, but most of all for the due exercise of the talents God gave them, and for fun'. *King George III and the Politicians*, p. 30.

George III's is illuminating. 'Ld. North', he wrote, 'cannot seriously think that a private gentleman like Mr. Penton is to stand in the way of the eldest son of an earl, undoubtedly if that idea holds good it is diametrically opposed to what I have known all my life'.[1] What was true of politics was true also of the professions. The higher branches of the law were almost exclusively reserved for gentleman, often younger sons or cadets of noble houses; so were commissions in the services. These were obtained by purchase or by influence. In the army the colonel acted as vendor, but to become an officer in a fashionable and sought-after regiment frequently required a combination of both money and influence, as Boswell, when he intrigued and badgered for a commission in the Footguards, found to his discomfort. Except in the circumstances of war there was little chance for a man to rise from the ranks, and if he did he rarely rose high.

In the navy the story was the same. Here the usual means of entry was to go to sea as a member of the captain's retinue. By tradition he was allowed four personal servants for every hundred of the ship's company. These were more than was necessary and the sinecure vacancies were filled by youths taken on to oblige a friend, or by the captain's own relations. Though a small naval academy was established in 1733 to give young officers a more scientific training, this did little to lessen the grip of patronage, for the entrants were to be the sons of noblemen and gentlemen. It was only when it became clear that the older way of entry, via the captain's retinue, was still preferred, that in 1773, in order to keep up the intake, the Admiralty assigned fifteen places to 'the sons of officers' who were presumably war-time creations.[2] In the Church, too, birth and connexion, if not indispensable, were very useful, a point neatly underlined in the following extract from Boswell's diary. 'Mrs. Cholmondeley, wife to the Honourable and Reverend Mr. Cholmondeley, came to tea. Her husband was an ensign in the Guards, and at the battle of Fontenoy fairly hid himself; for which he was disgracefully broke at the head of the Army. He turned clergyman, and being an earl's brother, has done very well.'[3]

---

[1] R. Pares: *Ibid.,* p. 57.
[2] M. Lewis: *England's Sea Officers: the story of the Naval Profession* (1939), *passim.*
[3] J. Boswell: *London Journal,* p. 92.

Though the professions were regarded as perhaps the most fitting careers for the gentry and the cadets of noble houses there was not that absolute barrier to their being employed in trade, and even industry, which prevailed on the Continent. As Voltaire observed, 'a Peer's Brother does not think Traffic beneath him. When the Lord Townshend was a Minister of State, a brother of his was content to be a City-Merchant; and at the Time that the Earl of Oxford govern'd Great Britain, his younger Brother was no more than a Factor in Aleppo'.[1] Often gentlemen without influential connexions were glad enough to apprentice their sons to local trades or, if they could afford the premium, to citizens of London. In 1713 Nicholas Langley, gent., paid £180 to place his son with Gabriel Smith, 'citizen and grocer'.[2] Local tradesmen demanded less. John Lade gave £40 when he bound his son Nathaniel to 'Giles Watts of Battell, mercer'.[3] Two years later he placed another son with a goldsmith in Canterbury.

Sometimes the trades chosen are unexpected, at least for a gentleman's son. Nathaniel Moore bound one son to a joiner, giving £30 with him.[4] Even more surprising is the indenture which enrolled the son of Thomas Lawndey, gent., as the apprentice of a wig maker for a mere £10,[5] while, in Bedford, a stone-cutter, one John Turner, took Thomas, the son of George Wakeman of Cople, gent., with as little as £5.[6] This was a sum more usually paid by craftsmen in binding out their sons. It certainly seems to imply either strained means on the part of the father or gratitude for past favours on the part of Turner. As the century wore on this tendency to look to trade or industry for a career seems to have diminished. The growing population and the increased openings in the professions may have been partly responsible for this. Earlier, apart from London and a few of the larger ports, opportunities for professional careers were very limited. Though it was the gentry who placed their sons out into what were essentially middle class occupations there was nothing derogatory in a nobleman engaging in large-scale enterprises. The Duke of Bridgewater stands out as a man of business, exploiting his coal mines and promoting the first canals in this country. But,

[1] Voltaire: *Op. cit.,* p. 71.
[2] Sussex Record Society, Vol. XXVIII, p. 112.
[3] *Ibid.,* p. 111.   [4] *Ibid.,* p. 111.   [5] *Ibid.,* p. 113.
[6] Mrs. Hilary Jenkinson: *Art. cit.,* p. 172.

in the main, by the close of the century industry and trade were recruiting fewer adherents from the gentry.

Though the gentleman faced by the need to earn his living might find that convention was limiting his choice of an occupation, the man of fashion, enjoying what amounted to amateur status, was much less restricted, particularly when his interests lay in the world of sport. Many a man of birth could have earned his living by his skill as a coachman, as a gamekeeper, and perhaps, even as a prize-fighter! In part this was due to the very close link between the ruling class and the land. The English landowner, whatever his deficiencies, was rarely an absentee, a mere receiver of rents. The country gentlemen were usually even more closely concerned with the business of farming, and kept at least some of their land for their own use, though the remainder was let out. Indeed the average squire, whose rent-roll was moderate, relied on the produce of his home farm and estate for much of the food that his household consumed; from it came the corn and milk, the butter and eggs, the capons and game, the mutton and beef, and above all the bacon, pork and ale or cider with which to wash it down. Even the greater families who controlled the destinies of the country and dominated the social life of London maintained a very close connexion with the life of the countryside, and did more than perhaps any other set of men to develop its agricultural potentialities. It has been rightly said that the great houses that they built or altered according to the fashionable Palladian architecture of the day, and surrounded by parks and gardens designed by 'Capability' Brown and his fellows, were the products of an urbanized aristocracy, but the experimental farms that often surrounded them were not. Men like Townshend or Coke or the Duke of Bedford, perhaps even George III himself, could have talked more intelligently and with more grasp of their subject, on the best local rotation of crops or selective breeding of cattle, than most of the whole-time farmers of their day. Arthur Young declared of the Duke of Buccleuch that he was 'a determined farmer and seems to like conversing on no other subject'.[1]

Yet these same men, who could give an expert opinion on manuring and marling, on turnips and horse-hoeing husbandry,

[1] A. Young: *Autobiography,* p. 261.

were often patrons of art and collectors of paintings and statuary. For the eighteenth-century aristocrat was not only a man of affairs, a man of the countryside, capable of a hard day's hunting followed by a night of heavy drinking, he was also expected to be a man of taste. One result of the Grand Tour was some familiarity with the art of France and of Italy. To collect and bring home paintings became one of the activities of the nobleman, just as the twentieth-century American tourist collects postcards and 'stickers' as the visible memento of his, or her, travels. But to collect presupposed knowledge. By the reign of George III, though the country gentry might remain ignorant enough and content only to adorn their walls with indifferent portraits of themselves, their wives and families, a man of taste, moving in fashionable London society, was expected to take an intelligent interest in the Fine Arts, and to be able to discuss with discrimination at least the better-known artists and their works. Though much of this criticism was bogus, and even more of it dominated by the accepted canons of criticism of the time, the great collections built up by men like the Dukes of Portland and Bedford, by Lord Bute, by Lord Lansdowne, or by Coke of Holkham, often better known for his interest in sheep, testify to the genuine interest and taste of the eighteenth-century nobleman. Nor should the influence of men like Horace Walpole, who, by his experimenting at Strawberry Hill, contributed something to the revival of the Gothic, or of Lord Burlington, be ignored. Such men were not only deeply and passionately interested, they were themselves critics of no mean ability. Lord Chesterfield, indeed, seems to have felt that they pressed interest and enthusiasm too far, almost as it were jeopardizing their 'amateur status', and warned his son that though it was fitting that he should be acquainted with architecture he should 'for the minute and mechanical parts of it, leave them to masons, bricklayers, and Lord Burlington, who has, to a certain extent, lessened himself by knowing them too well. Observe the same methods as to military architecture; understand the terms, know the general rules, and then see them in execution with some skilful person.'[1]

To the eighteenth-century men of wealth and rank, therefore, it is clear that the community gave much. Such material resources

[1] Lord Chesterfield: *Op. cit.*, Vol. I, p. 381.

as the country had yet developed were at their disposal for the creation of a beautiful and elegant background. The houses that they built were dignified and stately, furnished with comfort and luxury, their well-proportioned rooms a gracious setting for rout and ball and card party, while outside parks and gardens, where Nature herself had been subdued and trimmed into conformity with those rules of taste that the gentleman enforced, provided a harmonious frame. On such a stage the gentleman of wealth could play any part for which his ability, or even more his rank and standing, fitted him. Nor was he kept to one monotonous role, but could be at once politician, agriculturist and patron of the arts. To few men have so many doors been opened, on few has so little restriction been imposed. Yet if much was given to them, though many were idle, debauched, even stupid men as individuals, as a class they gave as well as received: they gave statesmen, soldiers, sailors, they led the way in adjusting and developing the agricultural wealth of the country, so that the industrial revolution that was to come was in a sense built on the foundations which they laid.

If the position of the nobility and gentry was fortunate, the great body of the middle classes had no reason to quarrel with their lot. An expanding economy was producing ever-increasing opportunities for making money, and ever-growing amenities on which to spend it. If, however, a boy were to make the best of the new openings in trade, in industry and in transport, he needed a different education from the old classical curriculum of the grammar school. The middling sort were beginning to look for something a little more in tune with the life their children would have to lead. For this reason middle class education tended to differentiate itself from that of the nobleman and the gentleman. This need was met by the private school. It fell to the Dissenters to blaze the trail towards a more modern system of higher education. Shut out as they were by the discriminating legislation that imposed religious tests on all who went to the grammar school or the university, they had to make some provision for the education and training at least of their own clergy. Hence the seventeenth century saw the rise of the Dissenting academies. Many were intended only for those entering the ministry; others opened their doors to any wno cared to enrol. Though such academies did not ignore the classics, which were everywhere still considered the basis of sound learning, they added to their curriculum more modern studies. Warrington, where for a short time Joseph Priestley taught, offered 'the principle branches of mathematics', and courses on 'natural philosophy, theoretical and experimental.' In addition there were regular classes in geography, history, commerce, the theory of languages, education and composition. A student who was intending to follow a business career could study such useful subjects as book-keeping: those with a scientific bent could concentrate on chemistry or anatomy. Individual students were not intended to read as widely as this syllabus might suggest. It was intended that the courses would be selected and dovetailed by parents or guardians.

These Dissenting academies did valuable pioneering in the educational sphere, though the worth of the contribution made by the individual academies varied. Just because the subjects offered were so many and the teaching staff often so few, in some cases, though certainly not in all, the standard attained was superficial. Even so, such schools fulfilled a real need in providing an education more in harmony with middle class requirements than either the grammar school or the public school. As a consequence they began to be patronized by the sons of Anglicans as well as by Dissenters. As the demand for this type of education grew, other private schools, without any particular religious bias, were started, thus supplementing and diversifying the older educational system. By the middle of the century advertisements like the following, inserted in the *Oxford Journal* began to appear.

At the Boarding-school in the Vineyard, Youth are commodiously Boarded; and taught writing in all Hands now practised, with the proper Ornaments; Arithmetic of Whole Numbers and Fractions both vulgar and Decimal; the Computation of Foreign Exchanges; and Book Keeping, either by the English or Italian Method; together with constant Instructions in the English Grammar. These several Articles taught, and Boarding included, for Twelve Guineas a Year and One guinea Entrance. There are also taught Geometry, Plain Trigonometry, and Mensuration of Superficials and Solid, also Surveying of Lands after the most accurate Manner by the Theodolite, or Circumferentor, lately purchased for that Business. But these Branches of Learning are distinct from the former, and taught for

Two Guineas each. . . . And those who have already learnt the first four Rules of Arithmetic, may be fully compleated for Business in one year.[1]

In the same town was a similar 'boarding-school for Young Ladies' where the pupils, according to an advertisement of August 1758, were

> boarded and instructed in the Rudiments of the English Tongue, and taught Dresden and all manner of Needle Work in the neatest Manner for £11 a year, and Two Guineas Entrance. The utmost Care and Attention are had to their Conduct and Behaviour in general, as well as to their Improvement in the above mentioned Particulars. Writing, French, Music and Dancing are also taught at the same school at an additional, but easy Expence.

Not all areas provided facilities for female education. Catherine Hutton, speaking of her own childhood in Birmingham, said: 'There was no boarding school in or near Birmingham at this time, none nearer I believe than Worcester, Stratford, and Litchfield.' All that was available was a dame's school kept by a Mrs. and Miss Sawyer. 'The mother taught spelling and reading in the Bible, the daughter needlework, useful and ornamental, for sixpence a week.' At the age of ten she was in addition sent for one hour a day to a writing master. As many of her school fellows had now 'been transplanted to Worcester' young Catherine grew restless and 'wrote a very handsome note to my father asking permission to go there'.[2] William Hutton, however, regarded boarding-schools as 'hives of contamination' and resisted even the cajolery of the 'handsome note'. The state of many of these boarding-schools for young ladies justified his apprehensions. After the death of his beloved daughter Robbin, Arthur Young wrote bitterly of Camden House School.

> The rules for health are detestable, no air but in a measured, formal walk, and all running and quick motion prohibited. Preposterous! She slept with a girl who could only hear with one ear, and so ever laid on one side, and my dear child could do no otherwise afterwards without pains, because of the vile beds are so small that they must both lie the same way. The school discipline of all sorts, the food etc., etc., all contributed. She never had a bellyful at breakfast.

---

[1] J. Townshend: *Op. cit.*, p. 23.
[2] C. Hutton Beale: *Reminiscences of a Gentlewoman of the Last Century* (1891), p. 4.

Detestable this at the expence of £80 a year. Oh! how I regret ever putting her there . . . they are all theatres of knavery, illiberality and infamy.[1,2]

Popular though the private boarding-school, both for boys and for girls, became, it supplemented rather than superseded the older grammar school. The number of these had been considerably augmented in the closing years of the seventeenth and earlier decades of the eighteenth centuries, so that between 1660 and 1730 more than a hundred and seventy new ones had been established. For the tradesmen's son or middle-class boy they represented the normal entry to the professions, and particularly to scholastic or clerical life, via the universities. The record of many of the northern grammar schools, of places like Sedbergh, later to pass into the ranks of public schools, or of Ravenstonedale, bears witness to the use to which the education which they offered was put by the sons of small farmers and local folk. Thus, whether they aimed at the world of money-making or at the professions, the sons of the middling sort were reasonably well provided with the educational opportunities suitable for their future careers.

If, as the century progressed, the kind of education thought most appropriate for a gentleman tended to differ from that most popular with the non-professional section of the middle class, in other directions the gap between their way of life was closing. As middle-class incomes rose with the expansion of the national economy the amenities and conveniences of civilized living came more and more within their reach.

Here the desire to ape the manners of those above them in the social scale produced beneficent results, making the middle class way of life, at least for its more wealthy and ambitious members, a fuller and more gracious thing, as aristocratic influence made itself felt. This was the great era of domestic architecture, and for one gentleman's seat that was built or altered or improved a dozen more modest dwellings were completed, and any traveller, particularly in southern England, cannot but observe the number of well-proportioned Georgian houses that grace her provincial

[1] A. Young: *Autobiography*, p. 263.
[2] Not all girls' schools merited this sweeping condemnation as he may have realized later when he crossed this entry through. For details of the school kept by Hannah More and her sisters, see M. G. Jones: *Hannah More* (1952).

towns. Of Nottingham, Charles Deering, the local historian, wrote,

> A considerable Number of handsome houses have of late been built by Wealthy Tradesmen, and more are daily building, a magnificent proof of the increase of Riches among the Inhabitants owing chiefly to a beneficent Manufactury.

And then, filled with local patriotism, he went on,

> And tho' Towns of considerable Business and a flourishing Trade seldom give Gentlemen great Encouragement to be fond of settling in them, yet this must be said for our Town, that the healthful Air, the pleasant Site, and the plenty of all sorts of Necessaries as well as Conveniences of Life, maugre all other Objections, has even very lately induced some Gentlemen to build themselves Mansion Houses in it.[1]

This was apparently not mere local patriotism, for Catherine Hutton, on a visit, commented on the fact that

> here it is the fashion to walk, and the first people in the town make a practice of it. The women are, many of them extremely elegant; I think but a few of them handsome; but there is an air in their dress and manner that is seldom seen at Birmingham.[2]

In London the contribution of the Georgian builder was even more substantial than in the provinces, for it was in the latter part of the century that the pattern of the squares and streets of the West End was laid out. Though many of these contained the town residences of the great, for, as foreigners remarked, there were few palaces in London, many more of these new houses were occupied by substantial merchants, by successful lawyers, and by all that host of people who, without either belonging to 'polite society', or even wishing to do so, were, nevertheless, making a sufficient income to command a very considerable degree of material comfort. If men like Lord Burlington or the Earl of Pembroke had not been prepared to finance the publications of architectural plans and books, such as Kyp and Knyff's *Noblemen's Seats*, or Paine's *Plans and Elevations of Noblemen's Houses*, the rules they laid down for good architecture might not

---

[1] C. Deering: *Nottingham Vetus and Nova.* Edited by G. Ayscough (1751), p. 16.
[2] C. H. Beale: *Op cit.,* p. 21.

have been either so widely discussed or so widely accepted. But, fortunately, at a time when the demand for houses was growing and the money to build was there, persons with any pretensions to education were usually in a position to pronounce a building 'good' or 'bad', according to the prevailing canons of taste, and these standards, imposed from above and so widely accepted, became part of the mental stock-in-trade of even the ordinary local builder, who, called upon to design a house, did so in accordance with the contemporary canons of good taste. And, therefore, though the designs of many were formal, limited, conventional, and though the builder relied on the general plans and suggestions available to him in published works, without himself either having received much training in the principles of architecture or being able to call upon the services of a professional architect, yet the growing number of the middle class were housed in dwellings that were both well-proportioned and dignified, and as such a stimulation to a more civilized way of life.

How far the elegancies of the upper classes permeated the way of life of the middling sort as a whole, by even the middle of the century, it is difficult to say. There is certainly evidence to show that the modest gentleman and the prosperous merchant, the better-paid clergy and the successful professional man, lived not only comfortably but with some refinement. Their houses were well designed and well furnished, well kept and clean, though with perhaps not quite the fanatical attention which the Dutch were wont to bestow on these matters. Still, since there was no lack of servants to polish and scour and scrub, for wages were low, even householders of limited means did not find it necessary to economize in this direction. Parson Woodforde kept a personal manservant as well as a farm man, and an upper and under maid. The Rev. John Warneford, writing about a living in which he was interested, asked, 'I suppose your house fitted for the commodious reception of a Family which, including three servants, consists at present of seven Persons',[1] and was informed that the previous incumbent's family had comprised the parson, his wife, four children and three servants. For a family as large as this, three servants was a modest establishment. On average, very ordinary families without any pretensions to gentility kept at

[1] G. Eland: *Op. cit.*, p. 44.

least one manservant to look after the master, as well as a cook-maid and one or two other female servants. Indeed, not to be able to employ at least one full-time maid might in itself well be used as the line of demarcation between 'the middling sort' and the great mass of labouring folk. But if some degree of elegance was to be found in many middle-class homes it was far from being universal. John Wood, describing Bath in 1727, commented on the fact that the floors of the dining-rooms were still stained with soot and small beer to hide the dirt, that the main articles of furniture were still cane or rush chairs, heavy oak tables, and coarse linen or woollen hangings, with a small mirror, on occasions, as the rooms' one concession to luxury. By the end of the century such simplicity was much rarer.

Even when furnishings remained simple it is probable that the middle classes, as well as their betters, over-ate. Men like Parson Woodforde, whose diary in this, as in so many aspects of eight-teenth-century life, illuminates the domestic practices of his age, dilates, with obvious satisfaction, on the pleasures of the table, recording with loving care his consumption of roast duck or roasted swan, or of a pike 'with a Pudding in his Belly', while his practice of serving gooseberries with his roast pork might well commend itself to the modern housewife, tired of the traditional apple sauce. Catherine Hutton describes another clerical meal while dining with the Rector of Aston in 1779.

> At three o'clock we sat down to table, which was covered with salmon at top, fennel sauce to it, melted butter, lemon pickle and soy; at the bottom a loin of veal roasted, on the one side kidney beans, on the other peas, and in the middle a hot pigeon pie with yolks of egg in it. To the kidney beans and peas succeeded ham and chicken, and when everything was removed came a currant tart. . . . After dinner we had water to wash, and when the cloth was taken away, gooseberries, currants and melon, wines and cyder. . . . At a little before five my mother, Sally Cocks, and I retired into the drawing room, where I amused myself with reading and looking at the prints till six, when I ordered tea and sent to let the gentlemen know it was ready.[1]

Many middle-class families, especially those in which children were numerous, must have had to content themselves with less

---

[1] C. H. Beale: *Op. cit.,* p. 15.

Scarborough, 1780

Bathing Machines at Brighton by Rowlandson

The Jubilee Ball, or the Venetian Manner of Masquerade at Ranelagh

varied menus. One estimate of the outlay on food for the establishment of a gentleman of more modest means, whose household consisted of himself, his wife, four children and two servants, excluding such basic necessities as bread and vegetables, suggested as adequate provision seven pounds of butter and three and a half of cheese weekly, a pound of meat per day, and an expenditure of two shillings on tea and three shillings on sugar as the basis of the weekly budget.[1] In addition, something like nine pints of milk and twelve gallons of beer were included, a proportion explained by the impure condition of much of the eighteenth-century water supply and the heavy drinking of the age. All indulged to a large extent, nor, among the middling sort, was drinking confined to beer and cider; the price of wine and spirits brought them within the reach of even moderate budgets. It is true that, because within the middle class very great differences of income and, therefore, of social habits were to be found, even the widest generalizations can be only approximately accurate, but even when every allowance has been made for this it would seem that the general standard of living alike in houses, in food and in clothing was good.

It was in the provision of entertainment that the effect of the fashionable world was most marked and social distinctions most blurred. In the earlier part of the century this was particularly true of London, where those well-known centres of pleasure, Vauxhall and Ranelagh, threw their doors open to all with well-filled purses. Here the nobleman and the citizen mingled, if not as individuals at least as classes. Here the citizen's wife could acquaint herself with the latest style of hairdressing, could copy the line of a cloak or the tone of a voice, could learn, if she would, to languish as a fine lady. The playhouse, too, catered both for persons of fashion and for the more thrifty citizen, and if the play or players had any kind of reputation it was often difficult to get places. Here again the two worlds mingled, though not so freely as at Vauxhall. Convention, as well as income assigned the former to the boxes or even to a place on the stage while the average Londoner was content with a seat in the pit. The riff-raff and the footmen, who had attended their masters or kept seats for them were relegated to the gallery. Those Londoners who were

G. E. Fussell: *Village Life in the Eighteenth Century* (1948), p. 39.

content with simpler amusements were equally well provided for
by the ring of pleasure gardens that surrounded the town. Here
they took the air, strolling between clipped hedges or drinking
tea round little tables in sheltered arbours. Some were pleasant
places where all was decorum. Others came to acquire a bad name
for rowdiness, for drinking and for debauchery: here the citizen
would not mix with the world of fashion but with the under-
world of highwaymen, thieves and their molls, the world made
familiar to us by Gay.

In the smaller towns recreations were limited to those which
people could provide for themselves. There were picnics and tea
drinkings for the ladies, drinking, cock-fighting, cards and gambling for the men, with an occasional visit from strolling players
and an infrequent ball organized by the local gentry, wherever an
assembly room or inn could supply a suitable room, large enough
for the formal dances of the day. Few towns had a regular theatre,
or even a regular assembly room in the first half of the century.
Yet, in spite of its lack of formal entertainment, the county town
had an importance in the social life of the district, of which it was
later to be deprived by the greater ease of travel. As a centre of
whatever society and gaiety there was it had no rivals. This very
fact often tended to emphasize rather than to obliterate social
distinctions. It was the local gentry who dominated its social life.
The assemblies were exclusive gatherings: the wife of a shopkeeper would certainly not be welcomed, though for the families
of the rector, the lawyer and the wealthy merchant there would
have been a place. When Arthur Young as a young man was apprenticed to a merchant in Lynn he found himself very much on
the fringes of local society, recording that, 'In this place monthly
assemblies were held, a major feast and ball in the evening, a
dancing master's ball and assembly at the Mart. It was not common, I was told, for merchant's clerks to frequent these, a suggestion I spurned, and attended them, dancing with the principal
belles.'[1] In Nottingham the distinction was so clearly recognized
that the town possessed two assembly rooms.

One of these places of Assembly [wrote Deering] is in the Low
Pavement, purposely built for this use, consisting of a handsome,
lofty and spacious Room, with a Gallery for the Music at the upper

[1] A. Young: *Autobiography*, p. 23.

End, the Room is 67 Feet long, and 21 Feet broad, to this belong two withdrawing Rooms and a Place where a Person attends who sells all kinds of Refreshments. This is called the Ladies Assembly. The other called the Tradesmen's Assembly, is held in a large Room 70 Feet long and 20 Feet Broad, where the wealthy Tradesmen, their Wives and Sons and Daughters meet for the same Recreation.[1]

As travelling facilities grew better and roads were improved by the exertions of the turnpike trusts, the most comfortably circumstanced and educated section of the middle class, as well as the gentry, became more mobile, though it was said of the majority of the well-to-do in Birmingham, even by the end of the century, that they did not travel far from home except on business. 'Comparatively few had ever seen London, near as it was; fewer still had ever seen a mountain or the sea, or had any idea of a ship, except from pictures. These things were read about and talked of as very wonderful indeed.'[2] Many middle-class families were more mobile. Though the educational advantages of the Grand Tour were not for them they broke the monotony of life and added to their own information by exploring their native country. The eighteenth century was the century of the watering-place and the Spa. Bath in particular was the very essence of the genteel and the civilized. Here persons of fashion, the minor gentry, the prosperous middle class, all accepted the discipline of its social routine. This was very largely the work of Beau Nash. A visit to Bath was a much more exciting and formative event to an ordinary middle-class family than it ever could be to the regular man of fashion, and did much to spread the observances of polite society among those who would otherwise have had little chance of such contacts. That there could be this intermingling, this apparent harmony of social life was itself highly significant of the place that the middle-class were coming to assume in the social structure of their country. They were no longer content to accept a purely utilitarian role in the national life: they wanted more than merely material satisfactions. By now they were claiming the more artificial pleasures of polite society. A visit to Brighton, that centre of Regency life, came into the same category, though here the social round was more informal and the fashionable cure sea-

---

[1] *Op. cit.,* p. 75.
[2] R. K. Dent: *The Making of Birmingham* (1894), p. 157.

bathing rather than taking the waters, a practice assisted by the new-fangled and experimental bathing-van.

The North had similar, if less sophisticated, resorts of its own. A journey to the South was a more formidable undertaking to most people than a trip to the Continent would be to-day. In Yorkshire both Harrogate and Scarborough rose to more than local fame. A visit to one of these places was an event important enough to be thought worthy of print and there seems to have been a steady demand for 'travel' books like Hutton's *A Tour to Scarborough*, describing for mere stay-at-homes both the incidents of the journey and life at the watering place, and in particular the new routine of sea bathing.

> There are thirty six machines for sea bathing, [wrote Hutton] which is a sufficient proof of their frequent use. I have often observed eight or ten in the water at the same time. The place is extremely convenient. The bathers are fond of a full tide; but I can see no evil in bathing at low water except the length of the way; for, as no river runs into the sea to weaken it the water must at all times have the same effect. Each time you bath is sixpence exclusive of perquisites.[1]

As for all new practices, much was claimed for this one; and sea-bathing was thought to be helpful for such varied complaints as epilepsy, palsy, disorders of the heart, debility, cutaneous complaints, gout, rheumatism and scrophile scurvy. It is little wonder therefore, that a class of persons not sufficiently wealthy or experienced to enjoy the experience of the Grand Tour should flock to avail themselves of amenities at once so novel, so pleasurable and so beneficial! Both Harrogate and Scarborough, because of their situation, were essentially more middle-class in their clientele than either Bath or Brighton, for they lay further from the hub of the polite world, London, and therefore attracted less attention from the world of fashion. Even so, they too helped to spread some of the conventions of polite society to a wider circle, for local families of good standing were among their patrons, and by their example helped to set a new standard of urbanity for those who frequented, either for pleasure or for health, the spas and seaside resorts of the North.

Some travellers were more adventurous in their search for air and scenery. Elizabeth Bennet, it may be remembered, exclaimed

[1] W. Hutton: *A Tour to Scarborough* (1803 edition), p. 170.

'What delight! What felicity!' when invited to join her uncle and aunt on a tour of pleasure to the Lakes. Catherine Hutton took her mother to Aberystwyth, and left an amusing record of the trials, and even perils of the journey: roads left much to be desired and the accommodation at some of the Welsh inns was more than primitive, even by eighteenth-century standards. On an other occasion they went to Blackpool, which made no very favourable impression on her. She described it as 'situated on a level, dreary, moorish coast, the cliffs are of earth and not very high. It consists of a few houses, ranged in a line with the sea and four of those are for the reception of company; one accommodating 30, one 60, one 80 and the other 100 persons.'[1] Of her fellow guests she has some amusing comments to make. 'The Boltoners', she declared, 'are sincere, good humoured, and noisy, the Manchestrians reserved and purse proud; the Liverpoolians free and open as the ocean on which they get their riches. I know little of the gentry but believe them to be generous, hospitable and rather given to intemperance'.[2]

In both their material standard of living and in their opportunities for amusement, rational or otherwise, the middle classes, and more particularly those of more ample means, had, therefore, little need to complain. If, however, the minor landed gentry are excluded, as not coming for this purpose within their ranks, comparatively few of their members could be described as being of independent means, and, therefore, what was most vital to them was not the entertainment or pleasure that was open to them but the scope that society gave to their talents for earning a living. This, as an earlier analysis of their composition showed, was very wide, and did not exclude the professions, though the plums were usually reserved for the gentry. In general, though a boy from a middle-class family might follow the Army, the Navy, the Church, the Law, or Medicine, there was a very real distinction between the upper and more honourable, and lower branches of these professions.

If the Law attracted him he might serve his apprenticeship with an attorney, but he was much less likely to become a member of one of the Inns of Court. If his inclination was towards medicine he would probably start his career as an apothecary's apprentice.

---

[1] C. H. Beale: *Op. cit.*, p. 55.   [2] *Ibid.*, p. 57.

This by the eighteenth century had become the backdoor to the medical profession. Originally the apothecaries had been attached to the Grocers, but in 1617 they separated and became a City Company in their own right. They had, however, no control or jurisdiction outside the London area and even within that area there were many practising apothecaries who were not members of the Company. Their original function had been merely to sell drugs, not to prescribe them or to presume to give medical advice. But qualified physicians were expensive and, outside London, not always to hand, particularly in rural areas. This is admirably illustrated by an extract from Parson Rogers' diary, where, on 16 May 1729, he made the following entry.

> Mrs. Gibbons being ill of fever intermitting, and the Gout in her stomach was so ill that 'twas thought another fitt would carry her off; so she desired me to write to Dr. Brown of Arlesley to make all hast he could to her assistance. No body being to be had, it being night, about 9 o'clock, I sent my son Thomas, who lay at Bedford and went early next morning to Arlesley, where he heard the Doctor was gone to Bath.[1]

It is pleasant to be able to record that on this occasion, despite the lack of a doctor, neither the fever nor the gout in her stomach carried poor Mrs. Gibbons off and that she lived to give Thomas five shillings for his fruitless journey.

In such circumstances it is understandable that the practice grew up of consulting the more accommodating and cheaper apothecary. Until Rose's case, however, he gave advice at his peril, for the physicians were jealous of their privileges. Even when the House of Lords decided that the apothecary might prescribe medicines he was still denied the right to charge for so doing. If he thought it safer to conform to the letter of the law the charge for his professional services had to be concealed in the price of the drugs he sold. He was in fact, in his own eyes and in those of his customers, merely a tradesman whose special knowledge enabled him to give advice on the use of drugs, and competent to treat minor accidents and ailments. Such training as he had was obtained in the traditional way, namely by serving an apprenticeship with a recognized master. In such cases the premium

[1] C. D. Linnell: 'The Diary of Benjamin Rogers, Rector of Carlton, 1720–71'. *Bedfordshire Hist. Record Soc.*, Vol. XXX, 1950.

demanded by a master of some reputation was considerable. This fact alone was a barrier to poor men's sons and explains why gentlemen were often willing to bind their sons to apothecaries. It was a respectable, and could be a profitable calling, which a gentleman might follow without complete loss of status, but it did not confer gentility, not even the rather threadbare and shabby gentility of the poor curate's cloth, on those who did not possess it by birth. In consequence though some apprentices were technically of gentle birth more came from the families of prosperous tradesmen. John Wells, for example, was bound out by his father, a draper, with a premium of £43 to an apothecary in Kettering. That the trade was a popular one is clear from the numbers of boys whose indentures were enrolled and whose names and premiums were recorded in local apprenticeship books. Many men went no further than this but, having served their time, set up for themselves doing the work of a country doctor.

For the ambitious or scientifically minded it was often taken as the first step towards study at the University and the attaining of a degree; a means in some cases of gaining a little preliminary experience and in others of acquiring sufficient funds to make further study at Edinburgh or Leyden possible. Provincial surgeons, too, seem to have been recruited in much the same way and drawn from the same social groups. The biography of John Dawson, the surgeon and mathematician, is illuminating in this respect. His father was a poor 'statesman' worth some £10 a year and young John was largely self-taught. After collecting some small funds by acting as a kind of itinerant schoolmaster he went as an assistant to a Mr. Bracken, a Lancaster surgeon, and there learnt enough to set up for himself in his native town, Sedbergh. When he had saved £100 he walked to Edinburgh and studied there until his hoard was spent. He then returned, earned a further £300 and with that continued his studies, this time in London, though he eventually returned to practise in Sedbergh. Obviously it was by no means impossible even for a poor boy, granted the ability and the persistence, to qualify as a doctor, while the son of middle-class parents, with some money to pay for his training, could do so with ease. Such men it is true rarely attained the dignity of admission as a Fellow to the Royal College of Surgeons. John Fothergill and John Lettson were only licentiates even when, at the height of their career, they were reputed to be making £5,000 a year. For the majority, even among the London doctors, their income was very much less. Even so, the practice of medicine, whether as a physician or surgeon, or as a mere apothecary, could be rewarding. John Knyveton, one of the new man-mid-wives, in 1772 reported: 'My financial state, thanks to God's mercy pretty sound: my business brings in about £400 a year, the lectures £100'. By 1778, as he began to attract a better-class patient, the figures were £600 and £150 respectively.[1] He was then able to buy a new chariot, employ a coachman in livery and have a servant 'to ride behind and knock flourishes on my patients' knockers'. Nor were the attractions of medicine only financial. There were fascinating opportunities to strike out new paths in medical treatments and to diagnose new diseases: many eighteenth-century doctors were men of considerable scientific interests and attainments.

Schoolmastering was another profession recruited mainly from the sons, and daughters, of the middling sort. Many schoolmasters were in Holy Orders and had turned to teaching to supplement inadequate stipends. Instances are common. John Redington, headmaster of Norwich Grammar School from 1732–7, had been first a sizar at Trinity, Cambridge, then a Fellow. In 1708 he had been ordained, and four years later was given the living of St. Edmund's, Norwich. His connexion with the city was, therefore, an old one.[2] Often clergymen ran schools of their own. Dr. Routh's father, who held the rectories of St. Margaret with St. Peter, South Elmham, in 1758 moved to Beccles, where he took charge of a private school. From 1764–74 he combined this activity with holding the rectory there for the Reverend Bence Sparrow. Finally he, too, obtained the headship of a grammar school, for in 1770 he was appointed to the Fanconberge Grammar School at Beccles.[3] Dissenting ministers also were often schoolmasters, and from the Dissenting academies came a steady stream of recruits to the profession. Joseph Priestley, in his *Memoirs* records how, 'Like most other young men of a liberal education I had conceived a great aversion to the business of a

---

[1] *Man Midwife*. Edited by Ernest Gray (1946), pp. 60, 76.
[2] H. W. Saunders: *A History of Norwich Grammar School* (1932), p. 303.
[3] R. D. Middleton: *Dr. Routh* (1938), p. 2.

schoolmaster, and had often said I would have recourse to anything else for maintenance, in preference to it.'[1] Nevertheless, the
poorness of his stipend and the unpopularity of his religious views
with many of his co-religionists drove him to this expedient.
When he moved to Nantwich he started a school, where, he con-
fessed, 'in this employment, contrary to my expectations, I found
the greatest satisfaction'.[2] Just as the increased interest in medicine
had multiplied the openings in that direction, so the rising standard of living, the growing complexity of industry and trade, and
the demand for some measure of education as a pre-requisite for
earning a living stimulated the demand for schoolmasters.
Though some of these teachers were very ignorant, knowing little
more than the rudiments of the three R's, others were men of a
wide culture and learning who brought to their profession intellectual curiosity, integrity and enthusiasm. If some ushers were
a badly paid and downtrodden race of men, many of the head
masters of the free grammar schools and the rising public schools
were making a very real place for themselves in the local society
in which they lived.

From the same social background, too, came growing numbers
of writers ranging from the man of genius, like Samuel Johnson,
to the ordinary ruck of ephemeral undistinguished authors, poets,
pamphleteers and political hacks, who catered for a new reading
public. The lapse of the licensing laws gave a new impetus to the
political tract, which the bitter political feuds of Anne's reign did
so much to encourage. The growing middle class themselves
created a demand for news, for curious information, for romances,
while many even of the labouring poor, instructed by the charity-
school movement at least in the art of reading, used their new
literacy to devour cheap quarto histories like *The Life and Death
of Mother Shipton*, which sold for sixpence or a shilling; or even
cruder, badly printed chapbooks, like *Penny Merriments*, or, more
edifying, *Penny Godliness*. As a result, even in the first half of the
century, there were a good many book-sellers in London, while
one estimate in 1704 speaks with some exaggeration of at least
another three hundred trading in the provincial towns. Here then
was a rich field for the middle-class man of parts, whether he

[1] J. Priestley: *Memoirs of Dr. Priestley to the year 1795, written by himself* (1806), p. 26.
[2] *Ibid.*, p. 28.

sought to earn his living as a book-seller, as a publisher, or as a writer, and to the professions of the doctor, the schoolmaster, the lawyer and the parson must be added that of the man of letters.

Another profession that by the eighteenth century was offering a public following, some reputation and, at times satisfactory, if uncertain, cash rewards, was that of the actor. The desire to act was confined to no one stratum of society, and the theatrical fraternity came from very different backgrounds and won very varying places for themselves in the estimation of their fellow men. Garrick might attain a national reputation and mix freely with the literary and even fashionable society of London, but the flavour of unrespectability still clung to the calling as a whole. The main body of players were not ranked much above the plausible vagabonds that wandered up and down the countryside, or above the jugglers and bear-wards that performed at local fairs, while for a woman to be an actress was, normally, for her to be placed among the ranks of the sisters of easy virtue. There was published in 1805 *The Thespian Dictionary*, which purported to give the biographies of the leading actors and actresses of the preceding century, and from it something, though it is revealing how little, can be gleaned of their backgrounds. Of many not much was known, apart from the fact that they came from Ireland. Of others, nothing is recorded of their early life or parents, in itself a significant fact, since where the background was respectable and known, it usually seems to have been given. For a youth from a comfortable middle-class home to take to such a way of life was hazardous. Nevertheless, young men of respectable, even well-to-do, parents were by the middle of the century sometimes turning to the stage for their careers. David Garrick was a case in point. His father was an army captain, and he had himself been educated at the Free School at Lichfield, where he had come under Johnson's influence. His father intended him to be a merchant, and he was sent to join an uncle who was a wine merchant in Lisbon. In a twelve month's time he was back in London, considering the law, and he was entered at Lincoln's Inn, though still dabbling with the wine trade. By now, however, his greatest desire was to become an actor. With the aid of Mr. Gifford, the manager of the theatre in Footman's Fields, he tried out his abilities at Ipswich, acting under an assumed name, and was sufficiently pleased both with the life and his aptitude for it, to forsake the idea of either trade or the Bar. By his reputation and the standing he achieved, he made it easier for other like-minded young men from similar homes to do the same. Yet, if the editor of *The Thespian Dictionary* is to be believed, many of the actors who came from better homes came to the stage because circumstances for which they were not responsible had already threatened or destroyed their domestic background. Charles Murray, the son of Sir John Murray, had had his family security ruined by the fact that his father had been the Pretender's Secretary in the 'Forty-Five'. True he had a livelihood at his command, for he had been placed under a surgeon in London, and had made several voyages as a surgeon's mate to the Mediterranean before the reputation, which he made in private theatricals, induced him to take up the stage professionally. Even then he thought it more discreet to assume the name of Raymur, an anagram of his own family name. Tate Wilkinson, who, for many years managed the Theatre Royal at York, had seen something of fashionable society and had formed some useful connexions. Sent by his father, who was Chaplain to the Savoy and to the Prince of Wales, to Harrow, he made as his closest friend George Forbes, who later became the Earl of Granard, and Lord Mansfield was sufficiently interested in the young man to give him a letter of introduction to Garrick, which got him an engagement at thirty shillings a week, and started his feet on the theatrical ladder. Yet here, too, there was the same element of a broken home in the background: his father was eventually transported for celebrating marriages irregularly!

Sometimes just the lure of the stage was enough. Charles Bannister, founder of the dynasty of actors, grew friendly with a group of strolling players while his father was working in the Victualling Office at Deptford, and joined them. Roger Kemble followed the same road, married the daughter of the manager, and, on his father-in-law's death, succeeded to the management of the company. Although both the Kembles tried to divert their sons from the stage (they apprenticed one to an apothecary and sent the other to the University of Douai) both sons eventually became actors. The same fate overtook Barrymore; he had been placed by his father in a counting-house, but he, too, joined a group of travelling players, though he did change his name to Blewit to save his family's pride.

Infrequently a young woman from a respectable home might be attracted to the stage. Mrs. Bannister, for instance, was the daughter of a mantua maker, and had been intended for the same trade until her talent for music promised more success in that direction, so that she appeared in oratorio at the Haymarket. She however quitted the stage in 1791, 'filling the more amiable character of a domestic wife and tender mother.'[1] Mrs. Barclay, who also came to the stage *via* music lessons, claimed to be the daughter of a clergyman. But the origin of most of the women who were actresses by profession is shrouded in obscurity, and of many of them it could doubtless be said, as it was said of Mrs. Barresford, 'She fell a sacrifice to dissipation.' For men at the best it was a career of doubtful standing, for women, at least in the public estimation, there was rarely even much doubt; though a certain number of men, who could be counted as coming from the middle ranks of society, did become actors, it was, until the close of the century, an uncertain and suspect profession. Boswell's verdict, when commenting on Johnson's habit of always speaking ill of actors, was that 'perhaps, there was formerly too much reason from the licentious and dissolute manners of those engaged in that profession' for this, but he added, 'In our own time such a change has taken place, that there is no longer room for such an unfavourable distinction'.[2]

It is sometimes forgotten that an expanding and rationalized agriculture was also providing the middle class with the possibility of new careers. At least one new profession emerged in the countryside, the creation of the improved agriculture of the day, the estate agent. Stewards there had been in plenty, many very inconsiderable men, like Nathaniel Chapman of Puddletown in Dorset, who was described as a yeoman, and who, for £12 a year, his board and lodging and 'his riding charges and reasonable expences in going aboute executing and attending ye severall occations and orders', was to act for Sir William Drake as 'generall

---

[1] *The Thespian Dictionary* (1805).
[2] J. Boswell: *The Life of Samuel Johnson, LL.D.* Edited by A. Glover, Vol. I, p. 103.

Bayliffe to buy and sell as occation shall bee, and to inspect his lands and tenements & take an account of his tenants in ye count-ies of Bucks, Linc and Cheshire'.[1] Such men may have been ade-quate where the estate in question was small and its owner was content to run it upon traditional lines, where, in fact, honesty and horse sense were all that was required. But more elaborate methods of farming were calling for more specialized estate management. Where there was a good deal of legal business to be transacted one expedient, of which increasing use was made, was to employ the services of a local attorney. Where he was honest, competent, and reasonably familiar with local farming conditions such an arrangement worked smoothly. The Deptford estates of Mr. Wickham of Grassington were so managed, first by Thomas Wellings and afterwards by Edward Currey, with ap-parent satisfaction on both sides.

But competent, honest service was not always easy to secure. Unsuspecting persons might well be the victims of unscrupulous exploitation. Women may have been particularly vulnerable in this respect. Such was certainly the experience of Mrs. Bent. She was a widow and was not apparently able to supervise the man-agement of her property which she entrusted to Thomas Carter, an attorney of Leicester. Thomas Carter, despite the fact that he was half-brother to a judge, proved most unscrupulous. Ap-parently he regularly returned as arrears rent he had received and pocketed and, just as regularly, charged up repairs that had never been done. Finally, Mrs. Bent, finding that her income was dis-tressingly and mysteriously dwindling, consulted an experienced friend. He, on going down to investigate, found, 'instead of little Pallaces (as one wou'd have judged by what had been charged), all ye Farm Houses miserably in disorder & ruin, & few or none of ye expences true'.[2] It is pleasant to be able to record that the defaulting attorney was brought to book and forced, under pain of exposure, to pay back his illicit pickings. Such episodes illustrate how difficult it could be for the landowner to secure efficient estate management where he was not able to exercise personal oversight.

By the close of the century the need for a specialist to undertake the supervision of any considerable estate was coming to be

G. Eland: *Op. cit.*, p. 56.　　　　　　　　[2] *Ibid.*, p. 66.

recognized. Nathaniel Kent, whose *Hints to Gentlemen of Landed Property* had been published by Dodsley in 1775, was undertaking a good deal of this kind of work. In 1788 he agreed to manage all Sir William Drake's estates on the following terms, 'For surveying, valuing, arranging, stipulating covenents, and new letting the estates upon the best terms possible . . . 6*d.* in the pound upon such Rents as may be established if done upon one view; but if it should take two views, then one shilling in the pound.' And he adds interestingly, 'This is a fixed and established Rule by which all men in my profession guide themselves'. He then stipulated,

> As to a recompense for my constant attention to your business, such as Auditing and Examining all accounts with your different stewards, seeing that no errors or impositions affect you, holding all necessary correspondence, and seeing that all Remittances are faithfully brought to account, superintending all contracts, bargains and sales . . . for one hundred pounds a year, provided such business be either transacted at your house in Town or at my office in Craig's Court. But if I am occasionally required to make a journey (which will not be very often) I shall expect a guinea a day & my Expences for the time I am out.[1]

As the £100 in question represented less than one per cent. of the rent-roll involved Kent was offering his services very reasonably; nevertheless, the handling of such business on these terms offered the prospect of a new, interesting and well-paid career to the man of business who was knowledgeable about country affairs.

But though the professions attracted those members of the middle class who had social ambitions or who were repelled by the cruder world of industry and commerce the great majority of them got their livelihoods through some form of economic activity, either in the actual production of the goods or in the handling of their distribution. Since the eighteenth century, though he was far from negligible earlier, the middleman had come to play an increasingly important part in the internal organization of the country. As towns grew larger, and as London absorbed more and more of the population the problem of transferring food and clothes to the places where they were most in demand was no easy one. In London, by Elizabeth I's reign, the old conception of buying and selling in the open market was

[1] G. Eland: *Op. cit.,* p. 68.

disappearing fast. Instead, country buyers were collecting stocks to sell to London wholesalers and retailers, London middlemen were at the same time challenging their monopoly of country produce by sending out their own agents to buy up commodities on the spot.[1] Everywhere there was a great network of such dealings, all of them very profitable, most of them open to men of little capital, and affording continual opportunities for the recruitment of the middle class. Though London offered the most spectacular field for such enterprises, all the great towns had the same needs to be supplied in a lesser degree. This was particularly true of the ports with the constant demand of ships to be victualled and crews to be clothed. The concentration of population, particularly in London, made the provision of transport another lucrative business. Dealers in cattle and sheep drove their animals from the grazing districts and sold them to London middlemen or to the London butchers. Heavy wagons brought in the malt and flour and country produce. Fleets of barges and small ships thronged the Thames, all bringing from the neighbouring counties the goods that London needed. Each of these activities offered openings to enterprising men, openings that called for only a modicum of resources for small beginnings but that might lead to the accumulation of considerable capital invested in wagons and horses, in pack trains of horses and mules, in barges and hoys and lighters. The transport of coal in the sturdy colliers down the East Coast was in itself a business of no mean size, for, by the eighteenth century, London was a coal-burning city.

The middleman found his openings, too, in looking after the needs of the country's growing industry, and particularly in the organization of the textiles. The small independent weaver who persisted in many parts, and particularly in the Yorkshire valleys, wanted to buy his wool in small quantities, and depended on the wool broggar to supply him. The Tudor government had frowned upon his activities, declaring that he put up the price of wool and, therefore, of the finished cloth, and so diminished the demand of the export market. Middlemen of any kind were indeed most unpopular in the sixteenth century; they came, one writer declared, 'between the bark and the tree,' and legislation expressly forbade

---

[1] F. J. Fisher 'The Development of the London Food Market, 1540–1640' *Econ. Hist. Rev.*, Vol. V, No. 2 (April 1935).

the buying of wool by dealers to sell again to the weavers or the
clothiers, who in turn put it out to their workers. But economic
pressure forced the government to give way. Special acts, such as
the so-called Halifax Act, had to relax the ruling for those localities where the independent weaver was forced to buy in small
quantities, and soon the wool dealer, buying whole clips to sell
again, become a common figure, even while legislation still tried
to hamper him and watch him at every turn. Nevertheless, since
his business was both necessary and profitable, he persisted, and
dealing in wool was another ladder by means of which the small
broggar might become the wealthy wool dealer.

Capital and contacts made in this way were frequently turned
to the organization of industry itself, and it was in this field that
the middle-class really built up the basis of that economic power
which was to revolutionize its place in society in the nineteenth
century. Textiles gave the earliest openings, and the rise of the
clothier from the fifteenth century is a commonplace of English
economic history. Even by the sixteenth century some of these
men were building up very considerable fortunes. They were
buying land, investing in sheep, employing agents to put out
their wool and to collect their cloth, and giving work to some
hundreds of spinners and weavers. With the proceeds they helped
to build churches and market halls, they endowed almshouses,
they bought estates, and often founded families of sufficient
standing to be counted among the local landowners.

In the North the linen drapers were doing for the new cotton
manufacturers what the clothiers had earlier done for the production of woollens. Their earliest and most essential service was
to act as middlemen. The raw cotton had to be imported from
abroad so none of the small manufacturers were in direct contact
with the source of supply. Consequently, middle-class merchants,
like the famous Chetham family of Manchester, found double
employment for their capital, first bringing the raw cotton from
London, and then distributing the finished fustian goods. Such
men were capitalists in a big way, for they supplied not the
weavers themselves but a whole host of smaller distributors who,
in turn, made contact with the actual workers. By the end of the
seventeenth century the merchant capitalist was using the opportunities afforded him by his control of this credit mechanism

Trade Card of a School for Young Gentlemen

Boarding School Education, or the Frenchified Young Lady

The Hopes of the Family—An Admission at the University, 1774

Nobleman and Fellow Commoner of Cambridge University, 1803

to develop a putting out system by which the small master became, in fact, a paid worker, usually on a piece-time rate. The continual demand for cotton goods, both at home and overseas, during the eighteenth century meant that the industry was constantly expanding, demanding more hands, more capital and better technical processes and devices to supply the greedy market. Here circumstances favoured the newer elements among the middle class. Established merchants were chiefly concerned with overseas markets and therefore mainly with the finished cloth. They were not primarily interested in the organization of production, and new men, taking advantage of new inventions were able to amass considerable resources.

Middle-class exploitation of production was by no means confined to the making of textiles. At the same time the heavy industries of iron and steel became increasingly attractive to enterprising men as the potential demand was released by the technical changes which freed the manufactures from the old hampering dependence on wood, and made available the native resources of the coal mines. Even before the inventions of the earlier part of the century had made this possible, considerable energy was being devoted to the manufacture of iron goods. Many metal workers were engaged in making such articles as nails, horseshoes, locks, chains and various kinds of tools and implements. Though the manufacture of nails was still a domestic industry, the iron rods from which they were made had to be turned out by slitting mills, which required capital for their erection and working. Areas like the district around Birmingham were already being associated with such activities and were fast building up a tradition of metal work. Round Sheffield in South Yorkshire, and in the north-east of the country, similar specialization was already to be found, and concentration around coalfields was already being favoured by the fact that the smith, like the forge worker, could use the neighbouring coal to produce the necessary heat for his work. After the combined inventions of men like the Darbys and Henry Cort made it possible to use coal in the manufacture of pig and bar iron, these craftsmen no longer needed to depend for much of their supplies on the Swedish and American iron imported for their use, and the consequent expansion offered still greater opportunities to the middle class.

The result of this activity was a greater concentration of population both in the centres of distribution and, where there was dependence on coal, in centres of manufacture, and though the growth of towns was less rapid in the first than in the second half of the century it was by no means negligible. Such developments encouraged the multiplication of the lower middle class because of the openings offered to the retail trader and to the middleman who supplied him. One of the outward signs of this change is to be found in the increasing number of shops that were to be found in all the towns. Men were concentrating on the retail trade rather than on selling the products of their own making. Houses were being converted into shops in some of the main streets, and even in the poorer parts the little shopkeeper was challenging more and more the preserves of the hawker. From this source still another ingredient was being added to the already rich and diverse growth of the middle class, the shopkeeper.[1] The point of view of the powerful capitalist and the petty retailer might be, and, indeed, was, very different, but both were even more sharply differentiated from that of the merchant and the agricultural labourer.

Money-making, though probably their main occupation, by no means exhausted the activities of the middle class. Although he could not hope to take any effective part in national politics there were plenty of outlets for the man with the itch to administer and organize. As the previous examination of the country's constitutional structure showed, the part that the middle class were called upon to play in local government was fairly substantial, both in the boroughs and in the running of the parochial machinery. In addition there still remained the great field of voluntary association. By the eighteenth century the gaps left in both the social and economic life of the country by the limited nature of government were becoming obvious. The answer was to form voluntary associations, financed by subscriptions, for certain definite and specific objectives which were intended to improve the social conditions. These associations fall mainly into two categories, those that aimed at some philanthropic or educational good and those whose aims were primarily economic. In either case the general framework was much the same. Some enthusiast for the

---

[1] The growth of shop-keeping in this period is well illustrated by the varied and delightful trade cards.

project, whatever it might be, interested a few people, like-minded with himself, and a committee was appointed in which further plans were discussed and the extent of subscriptions gauged. Next, if parliamentary authorization were required, which was often the case, steps were taken to interest the local member and to get a bill conferring the necessary powers.

It was in this way that necessary local improvements, so characteristic of the period, were secured. Where roads that linked the producing areas with their markets were impossibly bad the local gentry, who wanted a market for their crops and their beasts, joined with the merchants and the middlemen of the nearby town to set up a turnpike trust or to improve the facilities for water transport afforded by the local river. As the Industrial Revolution began to get under way, the insufficiency of what had already been done became more apparent, and men turned their attention to the possibility of providing canals. Here, though the pioneer was a nobleman, the new class of rising industrialists played a prominent part, as an examination of the scheme for the Grand Trunk Canal shows. In the improvement not only of communications between them but of the amenities of the growing towns themselves, the same sort of voluntary association was active. In 1775, for example, nearly £10,000 was easily raised for improving the entrance from the Market Place into St. Ann's Square in Manchester, everyone who subscribed being given one vote for each £5. This practice was general, and as the need for draining and paving and lighting the streets became more pressing it was to voluntary associations, empowered to act as Commissioners of Sewers by local Acts of Parliament, that the duty of providing them was entrusted. Even a cursory scanning of the Statute Book for the latter half, in particular, of the eighteenth century will reveal how frequently such rights were sought, and though it is true that the local gentry were prominent on such commissions there was still plenty of scope for all the middle-class business talent that was available.

The part which they played in schemes for local improvements was very far from exhausting middle-class energies, and one of the more interesting phenomena of the period is the spate of voluntary societies that were formed for moral or philanthropic ends. Thoughtful men and women had been increasingly

perturbed by the condition of the poor at the end of the seventeenth century. This perturbation was both moral and economic in
its origin. Gregory King may have exaggerated when he declared
that half the population in 1696 were dependent, or, at best, semi-
dependent, on some help beyond what they could earn, but the
mass of contemporary pamphlets dealing with the poor and the
need to organize and control them shows that the position was
at least serious enough to attract a good deal of attention.

This attention was chiefly drawn from two main sources, from
that large, solid and numerous body of men and women who
were animated by religious principles, and whose numbers in the
eighteenth century are frequently underestimated by those who
see only the debauchery of the age, and from the economists and
merchants. The former were shocked by the vice, the idleness, the
lack of moral and religious training that seemed to mark the poor.
The latter saw these vices not so much from the moral as from
the economic aspect. Valuable manpower was going to waste,
workers who might have been working for export and so securing
for their country a favourable balance of trade, were instead im-
pairing their efficiency by drink, seeking to maintain themselves
by gambling, by pilfering, or by a complete life of crime. Comments such as these are common. 'There is a general taint of
slothfulness upon our poor; there is nothing more frequent than
for an Englishman to work until he had got his pocket full of
money, and then go and be idle, and perhaps drunk, till it is all
gone'.[1] Contemporaries certainly felt that the great 'Law of
Subordination' was in danger, that the poor were no longer prepared to fulfil their part which a functional view of society
assigned to them, and that the situation was serious.

For this view there was possibly some justification. The rapid
economic changes and, perhaps, to some extent also, the more
extreme views of society put forward in the turbulent Civil War
and post-Civil War period, had raised a questioning, and often
insubordinate, spirit. The contemporary insistence on a low
standard of life for the great mass of the labouring poor had
robbed the workman, unless he were a man of quite exceptional
ambition and enterprise, of much incentive to over-exert himself

---

[1] D. Defoe: *Giving Alms No Charity* (1704), p. 448. Quoted E. S. Furness: *The
Position of the Labourer in a System of Nationalization* (1920), p. 100.

when employment was easy to find and the price of bread low. Though the writer on social and political economy and the man of affairs were apt to advocate stronger measures, religious opinion, both Anglican and Non-conformist, saw the main cause of this prevailing vice and idleness in the general misery of the poor and in the lack of any provision for their moral training. In accordance with these views the reformers were chiefly interested in trying to improve the moral standards of the poor. It was not a problem the State with its limited administrative machine either could or would tackle. Laws might on occasion be passed with the hope of dragooning the poor into frugality or industry or virtue, but the remedial measures that could alone hope to produce results of this kind were beyond its resources. If the problem were to be solved, voluntary effort would be needed. Here was a great field for middle-class activities, and, moreover, a field in which the women, excluded as they were from local government, could share. It is not surprising, therefore, that throughout the century numerous voluntary societies, directed towards social amelioration and financed by their members, were formed. The men and women who sponsored them were in no sense social revolutionaries. They accepted the class society of their day, and worked not to overthrow it but to humanize it. This moderation of their aims goes far to explain the widespread support that they received, and possibly also the lack of sympathy with which the eighteenth-century philanthropist is regarded by some schools of thought to-day.

One of the earliest of these societies to gain middle-class support was not directed towards any particular object but aimed at dealing with the general moral evils of the time. After the Commonwealth, licentious behaviour seems to have been on the increase, or at least it was so believed, perhaps because more men and women were aware of other standards. Archbishop Wake bewailed the 'Iniquity in practice' which, he averred, 'abounds too much among us, chiefly in the two extremes, the highest and lowest ranks of men'.[1] The State, in its capacity as guardian of public morals, had passed statutes enough against swearing and profanity, gaming and drinking, but there was no machinery, except that of the common informer, paid for his trouble with

[1] Quoted N. Sykes: *Edmund Gibson* (1926), p. 185.

a proportion of the fines, to put them into operation. Hence came the germ of the idea that the more respectable element in the population (it was the Archbishop's opinion that 'The middle sort are serious and religious') might form an association to perform that function which the common informer so often neglected.

The idea seems to have originated, like so many experiments in English social life, in local initiative. Social and moral conditions in the Tower Hamlets were such as to shock the more reputable inhabitants, some of whom started the practice of reporting breaches of the law. In 1691 a regular local association was formed for this purpose and this apparently inspired the campaign for the reformation of morals that marked the first two decades of the eighteenth century. The basis of the organization was the local association, and these became remarkably widespread, being found, according to one list, in Derby, Chester, Bristol, Morpeth, Newcastle, Alnwick, York, Leeds, Nantwich, Wigan, Warrington, Liverpool, Penrith, Kendal (a great Quaker stronghold this), Nottingham, Hull, Tamworth, Bedfordshire county generally, Lapworth, Wendover, Northampton, Newbury, Coventry, Shrewsbury, Leicester, Norwich, in Kent generally but especially at Canterbury, Kingston, Longbridge, the Isle of Wight, Portsmouth, Lyme Regis, Shepton Mallet, Gloucester, Staffordshire, Middleminster, and, in Wales, at Carmarthen, Bangor, in Pembrokeshire and the border county of Monmouthshire. Such a list illustrates how many people of the middling sort (it was joined by both Anglicans and Dissenters in its early phases) were prepared to take upon themselves the responsibility for reforming the manners of the community amongst which they lived. They had a measure of success. Between 1715–25 they were responsible for some 2,280 prosecutions.

The unsavoury business of collecting information and putting the law into operation could easily lend itself to abuse, and the reformers were far from popular even with men like Defoe, who was sufficiently aware himself of the many evils of his age. It was, moreover, a weapon used more easily against the poor than the influential, and, as Defoe wrote,

till the Nobility, Gentry, Justices of Peace and Clergy, will be pleased either to Reform their own Manners, and suppress their own

Immoralities or find out some Method and Power impartially to punish themselves when guilty, we Humbly crave Leave to object against setting any Poor Man in the Stocks, as the most unequal and unjust way of proceeding in the World.[1]

A little later he declared,

These are all Cobweb Laws, in which the small Flies are catch'd, and the great one break through . . . we do not find the Rich Drunkard carried before My Lord Mayor, nor a Swearing Lewd Merchant.

There was truth in these complaints, though doubtless many members of the Society for the Reformation of Manners would have been as glad to push their charges against licentiousness even in high places, but it was too often beyond their powers. Bishop Gibson had campaigned in vain against the practice of the Masquerade, so popular in the fashionable world, with all its opportunities for amorous intrigue, and a middle-class campaign against the evil of the time could hardly hope for more success. Members were unpopular, too, as 'spoil sports' and 'snoopers', and were accused, apparently unjustly, of informing for the sake of the fines to which they became entitled. Thus, for a variety of reasons, the number of prosecutions for which the Society was responsible declined markedly between 1725 and 1738. When sober opinion and middle-class energies were turned to more limited objectives, their success was greater, and most of the major achievements in the matter of social reform can be traced to the various voluntary societies which they instituted and financed.

One of the greatest of these great philanthropic movements was the movement to provide charity schools for the children of the poor.[2] It was argued, soundly enough, that from the ignorant little improvement could be expected. What the promoters of the charity schools desired was that poor children, before they had had time to become hardened in the looseness and debauchery of their parents, should be nurtured in the principles of the Christian religion, as they felt that this, and this alone, could give steadiness to the society of the day. The ability to read, as the Quakers had

[1] D. Defoe: *The Poor Man's Plea Concerning the Reformation in Manners* (1703), pp. 119, 120.
[2] M. G. Jones: *The Charity School Movement, A Study of Eighteenth Century Puritanism in Action* (1938), *passim.*

stressed, was the necessary foundation for the religious life; in that way the encouragement and influence of the Scriptures might be most widely spread. It was not by accident that the Bible and 'The Whole Duty of Man' figured so prominently in their educational syllabus. Charity schools were to fit the children they educated for the performance of their duties in that station of life to which they had been called, not to enable them to escape from it. Regular hours of attendance, often the provision of a special uniform, stern discipline, a familiarity with good works and precepts, would, it was hoped, inculcate in the young scholars the virtues of industry, self-restraint and, as befitted the grateful recipients of the charity, humility. The lease granted to the trustees of the Birmingham Blue Coat School, founded in 1724, makes this very clear. The foundation is described as being the work of

> several inhabitants of Birmingham and other pious people, considering that profaneness and debauchery were greatly owing to gross ignorance of the Christian religion, especially among the poorer sort, and that nothing was more likely to support the practice of Christianity than an early and pious training of youth, and that many poor people were desirous of having their children taught, but were not able to afford them a Christian and useful education, had, therefore, raised a considerable sum of money for erecting and setting up a charity school, and for a stipend for a master and mistress for the teaching poor children to write and read; and instructing them in the knowledge of the Christian religion, as taught in the Church of England, and such other things as are suitable to their condition and capacity.[1]

In the early years of the century the movement was both flourishing and popular. Many towns, whose citizens were animated by similar hopes, elected committees to set up and supervise a local charity school, and subscribers were actively sought. A few energetic persons, often the wives or daughters of the leading burgesses and professional men within the town, were enough to make a beginning, and that made, then supporters, at least in the first enthusiastic days, were usually not hard to find. In many places additional funds were raised by special services. A preacher, chosen for his eloquence and popularity, would deliver the sermon, the charity school children in their uniforms

[1] R. K. Dent: *Op. cit.,* p. 64.

would be paraded, and, stimulated by this living proof of their benevolence, the townspeople would be exhorted to be generous in their contributions. Thus, up and down the country the movement got under way and schools were set up. Their work in spreading education amongst the poor was one of the great contributions which the middle class made to the social progress of their age.

Like the charity schools, the movement to establish efficient workhouses owed more, in its early stages, to private association than it did to the local authorities. Earnest men were troubled by the apparent idleness of many of the poor. Such idleness was a double curse; it led to the demoralization of the unemployed, and it deprived the community of the benefit of their labour. Yet at times it had to be acknowledged work might be hard to find, because the parishes, once the pressure of the Privy Council had been removed, had given up all but the most desultory efforts to set the poor on work, as directed by the old statutes. The provision of workhouses, it was felt, would at once provide an opportunity for the industrious and deprive the lazy of an excuse. In this work, Cary of Bristol led the way. He organized with such success that the parishes of the town consented to act as one in the matter, got a local Act of Parliament, so as to have a legal basis for their experiment, and started a House of Industry that soon became famous. His experiment was the first of many; town after town got similar Acts, amalgamated their parishes and set up workhouses. So popular was the movement that in 1722 a general Act was passed, permitting the union of parishes for this purpose, and empowering the officials to refuse relief to any who would not consent to enter the workhouse and abide by its discipline. In this way workhouses became an integral part of the Poor Law.

Yet they remained in a very real sense the mark of voluntary associations, formed to supplement a gap in the Law and its administration. The actual parishes' officials were not much interested. Their main purpose was to get through their year of office with as little effort as possible, and without the pressure of energetic promoters very little would have been done. The old poorhouse, in most parishes, was in no sense a workhouse; it was merely a dumping ground and a scrap heap for paupers. Just as it was vital to their inauguration, so private enthusiasm was equally

vital to their successful continuance. To run such an establishment was no easy task. There were usually too few resources
available to classify the inmates in any detail. It was difficult to
find the right kind of work for them to do, still more difficult to
make the available labour pay even for the material on which it
worked, while the problem of finding the right kind of staff
seemed almost insoluble. So long as the local committees were
enthusiastic, some appearance of success was achieved. In *The
Account of Several Workhouses*, published in 1727, when in the
majority of places the broom was still new enough to sweep clean,
a picture was presented of well-run communities, where the inhabitants lived under strict discipline but were provided with
reasonable quarters and a diet that was probably in excess of what
their earnings outside would have bought. Even so early the
problem of providing suitable work was obviously formidable,
but something at least was being done to fit the younger inmates
for services or trades as soon as they were old enough to place
out.

Such satisfactory results were short-lived; novelty soon wore
off, the full difficulties of the situation became alarmingly apparent, the local committees of management grew slack, and
more and more the expedient of coming to terms with a contractor, who took the management of the workhouse off their
hands, was adopted. Something of the same kind had tended to
happen in the case of the charity schools, but in that experiment
the difficulties were perhaps less great, and the humanitarian and
Christian zeal of the few did at least keep the flame alight. In the
workhouse movement it flickered out, to flare up again in the
experiment for Houses of Industry in the rural South-east, for a
short time only, and once again to be extinguished as the voluntary workers grew discouraged.

Workhouses and charity schools were far from exhausting the
organized charity of the eighteenth century. Another enterprise,
akin in some ways to these, was the Foundling Hospital. It had
taken Thomas Coram seventeen years before he had organized
sufficient support to make the project practicable, but by 1739 he
was able to send two lists of signatures, one male, one female, to
George II, praying for a charter. After this had been secured, the
usual committee of management was set up, consisting of fifty

noblemen and gentlemen, with the Duke of Bedford as President
of the Governors. The enterprise started in a modest way, for
public opinion was only doubtfully convinced of the propriety
of establishing what they assumed, without any statistical evidence, was likely to be a refuge for bastards, and, therefore, merely
a pandering to social vice. The annual revenue for 1740 was estimated at £600 only, and this, it was thought, would not allow the
reception of more than sixty children a year.

In the early days of the Foundlings this limitation was a source
of strength rather than of weakness, for each child could be treated
as an individual and the governors were not swamped, as later
they were, with unmanageable numbers. Meanwhile, with adroit
publicity, the new buildings in Lamb's Conduit Fields, then just
on the edge of the dirt and smoke of London, were used to arouse
interest in the project, and its walls were made available to
artists to hang their pictures, a practice doubly useful in an
artistic, or, perhaps, better described as a picture-buying age,
when no public galleries existed. In consequence, the Foundlings
became a centre of artistic interests; Hogarth became one of the
governors and Handel gave concerts, which proved immensely
popular, to augment the funds. Meanwhile, in a decreasing death-
rate, the Hospital gave practical proof of its utility and good
management; between 1741 and 1756 only just half of the children
admitted died, as opposed to the three or four per cent. that would
have survived if put out by parish officers into the ordinary
London workhouses, or to nurse with the women employed by
the parishes for this purpose.

This success was ultimately to prove all but its ruin. In 1756
the government made a grant from public funds, subsequently enlarged, on the condition that the Hospital should admit children
from all over the country in whatever numbers applied. The
scheme, generous enough in its intention, was quite unworkable.
Children who would have stood at least some chance of surviving
in the purer air of the country were brought to London, and
dumped, often more dead than alive after the rigours of the
journey, into the basket that hung by the Foundling's gate. For
just under four years the stream of babies came, and during this
period the death rate rose to some seventy per cent. The task was
really too great, though the governors, amongst whom was Jonas

Hanway whose *Candid Historical Account of the Hospital for the Reception of Exposed and Deserted Young Children* is a mine of information as to their problems, did their best. By 1760, despite their efforts, the reputation of the Hospital was low, and in the March of that year parliament withdrew its grants and released the governors from the obligation to relieve and receive any children deposited with them.

But though on a nation-wide scale the scheme was an apparent failure, it certainly did not bring to an end the work of the men who were interested in the welfare of young children. Jonas Hanway, appalled by the gap the closing of the Foundling would cause, went on with dogged persistence in his efforts to get the laws touching pauper apprenticeship better regulated, to safeguard the health and lives of pauper children put out to nurse, and to improve the condition of the young chimney-sweeps.[1] In all these endeavours, he secured a very real measure of success, which illustrates how not only the voluntary association but even the private individual was contributing to the modification and softening of the harsh social pattern enforced by the law, so bringing it into closer conformity with the better opinion of the age.

The Marine Society was another notable achievement. This again provides one more example of how private effort was used to supplement the work of the government. In 1756 it had been founded by a group of businessmen inspired by Charles Dingley, a merchant of the Russia Company, who, since 1753, had been working at a plan for apprenticing poor boys to the navy and the merchant navy. Now, in 1756, facing the threat of war when the Royal Navy was far from well equipped or manned, the government was glad to avail itself of private help. Under the stimulus of war, funds were not difficult to collect, and by 1758 the Society had received £13,546 17s. 0d., and spent £12,811 10s. 10d. Much of this money was for the purchase of clothing, for at this date each seaman had still to provide his own. This charity, like so many of those of the period, expected very concrete results, and indeed aimed, as was usual, at killing more than one bird with its stone. In this case not only was the Royal Navy to be helped in

[1] For further details of his career, see J. H. Hutchins: *Jonas Hanway, 1712–1786* (1940).

time of war, and the merchant navy expanded in peace, but the idle and riotous youth were to be taken off the streets of London where they brawled and pilfered, and made useful to their country.

In all the charities so far enumerated, whatever the degree of success that they attained, the same desire appears, to secure social steadiness and to alleviate conditions, so that labour should be well trained and usefully employed, instead of being lost to the community. They cut, therefore, against no vested interest, and constituted rather a bulwark than a threat to the society of the day. The case of the slave trade was different. Here humanitarian and religious principles were the main driving force that inspired the reformers. The slave trade at this time was not only buttressed by charters, treaties, and an act of parliament, it was the foundation of many very respectable merchants' fortunes. Liverpool and Bristol, the two great ports which drew the greatest profit and business from the trade, had grown and prospered as a result, since their merchants were busily engaged in supplying the slaves to the American and West Indian planters, in handling the cotton and tobacco and other crops that slave labour produced, and in exporting the finished cotton cloth, so much in demand both in Africa and in the American and West Indian markets. The West Indian planters, too, always one of the best organized of the parliamentary lobbies, would be hard hit by any interference with their labour supply, and would resist it tooth and nail. The reformers here, therefore, were faced with no simple task of meeting with a few sneers and jeers from the flippant and the unfriendly, they were challenging one of the greatest vested interests of the times, and challenging it not on a material but on a spiritual and moral plane. It is little wonder that Granville Sharp, Clarkson, Zachary Macaulay and Wilberforce with their enthusiastic followers had to fight so fiercely and so long. Without the new moral values stressed by the Methodist and Evangelical movements, their results would have been still slower in coming. But by the second half of the eighteenth century the horrors of the middle Passage were being regarded by many earnest and religious people not as inevitable but as a crying sin shared by the whole nation. After the appointment of a Privy Council Committee to inquire into the conditions of the trade in 1788 hopes were for a time high, but the opposition proved too strong. When, therefore, the slave trade was finally abolished in 1807 this represented a triumph of voluntary association and organization, both financial and political, that can be appreciated only when studied against the strength of vested interests it had so successfully challenged.

Even so brief a survey of the wide variety of the voluntary societies is some indication of the breadth of interest of the eighteenth-century middling sort and of their sense of social responsibility. Too often this century is dismissed as one of drinking and debauchery, its ecclesiastical and academic standards are condemned with uncritical contempt, and the epithet 'materialist' used in no complimentary sense, is applied to brand it, yet the growing strength of the Methodists and the Evangelicals and the record of the middle-class contribution to the social and moral improvement of the age should check such hasty judgments. Mandeville, it is true, was most scornful of the motives that lay behind the 'enthusiastic passion' to improve. To him it was animated by a mere desire to ape their social betters, and perhaps to mix with them on committees. Because the social structure of the eighteenth century reserved to the aristocracy and gentry the right to rule and dominate in the traditional spheres of public life, it seemed to him that 'the middling sort' were deliberately creating the voluntary societies in order that they, too, might have their own fields of interference and control. But whatever their motives, and Mandeville's spiteful conjectures need not be taken too seriously,[1] the fact remains that, though individual members of the aristocracy and gentry could and did play their part in them, the majority of the members came from the modest middle element, many of them from Dissenting circles. In this way these societies provided an alternative outlet for those talents and interests which many a middle-class man might otherwise have found frustrated by the political arrangements of his day. And when to these philanthropic societies are added all the small activities of the growing towns, the management of the new circulating libraries, the foundation of literary and philosophical societies, it can be seen that the man of parts who was not a gentleman was not confined to a stultifying way of life.

[1] G. Mandeville: *On Charity and Charity Schools* (1723), *passim*.

Thus eighteenth-century society, though abundantly generous to the gentleman and nobleman, was certainly not niggardly in the rewards that it had to offer to its numerous middle-class members. The educational facilities open to them were adequate, within the framework of what was then considered to be education. The material conditions in which they lived, the houses they occupied, the clothes they wore, the food they ate, were, judged again by the standards of the age, good, and even by modern ones, very passable. Seven pounds of butter per week for eight persons can hardly be considered inadequate fare! Much, if not most, of the internal management of the economic life of the country was in their hands, most of the professions were open to their more academically minded members, and in some, reputations could be made that would take them out of their own class. Finally, even if the world of high politics was denied to them, in local affairs and in the numerous voluntary societies of the day, men with a turn for organization, for administration, for public affairs, could find ample scope for their talents. In short, the propertied classes, whether of gentle birth or not, though they made a very real, and probably decisive, contribution to the wealth of the country, had no real cause to complain, as had the middle class in France, of the way in which the society of the country was organized, or its rewards distributed.

Chapter Five

THE LABOURING POOR

THE great mass of the people, however, did not belong to the aristocracy, the gentry, or the middling sort, but were manual workers of one kind or another, the artisan, the petty shopkeeper and the labouring poor. To know, therefore, what satisfactions eighteenth-century society afforded to the majority of its members, it is necessary to know something of the conditions and way of life of this very large section of the population. Such an examination can only be very incomplete and essentially superficial; the variations within so large a class were almost endless, not only from the point of view of occupation and habitation, but also from the aspect of location. Their standard of life ranged from a crude sufficiency to the most absolute destitution that ended in death by exposure and starvation. The evidence available, too, is often unsatisfactory; instances of hardship and exploitation are common enough, but though common can they be considered typical? Moreover, it is only too easy to judge and condemn one age by the criteria of another. Bad as social conditions seem to the conscience of the twentieth century, the historian must record that they appear to have been improving, that a century of philanthropic effort and increasing production was having a beneficial effect on the standard of life of the labouring poor.

Contemporaries certainly appear convinced that the poor were better off in England than on the Continent, an opinion confirmed by foreign observers. Henry Meister, in an account of his travels in this country, declared 'I do not impose upon you when I say that though the English labourer is better clothed, better fed, and better lodged than the French, he does not work so hard. You will wonder at this the less, when you consider that the wages of the former are higher, and his diet more substantial; consequently that he has greater strength and activity in the performance of his

Subscription ticket for a School of Industry

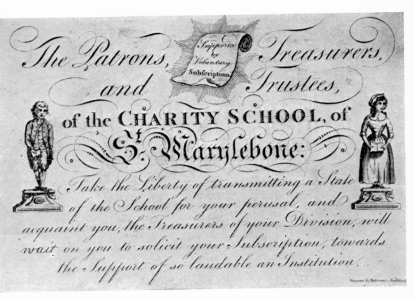

Subscription ticket for the Charity School of St. Marylebone

The Schoolmistress
by Opie

tasks'.[1] Remembering this and similar comments, a picture that seems intolerably grim to modern eyes must be seen against the background of its age. The business of the historian is to observe and record, not to condemn.

It is interesting to speculate how far the educational facilities available to the children of the labouring poor helped to raise their earnings and, therefore, their standard of life. Though illiteracy was widespread at the beginning of the century, the effect of the charity schools, promoted and supported by middle-class subscribers, must have been considerable: even by the middle of the century the ability to read was probably more general than is sometimes supposed. True, the education which charity schools provided was a limited one, since their aim was moral instruction rather than the imparting of knowledge. Instruction was, therefore, confined to what was conceived as being necessary for this purpose. To teach the children to read was the main aim, and for this purpose the chief texts were the Bible, the Catechism and the *Whole Duty of Man*. At the beginning of the century this choice might have been considered as to some extent inevitable, owing to the lack of suitable secular literature, but by its middle less heavy, more human, material was available. That provided by Hannah Moore could surely have been considered by the most carping as of exceptional moral tone, but little or no attempt was ever made to introduce this more interesting type of reading matter into the curriculum of the charity schools.[2]

The education provided for the majority was limited to reading, though to the most promising scholars, who could read competently, some attempt was made to teach writing and even, occasionally, arithmetic. But to this extension there was solid opposition from the small tradesmen, who were beginning to ask how they were going to set their own children up in life if the children of the poorest section of society were to be educated in such a way that they would be competent to do the work hitherto performed by their immediate betters. To meet this kind of criticism, and also to act as an inducement to parents to send their children (for it must not be forgotten that the system was

---

[1] J. H. Meister: *Letters written during a Residence in England*. (London, 1799). Edited by A. Geikie.
[2] *Vide* M. G. Jones: *Op. cit.*

voluntary on both sides), a good deal of stress was placed on manual activities. The children were frequently employed in spinning or knitting or, in the counties where such industries were widespread, in lace-making or straw-plaiting, or, indeed, in any simple repetitive task by which a few pence could be earned. At the same time lessons were conned by rote. This was particularly true where the pupils were girls, the object of such schools being mainly to turn out good, reliable, God-fearing servants. This pleased the parents, who were allowed the scanty wages so earned, and those critics of the system who clamoured that the children of the poor should be early inured to labour. If a working day that started at five or six in the summer and went on until eight or nine at night, with only short breaks for meals, or from six or seven in the winter until seven or eight, could achieve this end it should certainly have been most satisfactorily accomplished.

It is easy to criticize the educational facilities that the charity schools provided. Yet, limited though they were, it was at least something that some knowledge of reading should have been provided for a class that would otherwise have been largely illiterate. Intolerable as their regime seems to modern ideas it must not be forgotten that in any case industry or agriculture, with their long hours of toil, would have claimed them as soon as they were old enough to make any contribution to the family income. It was not a choice between leisure and school but between learning and industry. At the charity school, at least, labour was mixed with learning and some standards beyond those of the animal to eat, to sleep, to drink were suggested to them. Often they were clothed as well as taught, though care was taken not to choose a uniform that might pander to their vanity or give them ideas above their station. Even so, when many of their contemporaries went in rags, to be neatly and warmly clad helped to suggest the self respect that went with a higher standard of living.

Much depended, however, on the energy and competence of the managing committee. At a time when there was no source of trained teachers or social workers on which to draw the choice of staff was always difficult. Remuneration for such work was never high: too often it was life's failures who were attracted by such posts. For this reason the day schools were more successful than those that supplied board and lodging. Here the difficulties of supervising an unsuitable staff often led to all kinds of abuses. Too often the children went short of food and were left at the mercy of unconscientious teachers. But whatever their deficiencies in syllabus and training, and these were many, it can hardly be doubted that the charity schools did make some impression on the illiteracy of the country, though it may be doubted whether their moral effects were as considerable as their promoters had hoped. Certainly what they had to offer in the way of instruction must have been considered as worth having, or they would have been without pupils in an age when children were put to work so young. In some cases it is true that small weekly doles were offered to the parents to offset the wages the children might have brought in. In others they were given whatever the child had been able to earn while in school. The provision of free clothing was an additional bribe. But the most important inducement was that in the towns, with their greater openings for the child who could read, and perhaps write, education was seen to be of some practical value. In the country districts the charity schools appear to have had more difficulty in attracting and keeping their pupils.

The provision of charity schools was far from universal because their establishment depended on there being enough interested and enthusiastic people in the locality to get the movement going. Where they were not available there was often some other provision for the children of the poor, even if it were only the tiny dame's school where, for a few coppers a week, children could acquire the elements of reading. In country parishes poorly paid curates often taught in order to supplement their meagre stipends. Some men did this out of a love of learning and of their fellow men. The *Annual Register* of 1760 contains a charming picture of William Walker, the Lakeland curate-in-charge, who taught the local children in the parish church, charging nothing for his trouble, though grateful for the few pence or the payments in kind that might come his way. While he taught he spun wool to augment his slender emoluments; his school was a labour of love. In order to enable them to read the Bible many vicars paid some attention to the education of the children within the parish, particularly in rural areas where otherwise they would have gone untaught. In some of the older corporate towns there were endowed schools, whose foundations were older than the charity schools, which also taught the elements of the English language, having originally been intended as a sort of preparatory school for the grammar school with its concentration on the classics. By the end of the seventeenth century, Commissioners of Inquiry concerning Charities reported four hundred and sixty of these schools.

Towards the end of the next century yet another source of instruction had appeared in the Sunday school. Like the charity school the aim of the movement was religious. Started in Gloucester in 1780 its net was very widely flung in the growing industrial towns, where it catered for those children who, having been already absorbed into industry, could only snatch at education on the seventh day. In the crude industrial communities of the North, Sunday Schools added one spark of something that was not material, and helped to build up some feeling of corporate endeavour in a world where only too often the devil took the hindmost. Stockport, with its eleven Sunday schools and twenty-three teachers, instructed some eight hundred children, no inconsiderable achievement. As the hours were from nine to six, with an interval for dinner and divine service this attendance was no small tribute to the general belief that even the overworked children of the mills should at least be able to read.

That education was desired is further emphasized by the number of parents who were at pains to provide some sort of simple education for their children, even if they had to pay for it, as well as lose the child's earnings while at school. If one turns from generalizations to the biographies of poor boys who attained eminence of some kind, not necessarily economic, it is interesting to notice the educational facilities which first served to set their feet in the way of learning. Joseph White, later to gain some reputation as a theologian and orientalist, was the son of a journeyman weaver and received his early education at Gloucester Charity School. Lilley Wigg, the Norfolk botanist, was the son of a village shoemaker, and got his early education at the village school. With that slender equipment he taught himself some Latin, French and Greek. Then, removing at the age of twenty to Great Yarmouth, he set up a small school and, later, through the influence of men who were impressed by his ability as a botanist, he secured a clerkship in Messrs. Gurney's and Turner's bank.

Neither man ranks among the giants of his day and generation, but both achieved some reputation in their own line among the learned circles of the time. Their experience, which was not uncommon, illustrates the fact that whatever the eighteenth-century society failed to provide for its poorest members, it did at least make some limited attempt to cater for the simplest of their educational needs. In Hanoverian England to be poor was not to be totally deprived of all reasonable chance of being literate. This chance was, however, much greater in the urban areas. Chances in even these varied considerably according to the presence or absence of a group of people sufficiently interested in the problem of the poor children of the day to organize and subscribe for their education.

Much of the vice, debauchery and drinking, which the charity-school movement had hoped to check at its source by the inculcation of the habits of sobriety and hard work in the young, sprang from the general standard of living of the labouring poor. Housing, according to modern ideas, was deplorable, both with regard to its quality and its quantity. In the countryside a fear of attracting too many settled inhabitants, who, should they fall on evil times, or should they even produce too large a family, would become dependent on the rates, led to restrictions on the building of cottages. Many of those already in existence were too small for the families they housed; not only were they cramped, they were often dark and damp, with beaten mud floors and leaking roofs, while cooking facilities were limited to the open fire. Byng described the cottages at Alderminster as being 'mud without and wretchedness within',[1] and in many parts of the country, where brick was expensive and local stone not available, the mud cottage was a common feature. When, however, it was carefully constructed, it was not as uncomfortable and contemptible a building material as modern opinion might, over hastily, consider it. The lime workers, whose habitations and way of life St. Fond described, might well have preferred the mud cottage to their own habitations.

The whole tribe [he wrote], like moles lived underground. . . . They had preferred to scoup out their dwellings among heaps of cinders

[1] John Byng: *Torrington Diaries*. Edited by C. B. Andrews (1936), Vol. III, p. 155.

and lime refuse, which formed so many little monticules, or, if one may say so, mole hills. . . . Most of these habitations have three or four rooms, almost all of a round shape for the purpose of greater solidity. They are lighted from the side, when the position allows it, or merely from the chimney, which is a round hole in the roof to let the smoke out. Openings like dormer windows are also made by the doors of the places to admit a little light.[1]

But though much of the standard of rural housing was very bad, this was not the case everywhere: not all eighteenth-century cottages were hovels. Gilbert White, the naturalist, surely as careful and unprejudiced an observer of the ways and habitations of the human as of the feathered population of Selborne, about 1788 wrote: 'We abound with poor; many of whom are sober and industrious, and live comfortably in good stone or brick cottages, which are glazed, and have chambers above stairs; mud buildings we have none'. And to this pleasing comment he added: 'The inhabitants enjoy a good share of health and longevity; and the parish swarms with children'.[2] Arthur Young, too, in his *Tours* notes similar instances, recording after passing through Carrington: 'I should not forget to remark, that the village is one of the neatest, best built, and most lively I have ever seen, most of the houses and cottages are new built, all of them tiled, and many of brick, which with white pales and little plantations, have a most pleasing effect'.[3] Such cases may not have been common, but contemporary wills also suggest, at least for the rural craftsman, a modest degree of comfort within. William Briant, carpenter of Great Cressington, near Swaffham, in Norfolk, had in the 'low lodgeing room' two beds, a trunk, a chest, a little table, a buffet stool and a 'skreen', while his kitchen was provided with three pewter dishes, two old kettles, a skillet, four chairs, a stool, a table and two tubs, all of them described as old.[4] In the towns, particularly those of any size, and above all in London, living conditions were worse. The country dweller was able to collect some wood for firing and might have a garden or some scrap of land; nor was his cottage huddled into some airless court, while

---

[1] Faujas de Saint Fond: *A Journey through England and Scotland in 1784*. Edited by A. Geikie, Vol. II, p. 287.
[2] G. White: *Natural History of Selborne*. Edited by J. Fisher (1947).
[3] A. Young: *Northern Tour* (1770), Vol. I, p. 45.
[4] G. Eland: *Op. cit.*, p. 21.

the local well or neighbouring stream frequently provided him
with a purer or more abundant water supply than was available
to the townsman. In the towns new buildings spread only slowly
into the suburbs, and many of these were for the well-to-do, or,
at least, for middle-class occupation. The poor remained piled up
in the old congested area of the centre. This was particularly true
of London.[1]

The lack of transport increased this congestion. It was necessary for people to live near their work. Long hours absorbed
much time and energy, there was little enough of either left for
tramping to and from work. Nor, as the record of crime that
came before the courts showed, were the streets without hazard
once dark had fallen. It was desirable to get home soon. Because,
as Grosley pointed out, the facilities which the Thames afforded
for the transport of both raw materials and finished goods allowed
the concentration of industry along its banks, the heart of London
was a dirty, unpleasant place in which to live. He speaks of the
coals burnt in glass-houses, in blacksmiths' and gunsmiths' shops,
in dyers' yards 'which produced great clouds of smoke that en-
veloped the city like a mantle, a cloud which' he declared, 're-
coiling back upon itself, suffers the sun to break out only now
and then, which casual appearance procures the Londoners a few
of what they call "glorious days"'.[2] This black pall of smoke that
hung over everything was one of the characteristics of London
that most impressed foreign visitors. Few of them failed to comment on it with amazement and disapproval. It was not only the
coal-burning, smoke-producing trades of which complaint could
be made. Into the uncovered and incredibly filthy Fleet Ditch
went the offal of the catgut spinners, of the tripe-dressers, of the
sausage-makers, a mass of decomposing refuse which Pope
described as:

... Fleet-Ditch with disemboguing streams
Rolls the large tribute of dead dogs to Thames;
The King of dykes! than whom no sluice of mud
With deeper sable blots the silver flood.[3]

[1] For a graphic description of London housing, see M. D. George, *London Life
in the Eighteenth Century* (1925).
[2] Grosley: *Op. cit.*, p. 43.
[3] *The Dunciad*, Bk. II.

The smoke-laden air must also have been heavy with every kind of foul stench. Nor was the offence confined to eyes and nose: lice infected the houses, flies, bred by garbage, contaminated food. It was little wonder that fevers were endemic in many quarters of the town.

London in particular was considered as a devourer of men, but all towns of any size were filthy, insanitary places. In Manchester a local Act in 1765 gave Commissioners the power to appoint and pay scavengers to keep the streets and public places clean. Householders were ordered twice a week to sweep all the accumulated dirt and litter to the centre of the street, so that it could be the more easily collected, but little, in fact, was done. Sanitation, too, remained in a very primitive state. Privies were built over watercourses, providing a kind of elementary and most polluting water closet, or emptied into public middens, or were equipped with barrels that had to be emptied at intervals by the householder. The highest ambition of the Court Leet seems to have been to bully or persuade householders to empty them into the Irwell discreetly at night, so as not to impede the traffic. The correct procedure was to discharge them by the steps at the water's edge, but this too was often a counsel of perfection. Householders preferred the easier way of emptying them over Salford Bridge, or, even worse, tipping them into the streets or on to the public refuse heaps under cover of darkness. Even as late as 1841 one man was prosecuted for not attending to his privy at all until the stench became so offensive to his neighbours that they complained.[1] The state of the water supplies in these conditions can better be imagined than described. Such conditions affected all who lived within towns but they pressed most hardly upon the working population. The merchant and the prosperous manufacturer could live on the outskirts, and often had gardens, or at least larger and less crowded houses, as some alleviation. Shocking as the conditions of the eighteenth century seem to the modern reader, they were conditions that, as far as dirt and discomfort were concerned had been accepted as ordinary and normal for working people as far as the memory of man went. Nor should it be forgotten that only in the eighteenth century did the medical

[1] A. Redford and I. S. Russell: *The History of Local Government in Manchester* (1939–40), Vol. I, *passim*.

opinion of the day come to connect disease and dirt, and so provide reasons for an attack on both. Society was not giving to the great mass of the people less than it had been giving before, but it was still giving very little.

Overcrowding intensified these evils. Even respectable householders of the artisan or petty tradesman type seldom occupied more than one or two rooms for themselves. The rest of the house was let out. Garrets tended to be occupied by the very poor, often by a domestic worker who plied his trade and lived and slept with all his family in one room. Poorest of all were those who lived in the cellars. These were often separate from the main body of the house and were approached by steps from the street. Often they too provided a place of business as well as a home for a man and his family for, having an independent way of access, they were well adapted to the needs of the small cobbler, the petty greengrocer, the retailer of milk. They were nearly always dark and usually insanitary and damp, being liable in wet weather to flooding. In Manchester, in some parts of the town, cellars were described as being 'so damp as to be unfit for habitations' and in one street these dank holes, let out to lodgers, 'threaten', it was reported, 'to be come a theatre of disease'. In Birmingham, too, the long struggle of the Commissioners against people who would leave the flap, often the only means of air, open at night, bears witness to the numerous cellar dwellings in that town.

If it is difficult to draw an accurate picture of housing conditions it is even more so to draw any but the most general one of the average standard of food and clothes. Variations were very great both between the skilled worker and the labourer and also between town and country, between North and South, East and West. Examples of wages alone can overwhelm in a mass of figures but indicate little of the standard of living that they could secure. Prices varied considerably in different parts of the country. For many, their standard of living depended on the existence of commons, on scraps of gardens, on perquisites rather than on a bare money wage. Many trades, too, were seasonal, so that to know the daily or weekly wage is little help in casting the yearly budget. Both the unskilled labourer in the towns and the agricultural labourer in the country lived chiefly on bread, cheese, small beer, with meat, perhaps, once a week. Sir William Petty writing earlier had described the diet of the artisan as consisting chiefly of bread and cheese, neck beef and 'Inwards' twice a week, stale fish, old pease without butter.[1] In London in particular the lack of cooking facilities in one-room lodgings led to much dependence on cook shops and on the vendors of doubtful pies. Bread was the staple diet and the price of corn the decisive factor in the standard of living. In London before 1735 the labourer was spending about a quarter of his wages on bread, but as the trend of wages was slightly upwards between that date and the middle of the century the proportion decreased.[2] After 1750 the position worsened. Wages hardly rose at all before 1790 but prices rose steadily. As a result as much as one-third of the weekly wage had to be spent on bread and other expenditure had to be cut.

In other parts of the country the proportion varied, for the connexion between wages and the price of wheat is not as close as it is sometimes assumed. For the labourer in the metropolitan area the position was particularly difficult, for he had to meet London prices, not only for bread but for other commodities that were subject to more local variations in price than wheat, but he did not receive a full London wage.[3] Rural Kent, Surrey and Middlesex were never quite free of this metropolitan influence, and here the proportion of wages that had to be spent on food varied. From 1700 to 1730 it was about forty per cent., between 1730 and 1750 only thirty per cent., but after that date it rose again to something just over forty per cent. In that area, therefore, during the century, wages, in terms of wheat prices, only just held their own. In the West during the eighteenth century there was no improvement in the normal standard of living. Indeed there was possibly some retrogression.[4] Though the farming community was prosperous enough little of this was passed on to the labourer. All that he was allowed was a bare minimum and, with the rise of prices at the end of the century, even this was threatened.[5]

Incidental comments, culled from Gilbert White's letters, would seem to indicate that, at least in his part of the country, a

---

[1] Sir William Petty: *A Treatise of Taxes* (1662), p. 93.
[2] E. W. Gilboy: *Wages in Eighteenth Century England* (1934), p. 24.
[3] *Ibid.*, p. 56.　　　　　　　　[4] *Ibid., Op. cit.*, p. 130.
[5] It should be remembered that the practice of eating wheaten bread was not universal and that to calculate the expenditure on food in terms of wheat may exaggerate the proportion spent. Also rural labourers received some payments in kind.

considerable improvement in the dietary of the rural poor had taken place by 1778. Speaking of the disappearance of leprosy he suggested that one cause of the 'distemper might be, no doubt, the quantity of wretched fresh and salt fish consumed by the commonalty at all seasons as well as Lent: which our poor would hardly be persuaded to touch'. A significant comment this! He then went on to observe that 'The plenty of good wheaten bread that is now found among all ranks of people in the south, instead of that miserable sort which used in the old days to be made of barley or beans, may contribute not a little to the sweetening of their blood and correcting their juices, for the inhabitants of mountainous districts to this day are still liable to the itch and other cutaneous disorders, from a wretchedness and poverty of diet'. Stressing the new vogue for eating green vegetables he added,

> Every decent labourer also has his garden, which is half his support, as well as his delight; and common farmers provide plenty of beans, peas, and greens, for their hinds to eat with their bacon; and those few who do not are despised for their sordid parsimony, and looked upon as regardless of the welfare of their dependents. Potatoes have prevailed in these districts by means of premiums within these twenty years only, and are much esteemed here now by the poor, who would scare have ventured to taste them in the last reign.[1]

This was, perhaps, a fortunate corner of England, but the position of the labourer in the North was also far from desperate. Here, industry, though the East Riding and much of Lancashire remained predominantly rural, did affect the labour market by offering alternative employment. Therefore, though the trend of prices was slightly downward from 1710 to 1753, and then slightly upward, real wages were increasing. From 1700 to 1730 more than half the labourer's wage was spent on bread, a much greater proportion than the London labourer needed to lay out in the corresponding period. By 1730–50 it was a bare half and by 1790, despite a slight rise in the price of oats, it had dropped to a little more than a third. There were bad years, of course, such as 1709, 1722, 1740 and 1766, when the harvest failed. At such times almost the entire wage must have been spent on bread. But these

---

[1] G. White: *Op. cit.*, pp. 192–3.

were periods of exceptional hardship; on the average the standard
of living was rising steadily in the North. In many ways, too, the
Northern diet was more varied than that which prevailed further
South. A good deal of oats was consumed, though wheaten bread
was becoming more common by the end of the century, but
bread was supplemented by potatoes and more meat, usually
boiled, than in the South. Also more families seem to have been
able to keep a pig and there were more common rights so that
milk was not such a problem as it rapidly became in those parts
of the country where the growth of large-scale farming concentrated milk supplies in the hands of middlemen. These men were
concerned with supplying the big towns and had no interest in
meeting small local needs.

If the diet of the labourer of the North contained more healthful
variety, it included less of the so-called luxuries of the age. In the
eighteenth century tea and sugar were being consumed in increasing quantities by working people. Charles Deering, commenting
on contemporary customs in Nottingham, wrote:

> The People here are not without their Tea, Coffee and Chocolate,
> especially the first, the Use of which is spread to that Degree, that
> not only the Gentry and Wealthy Traders drink it constantly, but
> almost every Seamer, Sizer and Winder, will have her Tea and will
> enjoy herself over it in a Morning, not forgetting their snuff, a pinch
> or two of which they never fail of regaling their Nostrils with be-
> tween every dish; and even a Common Washerwoman thinks she
> has not had a proper Breakfast without Tea and hot buttered white
> Bread . . . being the other Day at a Grocers, I could not forbear look-
> ing earnestly and with some Degree of Indignation at a ragged and
> greasy Creature, who came into the Shop with two Children follow-
> ing her in as dismal a Plight as the Mother, asking for a Pennyworth
> of Tea and a Half pennyworth of Sugar, which when she was served
> with, she told the Shop-keeper: Mr. N. I do not know how it is
> with me, but I can assure you I would not desire to live, if I was to
> be debarred from drinking every Day a little Tea.[1]

Such indulgence was frowned upon. 'It may be said', exploded
Young, 'that wheaten bread, that beef, that mutton, that tea, that
sugar, that butter, are dear, but do not in the heat of an argument,
jumble them and the *necessaries of life* together'.[2] On one occasion

[1] Charles Deering: *Op. cit.*, p. 72.
[2] A. Young: *A Farmer's Letters* (1771), Vol. I, p. 205.

Young committed himself to what he thought was a suitable diet for a labouring man. On the first day he was to eat two pounds of bread made of a mixture of wheat, rye and potato, two ounces of cheese and two pints of beer. Next day he was to have three messes of soup made of lean beef, peas, mealy potatoes, ground rice, onions, celery and salt and water. A rice pudding made with a half a pound of rice, a little sugar and two quarts of skim milk was the fare for the third day. On the fourth he was permitted a quarter of a pound of fat beef and one and a quarter pounds of potatoes baked together, and some beer. Rice pudding reappeared on the fifth day and bread, cheese and beer on the sixth, while on Sunday he was again allowed to feast on fat beef, potatoes, beer and cheese.[1]

Few labourers' wages would, in practice, buy so much. In most parts of the country, as prices began to rise, the ordinary labourer could depend on his wages to procure no more than the barest living, bread, cheese and weak tea being his staple diet, as the pathetic budgets that Eden and Davies[2] collected testify. The unskilled town labourer and the agricultural labourer were hard put to it, therefore, to maintain even the necessary minimum. In one typical budget quoted by Davies a family of seven, apart from bread, bought per week one ounce of tea, three-quarters of a pound of sugar, half a pound of butter or lard and a pound of bacon. No meat was purchased and no milk. Yet even on this diet, by the end of the year the excess of expenditure over income was £8 16s. 0d., a gap presumably filled by the parish. In practice, until the end of the century, which was the period illustrated by these collected budgets, the position may not have been quite as grim as these figures suggest. Inventories of labourers' possessions in the way of household goods suggest a modest degree of comfort. So much depended on other circumstances that it is almost impossible to generalize beyond saying that the wages of the worker in industry were distinctly higher than those of the rural worker and that the wages of the village labourer were at their lowest in those districts where the new industrialism did not offer any alternative.

---

[1] *Ibid.*, p. 196.
[2] See F. Eden: *The State of the Poor* (1797); and D. Davies: *The Case of the Labourer in Husbandry* (1795).

On the other hand, the town labourer had much less chance of supplementing his wages from other sources. If common rights remained and the wife could keep her pig, some hens and geese, perhaps a cow, and if there were a scrap of garden where potatoes could be grown, then the rural family could command an adequate diet. The presence of by-industry, also, with the means that it afforded to the wife and the younger children of supplementing the family income without competing with her husband as a form of cheap unskilled labour on the farms, was of the greatest importance. But where these things were lacking, and the whole tendency of the eighteenth century was to remove them, then the material satisfactions that eighteenth-century society afforded to the agricultural labourer were, indeed, small. It must, however, always be remembered that in those areas where the small family farm predominated the numbers of the full-time wage-earning labourers cannot have been large and that to assess the position of the rural poor on the assumption that they were largely wage-earners in agriculture can be misleading.

For the skilled worker the position was easier, for a rather more ample wage afforded a margin that could be spent on more varied diet. Just how much they had to spend is difficult to calculate, for here again their earnings depended on piece rates and often, as in the case of the miners, on seasonal trades. Even so, there was a marked gap between what they could earn and what the labourer could earn. Where, in 1770, the rural labourer was earning 5*s*. to 6*s*. in winter and 7*s*. to 9*s*. in summer with a few well-paid weeks of exhausting toil at harvest that might bring in as much as 12*s*. a week, the average craftsman was some shillings a week better off, according to his trade. The Manchester cotton weaver got 8*s*., the Witney blanket weaver 11*s*. and the wool-comber 13*s*. In heavy industry the furnace keepers at Horsehay got 12*s*., the Sheffield cutlers 13*s*. 6*d*. and the Newcastle miners some 15*s*. By the end of the century the gap was even wider. True the agricultural labourer, working by the day, could make from 7*s*. to 8*s*. in winter and 8*s*. to 10*s*. in summer, but men in the cotton mills were taking home 16*s*. and the metal workers from 15*s*. to a pound. Less of the wage, therefore, had to go on bread. For the London craftsman the proportion at the beginning of the century seems to have been about one-fifth, and this by 1750 had

sunk to one-sixth, though for a man living in the metropolitan
areas who did not receive London wages, a full quarter would
still have to be necessary.[1] With the extra money it was possible
to buy more of the new luxuries, tea and sugar, but it is probable
that most of it went on additional meat and on drink. The miners
in particular were considerable meat eaters, partly because of the
heavy nature of their work, but, perhaps, even more because
they, unlike the greater part of the labouring poor, were not
afflicted by the scarcity and dearness of fuel. The miner, unlike the
agricultural labourer, could hope to come home to a blazing fire
and a hot meal.

Many wage-earners found buying clothes a real problem because only a very small proportion of the weekly earnings could
be set aside for this purpose. The small commoner might be able
to supplement with the wool from his own sheep and most
country women could knit and spin, but where, in the case of the
town worker, everything had to be bought the position was difficult. William Hutton's autobiography sheds a somewhat pathetic
light on what this could mean to the young. By his indentures he
was bound to his uncle, a stocking weaver. He had covenanted
to earn 5s. 10d. a week, which went to his master. Any earnings
beyond that were his own, but he had to clothe himself out of
them. It was not easy. Later in life he wrote of his experiences in
1759.

> Clothes came as sluggishly as food. I was arriving at that age when
> the two sexes begin to look at each other, consequently wish to
> please; and a powerful mode to win is that of dress. This is a pass-
> port to the heart, a key to unlock the passions and guide them in
> our favour. My resources were cut off: my sun was eclipsed. Youth
> is the time to dress: the time in which it is not only excusable but
> laudable. I envied every new coat: I had the wish to earn but not
> the power.

It took him two years, for all his desiring, but in 1741 he was able
to write,

> What the mind is bent upon obtaining, the hand seldom fails in ac-
> complishing. I detested the frame, as totally unsuited to my temper:
> therefore I produced no more profit than necessity demanded.

[1] Gilboy: *Op. cit.,* p. 24.

I made shift, however, with a little over work and a little credit, to raise a genteel suit of clothes, fully adequate to the sphere in which I moved. The girls eyed me with some attention: nay I eyed myself as much as any of them.[1]

But, alas, tragedy followed. His suit was stolen and it took him five years before its modest splendour could be renewed.

An amusing instance of the important part clothes played in the budget of an artisan comes from the *Oxford Journal* of 26 December 1761. Two footpads held up a traveller as he was returning from Abingdon market and demanded his money.

> To which he answered [says the account] that he had but Nine-pence, and if they took that from him, he believed he should be more highly honoured than any of his Brethren had been before, for it would be the first Journeyman Hatter that was ever robbed in the World. On this one of them said, 'Damn him, let's take his Coat'; but he begged they would not do that, since it would distress him much more than the loss of his Money; and after some little Hesitation they dismissed him, with Orders not to take any Notice of what had happened.

He was lucky to retain his coat: in London thefts of clothes were common. On the 3rd of January thieves broke into the room of one Ann Thornhill while she was upstairs gossiping with her landlady and took 'a Black and White Crape Gown, a Purple and White Lustring Gown, a Cloth-coloured Camblet Gown, a Grey Camblet Cloak, a Red Rug Coat, a Brown Cloth Waistcoat and a Banyan of several Colours', for which the thief, being later convicted, suffered death.

The countryman's clothes were coarse but warm, being chiefly made of homespun and locally woven cloth or linen that was heavy and durable. His breeches were frequently leather, again locally tanned, and clogs were commonly worn instead of shoes. His wife wore a short-sleeved gown and petticoat of flannel. New clothes were seldom bought. Unless they could be made at home, charity, the parish or the second-hand dealer were the usual source of supply. In the bigger towns and particularly in London the poor depended very much on the activities of the second-hand clothes dealer. These men drew their stock from thieves or

[1] W. Hutton: *The Life of William Hutton, F.A.S.S., written by himself* (1816), p. 30.

A Farm Kitchen by W. H. Pyne

The Village Ale-House, 1787

Easter Tuesday, or the Parish Meeting Dinner, 1785

Industrious Cottagers, 1801

from the servants of good families, one of whose perquisites was the right to their masters' or mistresses' cast-off clothes. Where the employer was a person of fashion the right was a valuable one and was the source of cheap finery for many Londoners. It had also other social repercussions, of which contemporaries were not unaware, in that it tended to iron-out class distinctions in the towns so far as these were stressed by differences in apparel. The complaint was made, as Defoe himself made it, that the maid, who used to be but as good as her mistress in the dark was not now her inferior in the daylight, and it was often felt that this trade in second-hand clothes was but another way of spreading luxury among the poor. But such complaints had little validity outside London or outside the range of those families whose sons or daughters were employed in fashionable households.

In Birmingham the artisan turned to self-help and co-operation for a solution. Thus breeches clubs were common, in which every member balloted for a pair worth a guinea, and when all were supplied the club was dissolved. Sometimes the initiative behind the organizing of one of these clubs came from a tailor. 'If a taylor be short of employment', wrote Hutton, 'he has only to consult a landlord over a bottle, who, by their joint powers, can give birth to a cloaths club; where every member is supplied with a suit to his taste, of a stipulated price. These', he adds, 'are chiefly composed of batchlors who wish to shine in the eyes of the fair'.[1] In Birmingham, such clubs were not confined to providing clothing for their members. The poorest paid into rent clubs where 'from the weekly sums deposited by the members, a sop is regularly served up twice a year to prevent the growlings of a landlord', while the more prosperous or provident paid into building clubs and balloted for the houses in turn as they were built, or into capital clubs where, when £50 had been accumulated through subscriptions, the lucky drawer was able with the sum thus acquired to set up for himself.

Another factor which, it is often pointed out, did help to raise the standard of the clothing and general cleanliness of the working poor was the increasing production of cotton goods during the century, an increase that became still more marked after the mechanization of cotton spinning that both removed a bottleneck

---

[1] W. Hutton: *A History of Birmingham* (1783), p. 138.

and cheapened the yarn. Before, except in those areas where the country folk spun and wove their own linen, woollen cloth had been their common wear, the linsey petticoat and the flannel gown. When these were worn, unlike the lighter cottons, whose filth was at once more apparent and more easily removed, it was not customary to indulge in frequent washings, and the majority of the garments of the labouring poor must have been stale with odours and stiff with dirt before they finally rotted to pieces and were thrown away.[1] Yet, whatever the difficulties were, foreign visitors seem to have been impressed by the standard of clothing that many, if not most, of the labouring poor achieved. Thus Grosley commented on the fact that the drivers of the wagons whom he saw on the road were 'dressed in good cloth, a warm great coat upon his back, and good boots upon his legs', while Kalm was amused by the number of peruques he saw. Wearing them he found to be a universal custom in those parts which he visited, so that, he declared, 'It did not strike one as being at all wonderful to see farm servants, clodhoppers, day labourers, farmers, in a word all labouring folk go through their usual everyday duties all with Peruques on the head.' It was an extravagant custom, since, he adds, 'They were dear enough. For one guinea it was passable and did not look very handsome.'[2]

But though bad housing and overcrowding meant little comfort in the home and clothes were a drain on most working people's resources, society, in return for their labour, did provide some sort of roof over their heads, clothes that were some protection against the weather and, except in times of dearth, enough food to prevent hunger, even though their diet was deficient in vitamins and monotonous in the extreme. No society that was known to Englishmen provided more than this: most gave to their workers considerably less. That the eighteenth-century social conscience was so little disturbed by the low standard of living of much of the population was due, at least in part, to the

[1] It must be remembered, as against this view, that in the towns, at any rate, water supplies were quite inadequate in the poorer districts, and frequently contaminated, which made constant washing difficult. Also, as Engels points out in *The Condition of the Working-Class in England in 1844*, heavy cotton goods give less warmth, and protection against cold and wet than woollen ones and are less well adapted to the English climate.

[2] P. Kalm: *Account of his visit to England on his way to America in 1748*. Trans. J. Lucas (1892), p. 52.

mercantilist beliefs of the time. These definitely and clearly called for low wages.

Economic policy was constructed to serve national not individual ends. It was quite possible for it to envisage a situation in which the mass of the people would be both ill-housed and ill-fed, and yet, because the export trade was thriving, the national wealth could be considered as increasing. What was important was that we should have sufficient man-power available to produce not only as much as possible of what we needed as consumers, but also to work up for export commodities whose value had been increased by the labour expended on them. It was argued that if the raw material were produced here and English labour employed in working it up then the difference between the cost of the material and the price the foreigner paid for the finished product was clear gain. Such a theory, which placed so much stress on the export trade, called for a large population that would be content to work for low wages. Thus Petyt wrote in 1689, 'Plenty of people must also cause cheapness in wages, which will cause cheapness of manufactures; in a scarcity of people wages must be dearer, which must cause dearness of manufacture. . . . The populacy I intend and which can only be serviceable to manufacture, are those exuberant numbers which cannot find employment in husbandry or otherwise but in trade.'[1] In this spirit suggestions were made for augmenting the labour force by encouraging immigration or making the process of naturalization easier, with the avowed purpose of increasing competition and so forcing people to labour.

Not everyone accepted such statements uncritically. On one occasion Adam Smith observed that

Our Merchants frequently complain of the high wages of British labour as the cause of their manufactures being undersold in foreign markets, but they are silent about the high profits of stock. They complain of the extravagant gains of other people, but they say nothing of their own. The high profits of British stock, however, may contribute towards the raising of price of British manufactures in many cases as much and in some perhaps more, than the high wages of British Labour.[2]

---

[1] Quoted E. Furness, *Op. cit.*, p. 31.
[2] A. Smith: *Op. cit.*, Vol. II, p. 100.

Nor were prolific and much quoted writers like Arthur Young consistent in the views they expressed on this topic. Thus, if in a moment of exasperation he could write. 'Everyone but an idiot knows that the lower class must be kept poor or they will never be industrious;'[1] speaking of the effects of high wages he could also write, 'In a word, idle people are converted by degrees into industrious hands; youths are brought forward to work, even boys perform their share, and women at the prospect of great wages clap their hands with cheerfulness and fly to the sickle. Thus a new race of the industrious is by degrees created.'[2]

Generally, however, it was argued that higher wages would lead to a falling off of industry, and that high prices for the necessaries of life were no bad thing since they forced the poor to labour steadily if they would not want. In evidence of this viewpoint it was widely averred that workmen were more regular and steadier in their conduct when the price of food was high. Petty's comment on the matter was widely shared. 'It is observed', he wrote, 'by Clothiers and others, who employ great numbers of poor people, that when Corn is extremely plentiful, that the Labour of the poor is proportionately dear: And scarce to be had at all so licentious are they who labour only to eat, or rather to drink.'[3]

The need of a large labour force willing to accept low wages and long hours was also one of the reasons advanced for denying education to the poor. It was not only Mandeville who asked who was going to perform the drudgery of society if everyone were well educated. Typical of much that was written and said along these lines is the explosive outburst of a die-hard contributor to the *Gentleman's Magazine* in 1801, who wrote,

> The young scholars, instead of confining their reading (as their patrons and patronesses intended) to the religious works, eagerly learn the obscene songs hawked by ballad singers; and if they go out to service, become subscribers to the abominable circulating libraries that are now established in every petty town, from whence they obtain books that corrupt both their morals and political principles.

[1] A. Young: *Eastern Tour* (1771), Vol. IV, p. 361.
[2] A. Young: *Northern Tour* (1770), Vol. I, p. 196.
[3] Sir William Petty: *Political Arithmetick* (1690). Edited by C. H. Hull (1899), Vol. I, p. 274.

Of writing they make little other use than to carry on gossiping and amorous correspondences; . . . Scholars are above receiving instruction, and scorn handling ploughs and spades, scrubbing brushes or mops.[1]

Dr. Johnson, on the other hand, when consulted by Mr. Langdon, who was contemplating setting up a school on his estate, and who had received the usual pessimistic prophecies on the theme of education promoting idleness, replied with robust common sense,

No, Sir. While learning to read and write is a distinction the few who have that distinction may be the less inclined to work; but where everybody learns to read and write, it is no longer a distinction. A man who has a laced waistcoat is too fine a man to work; but if everybody had laced waistcoats, we should have people working in laced waistcoats. There are no people whatever more industrious, none work more, than our manufacturers, yet they have all learned to read and write.[2]

The propensity of the labouring poor to work irregular hours, putting in violent bouts of work and balancing them by days of idleness, when funds permitted, was also in general deplored by the economists of the day. To them there was something immoral in such behaviour. It was argued that the wealth of the nation was increased by the amount that labour, employed on the raw materials, added to their value. It followed that the sum of the daily wages lost through this self-regarding, irresponsible idleness or excessive holidays was the sum by which the national wealth might have been increased, and was not. If the maximum national wealth was to be attained then the labour of the people must be fully utilized, and this, most writers recognized, was only possible when money was circulating freely and trade was brisk. Even though the cruder idea that money itself was wealth was disappearing, it was generally felt that a favourable balance of trade was necessary to bring money into the country and so make full employment possible. The trading balance, however, could only be favourable so long as exports were increasing, and this again, it was thought, was only possible when wages were low and our goods cheap in foreign markets. Thus the full exploitation of the national resources depended on the steady labours of

---

[1] *Gentleman's Magazine*, LXX, p. 491.
[2] J. Boswell: *Life of Johnson*, Vol. II, p. 22.

the poor, and idleness meant the shirking of a moral obligation
on the part of the workman.

Excessively long hours, therefore, could be defended as easily
as low wages, and few writers, who had not themselves experienced the fatigue they occasioned, realized how greatly they
contributed to the so-called slothfulness of the labouring poor.
Francis Place, in his autobiography, recalls the days when, after
a bout of unemployment, he and his wife were forced to work
sixteen to eighteen hours a day, barely stopping to snatch the
minimum amount of food and sleep, until they could get out of
debt and redeem their pawned possessions. Even when this
emergency was passed it was their practice to work so unre-
mittingly that they hardly had time to stop for meals. Only at the
weekend did they relax. On Saturdays they tried to finish by
three o'clock, then, putting on their best clothes, they went for
a stroll and on their return had their first hot supper of the week,
usually a beef steak or a mutton chop. For most people the day's
work began at six and, with no more than a hour or so allowed for
dinner, went on until eight or nine at night. This represented the
normal working day of the apprentice and journeyman, and for
the domestic worker piece rates were calculated on a similar
basis.

The low standard of life endured by many of the labouring poor
cannot, however, be explained solely in terms of low wages and
long hours. There were other important factors which created a
feeling of insecurity and uncertainty in the average worker's life.
Some of these were economic, others were social and legal, but
the different strands are so tightly intertwined that it is not always
easy to disentangle them. Steady jobs were few and the irregularity of work was apt to produce an 'eat, drink and be merry for
to-morrow we die' attitude. This irregularity was very pronounced in many trades where the daily or weekly wage seemed
relatively high, and explains much of the misery that the observer,
unaware of this fact, would not expect to find. The weather was
often responsible for seasonal employment. This was certainly
the case for certain types of farm work and for building. It influenced, too, the miner, partly because the domestic part of his
demand was seasonal, but mainly because of the effect of bad
weather on an indifferent transport system. The coal from the

Midland and other inland pits had to be carried by pack-horses and when winter rain or snow made roads impassable the miners were stood off. In Northumberland and Durham it was not a question of roads but of stormy seas. When the colliers were port-bound, stocks piled up at the pit-head and the miners went on short time. Not all irregularity of employment was caused by the weather; in many of the luxury trades changes in fashion or an unexpected Court mourning could spell disaster. War and peace were equally unsettling, cutting off the demand for some articles and stimulating the production of others.

If economic factors often made it difficult for the steady work-man to find and keep permanent employment it must be admitted that many workmen were not steady. On this point contempor-aries pour out a stream of complaint and abuse. In extenuation it might be pleaded that there was very little in the general circum-stances of the labouring poor to encourage either forethought or thrift. Convention had limited their wants to the simplest foods and frowned on even their inclination towards tea and wheaten bread. Wages were too low for there to be much hope of their saving enough to secure a decent and comfortable old age. If their children could not provide this then the parish was the normal resource. What reason, therefore, was there to make them work for more than their immediate needs?

This attitude was no doubt further encouraged by the extent to which the drinking of beer, porter, and, particularly in the early decades of the century, gin in London, was part of the ordin-ary routine of the workman's life. Drink was an indulgence that broke up the monotony of the over-long working day. In addi-tion beer and porter may have helped to balance an inadequate diet, though the same could hardly be claimed for gin. It was more important to have a pint now than to save for a future which a high death-rate in most cases made problematical. In London the temptation was increased by the numerous beer-houses and taverns that functioned as places of call where out-of-work craftsmen or domestic servants could hear of new masters. Often wages were paid out to domestic workers in public houses.[1] They were the headquarters of innumerable fraternities and clubs.

---

[1] See M. D. George: *London Life in the Eighteenth Century*, for a full account of the temptations and insecurity of the London worker.

Nor was drink the only temptation to assault the workman's pocket. Gambling was nearly as popular and nearly as ruinous. Every class in the eighteenth century gambled: it was the national vice. At fashionable clubs like White's estates changed hands with the chance of the game, and his gaming debts were the only debts that a gentleman would inconvenience himself to pay without the threat of a debtor's prison looking over him. Betting, too, accompanied every kind of sport, and if the gentleman backed his fancy in racing, in prize-fighting and in cock-fighting, so did most men who came within the orbit of the game and had a coin in their pockets. With every temptation to spend and little inducement to save it is hardly surprising that so many men lived carelessly.

It might have been expected that this tendency would have been held in check by the habits of industry acquired while serving an apprenticeship, but whatever the earlier position might have been by the eighteenth century this was not so. It is true that most men did serve an apprenticeship if they intended to follow a craft or enter the ranks of the shopkeepers, though for many kinds of employment this was no longer necessary. But the old picture of the moral training in good living and citizenship, if it was ever honoured in the observance rather than the breach, had largely disappeared. Apprenticeship had become more a source of cheap labour, and of income *via* premiums than anything else. Here again William Hutton's experience is illuminating. He served his first apprenticeship in the silk mills of Derby, starting when he was too small to reach the machines without the aid of wooden pattens fixed to his feet. But apprenticeship of this kind was more equivalent to the child labour of the later textile factories than anything that the Middle Ages would have understood by the term, since young William lived at home, and his term when served left him without a training that he could follow as a man. His next apprenticeship was to his uncle, a stocking weaver. It brought him as little contentment as his first. Indeed, as he wryly observed, Jacob though he did serve fourteen years in all before obtaining Rachel for his wife, did at least obtain his objective in the end, whereas he, after fourteen years of hard and uncongenial toil, was still without a training that would bring him in a reasonable competence! During his second apprenticeship his aunt grudged him every mouthful of food that he ate, while his uncle, though usually sweet tempered enough, on one occasion beat him so severely that he ran away, and when he was out of his time did nothing to help him to set up on his own. Some apprentices were luckier. Samuel Roberts, of Sheffield, records that his father's and grandfather's apprentices were well fed and well treated and always dined with the family, but he admits that this was not always so and that 'apprentices and even journeymen, were not infrequently beaten by their masters'. Certainly on balance it does not seem as if the institution of apprenticeship did much to create habits of steadiness among the rising generation.

Another institution which, combined with irregular employment, drinking and gambling, produced an attitude of irresponsibility was that of imprisoning for debt. In the eighteenth-century prison, people who could not pay goalers' fees and buy comforts starved and frequently died. To be imprisoned for debt was, for the poor man, the final disaster. Yet with irregular employment, scanty wages, habits of drinking and gambling, debt was a net spread before most of the labouring poor. Often the debt was genuine enough though instances are disconcertingly common of trumped-up charges preferred out of spite. To swear a debt or a bastard to a man was to place him in a position where, though innocent, he might find it difficult to defend himself. In consequence when faced by the threat of either of these charges the average man took refuge in flight. Sometimes whole families contrived to slip away. All too often only the husband disappeared leaving his wife and children to fend for themselves, as, indeed, they would equally have had to do if he had stayed to be shut up in the Marshalsea. No one can study the history of any parish without coming across the familiar case of abandoned children or deserted families for whom the overseer had, most reluctantly, to provide.

No attempt to evaluate the position of the great mass of the population can afford to ignore the Poor Law. Apart from private charity, which from its very nature was intermittent and badly distributed, it was their only resource, except crime, in times of emergency and want. In theory the provision made was adequate when judged by any eighteenth-century standards. Indeed, many contemporaries felt that it was dangerously generous, that the knowledge that the parish was bound to provide for them in old age, in sickness or any other emergency, prevented the poor from working as hard as they might, to the detriment of the national income. The foundation of the Poor Law had been laid by the great codification of earlier, experimental legislation under Elizabeth I. By its provisions overseers of the poor were to be appointed in every parish by the justices of the peace. They were to work with the churchwardens and the parish was entitled to levy a poor rate, also to be confirmed by the justices, to provide the necessary funds. Their duties in theory were threefold. They were to relieve the sick and aged, to apprentice poor children and to find work for the able unemployed. This last side of their activities soon fell into disuse, once the coercive power of Star Chamber and the Council Table were removed. By the eighteenth century the average parish official was concerned only with the relief of the sick and the aged and the care of orphans or other abandoned children.

From the point of view of the labouring poor there were serious limitations on the help that was given. It had always been recognized in a somewhat general way that a parish need only relieve its own poor. More precise definition had been provided by the Act of Settlements and Removals in 1662. By its provisions, together with later amendments, a person obtained a settlement by birth, by serving an apprenticeship within its boundaries, being hired for a year, paying parish rates and, in the case of a woman, through marriage. Persons not covered by any of these provisions could gain a settlement by renting a house of the annual value of £10 a year, or giving a notice in writing of their intention to acquire a settlement followed by forty days' residence. As the average rent paid by the labourer, the artisan or the small trader never approached this figure the first of these provisions was of academic interest; it had no bearing on the settlement of the labouring poor and was, indeed, designed to prevent rather than facilitate it. But the other provision, that of forty days' residence, which after 1693 commenced only after the delivery of a notice in writing, was accompanied by a clause empowering the parish officers, with the sanction of two local justices of the peace, to send back to their place of settlement any person trying to settle in the parish whom they thought 'likely to become chargeable'. Moreover the Act contained no definition of what constituted such a likelihood; that was left to the parish officials and the justices, neither of whom were likely to be over-generous in their construction when an error might saddle the parish with new paupers to be provided for out of the rates. Therefore, though every poor person had a right to relief, that right was confined to a single parish which could not easily be changed if suitable work could not be found locally.

Such legislation must have contributed to the immobility of a great part of the population. People could move, but they could only move at the expense of risking their right to poor relief. This is in practice what happened. At a time when industry was increasing, towns growing, and the population shifting its centres of density, it was quite impossible that every newcomer to a parish should be moved back to his, or her, place of settlement. To attempt to obtain a regular settlement by forty days' residence was usually fatal, but the newcomer to a parish who made no such attempt was seldom molested unless he, or she, fell into certain categories, which the parish officers knew from personal experience were particularly vulnerable to economic pressure. In the country districts, the labourer 'overburdened with children' was always suspect and unwelcome since agricultural wages, even when reinforced by some by-employment on the part of the wife, were seldom sufficient to support a large family without at least some trifling allowance from the parish. Both in town and country alike, single women were apt to prove a liability, unless they were engaged in service, while the widow or woman with children was almost bound to require some relief. Parishes concentrated, therefore, on moving these types of persons, and the single man of ordinary strength and ability was generally left alone unless disaster overtook him or he was injudicious enough to marry a woman of the parish, in which case, as his wife now acquired her husband's settlement, there was a great temptation to remove the newly married couple back to the man's legal place of settlement, if this were known.

The effects of this system on the poor were almost wholly unfortunate both from an economic, and even more, from a social point of view. It meant that freedom of movement was something to be purchased at a great cost which often involved personal suffering and degradation. Thus, a man who had left his parish in early youth and spent all his working days elsewhere might in sickness or old age be bundled into the parish cart and returned to a parish where he had no friends or ties, and whose officials would most certainly receive him unwillingly.[1] It was also a system that led to much interference with the private lives of the labouring poor in many other ways. Men were bribed to marry unwanted women in order to procure them a settlement in another parish, putative fathers of bastard children were forced into matrimony, sometimes even being brought to the church in chains, not in the interests of morality but 'to save the parish harmless', while, since bastards took not their father's settlement, which was the practice of legitimate children until they were seven, but that of the parish where they were born, women who were suspected of being about to give birth to illegitimate children were openly bribed or bullied to go from parish to parish, as in some monstrous and nightmarish game of musical chairs, until the woman could go no further and the child was born. In the same way, the apprenticeship clauses, particularly in the towns, were grotesquely distorted.

The original purpose of the law had been the praiseworthy one of seeing that no child for whom the parish was responsible should be thrown out upon the world without a trade by which it could earn its living, a very necessary provision at a time when so many trades could be legally practised only by those who had served their seven years' apprenticeship. Parishes could, therefore, do one of two things; they could either bind a child within their own parish, in which case they paid no fee and the prospective master could only refuse if he were willing to pay a fine instead of taking the child, or they could use parish funds to bind the child apprentice outside the parish. Though this was in the first instance the more expensive method to follow, it had the advantage that the child then gained a settlement in the new master's parish, and, therefore, the original parish was freed of all further responsibility.

This method was generally more characteristic of the towns than the country, where children bound to the local farmers constituted a cheap and not unwelcome labour force, and

---

[1] The responsible parish could avoid such action by making a financial contribution to the support of the said pauper, so removal was not invariable.

the individual knowledge of the overseers acted as some kind of brake in a rural community in which everyone knew everyone else's business. But in the town parishes, particularly where the poor were huddled into crowded tenements, no-one cared particularly what happened to the children of the nameless poor, and the supposed interests of the parish were paramount. It was from this source that the helpless parish apprentice came, and once he had been bound over, those who should have been the guardians of his interests cared for them no more, while his new master, once the fee had been secured, either exploited him unmercifully or treated him with the brutality necessary to force him to run away and so join the ranks of wandering and abandoned children. It is true that legally after 1767 for London, and after 1778 for the rest of the country, owing to the strenuous efforts of the philanthropist Jonas Hanway, conditions were somewhat tightened up, the amount of premium paid was increased and was now to fall due in two instalments rather than to be given in one lump sum at the beginning. But in the literature of the period, in the records of Quarter Sessions, and, later, in the state of the poor apprentices bound to the cotton masters of the North, there is plenty of evidence to show how illusory a benefit the right to be apprenticed by the parish often was to the children of the poor.

So monstrous were some of the abuses connected with the administration of the Poor Laws that it is too easy to forget that in many ways the right to claim parish relief did provide some safeguard for the poor against the disasters and general insecurity of their life: that if wages were kept low in the interests of the export trade, there was some public provision for sickness and old age. According to the standards of the eighteenth century this was often not ungenerous. Most parishes recognized their obligation to help in cases of sickness, and, in some, fairly elaborate arrangements were made for this kind of assistance. Thus, by the close of the eighteenth century, it was not uncommon for a parish to enter into a definite contract with a local doctor to supply medicine and attendance for the parish poor. Sometimes these contracts were all-embracing, in other cases outbreaks of epidemics were definitely excluded. Other parishes were less systematic and employed the local doctor, the local wise woman, or the local bone-setter, as the occasion seemed to require. Nor

were the parish activities in sickness confined to supplying medical
attendance. At Cowden, where Robert Still and his family con-
tracted smallpox, the parish supplied a nurse for five weeks,
faggots for his fire, and a lavish assortment of food, including
beef, cheese, mutton, butter, milk and beer. Altogether the parish
incurred a pretty bill which the justice who finally passed the
account stigmatized as 'most unreasonable'. Funeral expenses of
the poor, too, usually fell on the parish, and these again were not
always the sordid affair of 'rattle his bones over the stones, only
a pauper that nobody owns'. Westbury paid 'for drink and
Biskett' for the bearers, while Coddenham tolled the bell, for
which the sexton was duly paid, and consoled the presumably
desolate father of one pauper girl with a shilling for beer! But
here again the practice of town and country parishes was very
divergent, and in the former the sordid impersonality of tradition
undoubtedly prevailed.

Apart from its sick, the other great responsibilities of the
parishes were its aged poor and those too young as yet to be apprenticed. Here again practice varied and much depended on
whether the parish had any kind of workhouse or humble poorhouse for the employment or housing of its poor. If it had, their
situation was often grim enough. After a few years of energetic
management by enthusiastic committees of local worthies, determined to see that workhouses were well-run places of employment, most of them fell into the hands of contractors. In that
case the fate of the poor within their walls depended on the character of the contract. If the contractor received a lump sum to
cover all contingencies his policy was to make the workhouse so
repellent that none but the desperate and destitute would enter
its walls. If he was paid so much per head his policy was to attract
rather than repel, and the slackness and immorality of the house
was then such as to make it a penance for the more self-respecting
poor to drag out their last years among its disorder and dirt.

In country parishes tiny poorhouses were more common. In
these the aged poor were provided with the shelter of a roof,
little more, and some scanty allowance for diet: here again discomfort and squalor reigned supreme. In those parishes where the
officials contented themselves with paying the rents of their aged
poor, or of putting them in small cottages on the waste, or of

boarding them out with more active neighbours, things were decidedly better. This was true also in the case of children who were boarded out instead of being 'a slave of slaves, the lowest of the low' within the workhouse. For both classes, in addition to house rent, fuel, clothes and some small allowance for diet were usually made, and again this was often not ungenerous, and in many rural parishes the provision made for the aged poor was probably not greatly below that which their labour had previously provided; though here it should not be forgotten that this was in too many districts hardly above subsistence level.

From the point of view of the labouring poor, therefore, the existence of a Poor Law did help to alleviate the insecurity of their lives. In childhood, in sickness, in old age, at least something was done. If the theories of the mercantilists denied to the majority of the nation such wages as made it possible for them to enjoy a fair standard of living, and still be able to save for illness or old age, the state did, in the form of the Poor Law, attempt to make some recompense. In the case of the poor labourer 'overburdened with children' it even, to the extent to which it supplemented his wages by an allowance, provided assistance in the nature of family benefits, though this was an expedient that grew up without direct legislative sanction in response to the impossible economic situation of some of the rural workers. Yet what was done was not, for the most part, well done. The original structure of the Poor Laws had been contrived to meet the needs of a very different England, an England that was rural rather than urban, an England that was dominated by the Privy Council, not one in which local interests, as represented by the justice of the Peace, had full sway. As the industrial changes of the eighteenth century gathered momentum, so the strain on this out-of-date structure increased, and in assessing the impact of the so-called 'Industrial Revolution' on the lives of the working population of the country careful consideration will have to be given to this factor. For the Poor Law played too important a part in the lives of so many people for it ever to be ignored.

Nor should it be forgotten that there were depths of destitution below those to which the settled poor might sink. In the average country parish the inhabitants were not so numerous that the destitute among them could not be either relieved or removed to

their rightful place of settlement, but in the bigger towns, and
above all in London, a labyrinth of courts and alleys made this
almost impossible. Here the dregs of the population, who
scrounged or begged or stole for a living, existed precariously.
Dr. Johnson, describing the wretchedness to which Richard
Savage's spendthrift ways had reduced him, portrays graphically
the shifts and contrivances of this kind of life.

> He lodged as much by Accident as he dined, and passed the Night
> sometimes in mean Houses, which are set open at Night to any casual
> Wanderers, sometimes in Cellars among the Riot and Filth of the
> Meanest and most profligate of the Rabble; and sometimes, when
> he had no Money to support even the Expences of these Receptacles,
> walked about the Streets till he was weary, and lay down in the
> Summer upon a Bulk, or in the Winter with his Associates in
> Poverty, among the Ashes of a Glass house.[1]

And when sickness, which, with filth, hardship and under-feeding,
came soon, or old age overtook such people, they had no resource
but to creep into the shelter of some abandoned and derelict
house and there, like a sick animal, die. Dr. Johnson, when on one
occasion discussing the state of the poor in London, told the
assembled company:

> Saunders Welch, the Justice, who was once High Constable of Hol-
> born, and had the best opportunities of knowing the state of the
> poor, told me, that I under-rated the number, when I computed that
> twenty a week, that is, above a thousand a year, died of hunger; not
> absolutely of immediate hunger; but of the wasting and other dis-
> eases which are the consequences of hunger. This happens only in so
> large a place as London, where people are not known. What we are
> told about the great sums got by begging is not true; the trade is
> overstocked. And you may depend upon it, there are many who
> cannot get work. A particular kind of manufacture fails: Those who
> have been used to work at it, can, for some time, work at nothing
> else.[2]

Because the hours of work were long and living conditions
hard would it be true to describe 'the labouring poor' of Georgian
England as a down-trodden and victimized majority? Nothing is
more difficult than to make objective judgments about another

[1] Samuel Johnson: *Life of Richard Savage* (1748), p. 127.
[2] J. Boswell: *Life of Johnson,* Vol. III, pp. 58-9.

A Midsummer Afternoon with a Methodist Preacher by de Loutherbourg

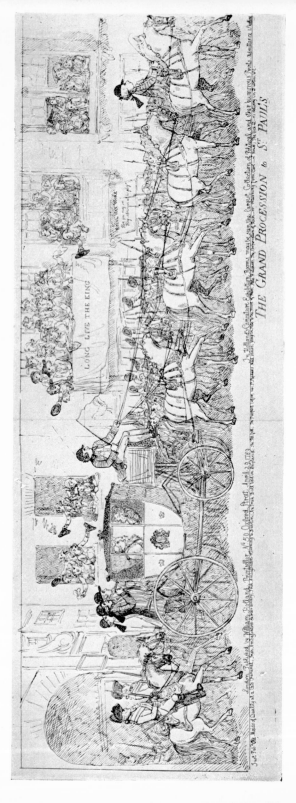

THE GRAND PROCESSION to ST PAULS

London. Published by William Richard, Printseller, N° 50 Oxford Street, April 29, 1789

The Grand Procession to St. Paul's on St. George's Day, 1789

age whose standards and values are no longer accepted. The twentieth century has experienced a tremendous revolution in the attitude of most English people to the society in which they live. The great mass of the people are no longer a submerged nine-tenths, and a society that judged them to be only hewers of wood and drawers of water is being fairly rapidly replaced by one that is groping towards something more in the nature of an economic democracy. It is, therefore, easy for the twentieth-century reader to exaggerate the impact of the brutality, the prevailing squalor, the poverty on English folk who lived two hundred years before.

Yet there is little evidence to show that the average member of the labouring poor was filled with bitter resentment or economic despair. Certainly the first part of the eighteenth century, while food prices remained low, was marked by much less discontent and unrest than the sixteenth had been. If the standard of life was simple it was also traditional and accepted. Nor was the working population without its pleasures. Drinking and gambling provided some colour and excitement, the almost inevitable reaction to the social and economic pressure that bad conditions were exerting. Kalm commented with some amazement on both the time and the money that the rural labourer was able to devote to his own pleasure, observing of farm servants that 'as soon as they entered the cottage in the evening, they did not apply themselves to the least work, more than that they ate, sat and talked till eleven o'clock in the evening. They never troubled themselves to make waggons, or agricultural implements.'[1] And in many cases their time was even less profitably employed, for drinking, either at the local ale-house or in the company of friends, or gossiping with their fellows, was the common practice, so that Kalm often 'wondered over this, that folk who could only provide food for themselves, their wives and children out of daily wages, could spend time and money in this way'. It was, he noted, 'customary at all the places I travelled through in this country.' However, he added, that he 'seldom saw any one imbibe so much, that he became drunk from it'.[2] A good deal of drunkenness however, there undoubtedly was, and after a good season for apples in 1776 his steward wrote to Sir William Jerningham informing him that 'syder has been offered for 10s. per hogshead',

---

[1] P. Kalm: *Op. cit.*, p. 173.   [2] *Ibid.*, p. 334.

a hundred gallon to each hogshead, adding significantly, 'so we may expect to see much drunkenness amongst the lower sort of people'.[1] Their taste lay mainly in the direction of crude and brutal diversions. When the gentleman fought his cocks the yokel was looking over his shoulder and, just as the nineteenth-century miner had his whippet, so many an eighteenth-century country-man had his own birds. Bull-baiting was both common, as the survival of the name 'bull ring' shows, and very popular. So were the displays put on by the bruisers, who fought without gloves and aroused enthusiasm in proportion as they drew blood. Local fairs provided side-shows and the excitement of pedlars' packs and the gaiety of dancing, of drinking and noise.

Even some crumbs of public entertainment came the way of the poor. In the towns at all events it was customary to celebrate im-portant public events, coronations, royal births and marriages and great victories with general rejoicings in which windows were illuminated, giving the dramatic contrast to the usual mirk of the night that a sudden lifting of the blackout precautions brought to their war-weary descendants two hundred years later. Fireworks were let off, drink flowed freely, and those who had heavy pockets treated freely those whose purses were lighter. Another, and grimmer, spectacle was provided by the public punishment of malefactors, people placed in the pillory or whipped through the streets until 'their backs were bloody', and, most exciting of all, a hanging. For the populace of London this was a commonplace, but a really important hanging at Tyburn always brought a con-course of people together, men of fashion as well as the London mob; provincial towns were sometimes equally fortunate. When this happened the public flocked to the execution as their descend-ants do to a football match, and even employers like Parson Woodeforde gave their menservants time off to enjoy the excite-ment when two notorious highwaymen were hanged at Norwich! Though to a large extent the really rural population were excluded by their isolation from the amusements that were available for the townsman, they, too, were not left without their simpler diver-sions. Rowdy and traditional games of football up and down the village street, to the terror sometimes of the more respectable part of the inhabitants, celebrations accompanied with much eating

---

[1] W. St. Clair Baddeley: *A Cotswold Manor* (1929), p. 220.

and drinking for Harvest Home, for May Day, for the traditional great feasts of the Church, all helped to break up the monotony of daily toil.

Nor was the eighteenth-century Englishman a completely helpless victim of the authorities. It is true that the countryman found his freedom limited to a very large extent by the administrative framework of society. The Act of Settlements and Removals threatened his freedom of movement. The constable could arrest him for minor offences and put him in the stocks or the village cage, while the justice could fine him for tippling in the ale-house or using profane language; he could have him arrested on suspicion and have him committed to gaol until the next Quarter Sessions; he could be fined for not going to Church; he could be arrested for poaching. There was certainly opportunity enough for plenty of local bullying, and no doubt much took place. But villages have their own methods of self-protection. The constable was a local man and a near-equal once his year of office was over; even the squire was not completely invulnerable to local opinion. And if times were too hard, the price of bread too high, the poor had the tradition of riot on which to fall back. Certainly they did not starve in silence. The year 1766 was such a period of distress, and trouble was widespread. At Birmingham special constables had to be appointed to prevent farmers and others who were bringing produce to sell in the market from being molested. It was certainly not an unnecessary precaution, for in Abingdon market on 4th of October 'Some Parcels of Grain, said to have been illegally purchased, were by the Populace sold in the publick Markets at 5s. a Bushell.' It was the sort of thing that happened often. The crowds were orderly enough unless molested, and their conviction of the rightness of their actions is illustrated by the fact that the seized produce was so often sold for what was felt to be a reasonable price, not merely looted. Nevertheless, the resentment of a hungry mob against a middleman blamed for profiteering, could be an ugly thing, and that very day a local trader, Joseph Butler, thought it worth his while to make a public declaration to the Mayor of Abingdon that the report put about by 'some malicious Persons . . . that he had corn stored up in Oxford and had bought up cheese, to the amount of Eighty Tons was false'.

Where the authorities took strong measures to resist the action of the hungry mob sometimes violence followed which resulted in tragedy. At Pagenhall, in the Cotswolds, the crowds were dispersed by the magistrates and some of the rioters later hanged. Such episodes were not infrequent. On 10 January 1766, the *Oxford Journal* reported that

> On Tuesday last David Ecland, one of the Abingdon Rioters, was executed at Reading (conformable to his sentence at the late Assizes held there under a special Commission), in pursuance of Orders received by Express, last Friday, from the Secretary of State's Office. . . . It was [went on the report] a most affecting Scene; Ecland's wife, with his six poor Children, attending to take their last Farewell, under these deplorable Circumstances, and to bring away the Body after Execution, with which they next Day arrived at Abingdon, having rode in the same Cart all the way. The Spectators, at this Execution, appeared greatly affected, as it seems Ecland had always sustained an unblemished Character before he unhappily joined in the late Outrage.[1]

Such scenes underline the grimmer side of Georgian England. Yet society was not oblivious of its responsibility for its poorer members in times of scarcity, and ruthless action to stamp out disorder was often accompanied by charitable organization to alleviate distress. In places like Birmingham, subscription lists were opened both in 1766 and in the following year, when a fund was set up to transport rice, described as 'a cheap and hearty food', to the town. It was an all too familiar circle. When the poor starved they rioted, and when they rioted, though the ringleaders might suffer for their courage, both public authorities and private individuals, made thus conscious of the distress about them, did what they could to relieve it. Though the twentieth century must condemn the execution of men who rioted for food, it might well pause to reflect that the hangings were at least accompanied by subscription lists, and to ask in how many countries in eighteenth-century Europe that could happen?

Certainly when pushed too far the eighteenth-century Englishmen, and women, lacked neither courage nor initiative, and if they took a modest view of their rights, and demanded little beyond a roof for their heads, sufficient food to fill their bellies, and clothes

[1] Townshend: *Op. cit.*, p. 60.

that would cover them, with a sauce of drink and idleness to give a relish to the monotony of life, when these things were jeopardized their protests were vigorous enough. That they should have been so sporadic, taking place only in times of sudden worsening of conditions or when the mob to satisfy some political rancours had been stirred to life by its betters, is some indication that in ordinary times the mass of the labouring poor felt no great sense of injustice against the social order of their age.

Chapter Six

AGRARIAN AND INDUSTRIAL DEVELOPMENTS

THE great difficulty of making an analysis of any society is that unless such a study is pinpointed in time to a certain year, or even month or day, it is never static but always in a state of flux. New factors are always subtly influencing old institutions, undermining traditional acceptances, altering the pattern even as we study it. This is always so, yet at some times the stream of change seems to flow so sluggishly that it would take an observant eye indeed to perceive the slight alterations that twenty, or even fifty, years have made to its course, while at others the waters swirl so swiftly that even the half-attentive watcher cannot but be struck by the differences that the same period has made apparent. The eighteenth century, and most particularly the latter part of it, belongs to the second and not the first of these categories, so much so that the historians of the nineteenth century, looking back, have labelled its closing decades 'The Industrial Revolution.' Historians to-day use the term with more reservations as the mounting evidence of subsequent research has revealed the degree to which the foundations, of what appeared as dramatic change, were laid in the sixteenth, seventeenth and early eighteenth centuries. Evidently the early part of the stream was not so sluggish, the latter not so contrastingly rapid, as had once been thought. Yet when all reservations have been made, the economic changes of the eighteenth century, and particularly those that seemed to occur with increasing frequency towards its close, were strikingly significant and important. So significant and so important that it was inevitable that they should have very definite repercussions on the structure of the society which was forced to adjust itself to them.

To attempt to assess these repercussions is a fascinating, but not an easy, task; their ramifications are so often both entangled and obscure, and to isolate and simplify is inevitably also to falsify. Yet such generalizations are interesting and worth attempting, though their essentially superficial nature must never be forgotten. It is only the surface of things, their appearance, rather than the subtle interweaving of the forces that created and shaped them, that the historian can measure and describe with any degree of confidence. To do even this it is necessary to examine, though briefly, for it is a well-trodden road, the nature and extent of the major changes in both agriculture and in industry which were the outstanding features of the age. Here it is probably most satisfactory to study first the economic developments that chiefly affected the countryside, since most people at the beginning of the century were either country dwellers or had some connexion with the land. King calculated that out of a population of five and a half million some one million, four hundred thousand could be counted as urban, while the rest were living in rural areas. Town and country were not, however, and never could be, isolated compartments into which economic facts can be tidily sorted; throughout the century changes in agricultural practices affected the course of industry, while at the same time developments in the technique of manufacturing altered the way of life of the countryman.

It is never at any time easy to paint a picture of English agriculture which is at once general and reasonably accurate. The opening years of the eighteenth century are no exception to this statement. Local studies, the importance of which are becoming increasingly obvious, have emphasized the varieties in farming practices occasioned by differences of soil and climate. Pasture farms and scattered homesteads had always predominated in those parts of the country which were physically unsuited to open field farming. In other areas the open fields had long disappeared. Sometimes this was due to the pressure of a commercially minded lord of the manor, anxious to increase his rents. More often than is always realized, it was the result of agreements made by many small farmers. It was not only the large farmer who found it convenient to hold his land in severalty.[1] By the beginning of the eighteenth century the older arrangements had been modified; they had not been eliminated. In spite of the great wave of enclosure that had swept over Tudor England, shocking conservative opinion into a wave of protest that poured forth from pulpit

[1] This term is used to indicate that the farmer had exclusive rights over the land he owned or rented, that he could enclose it with a hedge or wall, and could organize his farming routine independently of his neighbours.

and press alike, in spite, too, of the failure of the somewhat equivocal and dubious efforts of the Stuart kings to impose barriers to the flood, much of England, possibly half the arable land, still lay in the great open fields.[1] Changes in their management and in the organization of rural life since they had first taken shape in the obscurity of the so-called Dark Ages there had certainly been. The old equality of holdings, enforced from above, had long disappeared. Some farms were comparatively large, others mere fragments, while the tenants of any estate were a jumble of copyholders, leaseholders, tenants at will, and freeholders. The latter had by now shaken themselves free of all but a nominal connexion with the manor, and their holdings formed something like independent enclaves. Yet as long as some form of the open-field village remained, and England was a country of commons and wastes and contained much unreclaimed land, the social structure, which had grown up within this agrarian shell, would remain also.

The open-field villages tended to foster and shelter the peasantry. Their economy was particularly suited to the needs of the small farmer. Land could be bought and sold in tiny lots; adding strip to strip was easier than adding field to field. The existence of commons helped him, too. It is true that the benefits derived from them can easily be overrated. The pasture that they provided was often very poor. Frequently they were grievously overstocked, for the richer farmer, with closes of his own, often turned his sheep and cattle first out on to the commons, and, when these had been eaten bare, he moved them back into his own closes, where the pasture had been husbanded for this purpose. Meanwhile, the beasts of the poorer farmer, who often had no other pasture available, became thin and half starved. Nevertheless, even at their worst, commons represented some extension of the small open-field farmers economy, though it might well be true that five acres of enclosed pasture were more valuable than grazing rights over 250.[2] Deficient though they were they enabled him to carry on. In other ways, too, the system favoured small-scale farming. Markets were local and methods very simple. There were few advantages to be gained from either large-scale production or

[1] R. E. Prothero (Baron Ernle): *British Farming Past and Present* (1912), p. 154.
[2] *Ibid.*, p. 158.

marketing. The small farmer had less to sell, the time he could wait for a return on his money and labour, particularly the latter, might be shorter but his costs of production and the efficiency of his methods were not likely to be very different from those of the more substantial farmer.

In the early eighteenth century, however, factors were at work which were to change this situation considerably. The trend of land purchases altered. The sixteenth and seventeenth centuries had seen accumulation by the gentry, the building-up of the squirearchy, the predominance of the moderate estate. Now the process was again being reversed. By the early eighteenth century, land, as it came into the market, was being added to the great estates rather than going to the formation of new moderately-sized ones.[1] The reason for this seems, in the first place, to have been not so much economic as social, not, that is, the desire to accumulate land for the sake of the profits to be got from its management. Land was wanted for the prestige and political power that accrued to its possessor. But though the original motive for purchasing might not be economic, few landowners could afford to ignore financial considerations. Unlike the merchant, the average gentleman and nobleman depended for their revenue on their estates. The expenditure required to sustain their way of life was considerable and this meant tackling problems of estate management seriously. Though the nobility and gentry were by no means urbanized or absentee landlords, they were landlords rather than agriculturists. That is, their revenue came for the most part from their rent rolls, and not, like that of the Prussian Junkers, from the direct farming of their land. Indeed, foreign visitors commented on the fact that the gentry 'hardly ever cultivate their fields or landed estates themselves, but let them out to farmers and live on the money flowing in from their tenants'. This was the reason which Kalm thought explained the damage which rooks were allowed to do to the crops. The crops were the property of the tenants while the rooks were

> so sly as to build their nests in such trees as stood in front of gentle-men's and noblemen's houses and belong to them ... because it was very seldom any gentleman allowed any to shoot or molest them in

his trees, but seemed to consider himself entitled, as it were, to shelter them because they had taken refuge with him, and, as it were, solicited his protection.[1]

Estates that were largely farmed on the open field system were awkward to manage and difficult to exploit. This was largely due to the mass of small farmers that made up the majority of the tenantry. At best it was more troublesome to collect the rent in driblets and cost more in overhead expenses. The smaller farmer, too, generally farmed more for subsistence than for the market, though he usually had one or two lines that brought in enough to pay the rent and buy such necessaries as he and his family could not provide themselves. In bad seasons such men had little behind them in the shape of cash reserves, so rents became difficult to collect and often tended to fall into arrears. From the point of view of the landowner the fact that many of the small open-field farmers were copyholders was an additional disadvantage, since copyhold, with all the traditional restraints upon it, meant that the lord was only in about half effective possession of the land that was nominally his own. As a result progressive estate agents pressed for the elimination of the old-fashioned farmer and the substitution of more substantial tenants who, because they were farming for the market, would be able to pay bigger rents. This was one reason why an attack on the peasantry was likely to be one of the features of eighteenth-century rural development. 'The people who suffered were the smaller tenants with ten to thirty acres.'[2] But if the small tenants were to be replaced by bigger ones conditions had to be created in which a supply of this kind of tenant was forthcoming. This meant that farming profits must be sufficiently high to attract men with some capital and make them willing to compete, by the offer of increased rents, for the land that the aristocracy and gentry now controlled.

Unfortunately, farming in the early part of the eighteenth century was only moderately prosperous. Except in years of dearth the price of wheat was low and the subsidy of 5s. a quarter paid when wheat was exported for less than 28s. a quarter was of debatable value.[3] Pasture farming promised better, for the demand

---

[1] P. Kalm: *Op. cit.*, p. 143.   [2] H. J. Habakkuk: *Art. cit.*, p. 16.
[3] T. S. Ashton. *An Economic History of England: The Eighteenth Century* (1955), p. 49, for a discussion of this point.

for wool and, to a lesser but increasing extent, for both mutton and beef, was steady. Here, too, the existence of the open fields seemed to block progress. Winter feed for the cattle had always been one of the worst problems the farmer had had to face, and until it had been solved, it would not be easy, and was, perhaps, impossible, greatly to extend dairy farming and the production of meat for the market. It was not so much a lack of knowledge as the lack of incentive to apply it that prevented progress. Holland, with its large commercial and industrial population in relation to its arable acres, provided an example of what could be done in these ways. Men like Weston, who had been forced to spend years in political exile, wrote up their observations, advocating the use of new crops like turnips and artificial grasses. At the same time scientific curiosity was growing, and theorists like John Evelyn were studying the composition of soils and the methods by which plants obtained their food. Works like his *Terra*, and Nathaniel Grew's *Physiology of Plants* disposed of many of the unsound speculations of the past, and gave to newer methods of cultivation the backing of an authoritative science. As a result, more attention was paid to those crops that could be used to augment the winter feed for cattle. By the early eighteenth century the progressive farmer was sowing grass seeds with the last crop of grain, white clover, which was native, and foreign fodder crops, like sainfoin and lucerne. More spectacular in many ways was the increased use made of root crops. By the beginning of the eighteenth century progressive farmers, particularly in Norfolk, were growing turnips as a field crop. Sown in quantity they would obviously provide a valuable winter feed for cattle. But the practice was far from universal. Even in 1727 Edward Laurence was still advocating the substitution of a four-fold rotation of crops, with the turnip taking the place of the fallow field, for the traditional three-fold one. As a field crop the turnip made slow progress until the middle 'thirties. Even then it was sown broadcast, and the sheep and cattle were turned out into the fields to eat the crop there.

With the new stress on food for cattle rather than food for man, combined with the newer rotation of crops, which Townshend was advocating so strenuously in Norfolk, and with the new scientific knowledge of the composition of the soil and the nature of plants, came an increased interest in the problems of cultivation.

Here the name of Jethro Tull stands out as a pioneer. It is true that his own scientific premises were unsound. He advocated correct practices for the wrong reasons, and, though he created a furore with his writings on horse-hoeing husbandry, his theories underwent an eclipse until they were reintroduced into this country from France many years after his death.[1] Despite these things, his emphasis on the use of drills, the more economical sowing of the best quality seed available, and the constant application of the 'iron among the roots' made a great contribution to English farming. Previously it had been customary when sowing wheat, of which there were about four main varieties by the mid-century, to use three or four bushels to the acre; Tull showed that two bushels sown in accordance with his methods would yield twenty-two bushels and that the use of an extra bushel of seed would only increase the yield by another one and a quarter bushels. By careful cultivation during the period of growth, so that the soil was thoroughly broken up, he thought that it would be possible to grow the same crops on the same land indefinitely without the use of manure. His methods, less good for the wheat, for which they were intended, revolutionized the efficiency of the turnip as a field crop, since it grew to advantage in the long rows which could be kept free from the entangling weeds.

His refusal to believe in the necessity of manure when the land was kept clean and the soil well broken was fortunately not shared by other farming pioneers. Townshend, whose name is so firmly associated with turnips and the rotation of crops, was equally active in demonstrating that poor land could be brought into cultivation and made productive by the right use of the right manures. In particular he showed the importance of the practice of marling on the sandy soil of Norfolk. Marl is a soft, soapy substance, deposits of which are found some times as little as eighteen inches from the surface and sometimes several feet down. When it is spread on the land it has the effect of increasing its fertility for as much as twenty years. On other soils, or where marl was not found, lime was used or burning resorted to, partly to clear weeds away, partly to enrich the soil with the ashes so obtained. Thus, by better farming methods it was clear that the English country-

[1] T. H. Marshall: 'Jethro Tull and the "New Husbandry" of the Eighteenth Century'. *Econ. Hist. Rev.*, Vol. II, No. 1 (January 1929).

side could be made much more productive. The fallow year, hitherto considered indispensable if crops were to be raised, was eliminated, so automatically bringing a third more of the cultivated land into use each year. On this land, too, by better methods, heavier crops could be raised. Also sandy wastes or boggy swamps that had before been considered unsuitable for either arable or pasture farming, were shown by correct manuring or careful draining to be capable of growing good crops, as when Coke raised good wheat where before 'two rabbits had struggled for one blade of grass.'

With better agriculture and more fodder crops came a greater concentration on the breeding of livestock. Hitherto, sheep, valued as mobile dung-carts, had been bred for their fleeces, and cattle for the pail and the plough. Meat had been a very secondary consideration; it was the oldest, skinniest animals that had been killed at Michaelmas. The prosperity of the eighteenth century was, however, providing a new market for butchers' meat. The middle class and the more prosperous artisan in the towns were eating mutton and beef more frequently, even if the countryman still had to be content with his pig. But to exploit this market a very different kind of beast was required, one which matured quickly, so that the cost of its keep did not eat away the profits of its sale, and which was best covered on those joints that made the most tender and sweetest eating. To achieve this result was very largely the work of Robert Bakewell, whose methods of inbreeding, rather than cross-breeding, produced, in the new Leicestershires, a sheep that was ready for the table in two years, and whose growth was small, compact and well covered. Though he was less successful with cattle, since the Longhorns with which he experimented were so soon to be superseded by the Shorthorns of the North, others followed his methods, and the scientific breeder and the conception of pedigree stock came into being.

It was, perhaps, not inherently impossible to combine these new methods with the open fields. An Act of 1776 empowered any open-field community, where a two-thirds majority could be obtained, to bind the unprogressive minority to follow the new rotation of crops. Also in many open-field villages, arrangements had been modified to the extent that many farmers possessed closes and individual enclosed fields, as well as a share in the open ones and grazing rights on the waste. In such circumstances it was not at all impossible to practise mixed farming according to the new ideas. But though the change could have been made it is not likely that it could have been made quickly. The average farmer was bound to the old traditional ways; he had little desire to experiment and, while he depended on his holding as much for subsistence as for profit, he saw little need to do so. In consequence there was not much prospect of extracting increased rents, particularly in an era of steady, and even falling, prices, from this type of farmer. Yet, before farmers were prepared to take up more land and by their increased demand make higher rents possible they had to be convinced that it would be to their own interest to do so. Since nothing succeeds like success, it was, therefore, necessary to afford a practical demonstration that the new methods did, indeed, pay. To afford this proof was largely the work of the great landowners. The advice of the professional writer was, often with much justice, distrusted. Sound agricultural ideas were mixed up with wild-cat, unproven schemes, and the failure of the one often discredited the other. But the practical experimental work of men like Townshend and Coke could not be gainsaid. It demonstrated that the sinking of capital in new buildings, better ploughs and drills, manures, better seed, better cultivation and better stock, all paid.

This stress on new methods, a more flexible attitude to the problems of agriculture, the employment of more capital and an emphasis on higher productivity was not confined to agriculture. Industry, too, was expanding with a new rapidity, and becoming an increasingly important factor in the economic life of the country, which was, in its turn, to have considerable repercussions on rural England. At the close of the seventeenth century industry was, for the most part, still organized on traditional lines. The greatest proportion of its production was for home rather than for foreign consumption. Most of the work was still done in the home of the worker rather than on the premises of the employer. True there were considerable exceptions to this statement. Certain industries, by their very nature, had always been under the direct control of the capitalist. Coal-mining around the Tyne and the Wear had already been extensively developed by the close of the sixteenth century, while early in the seventeenth the coalfields of the Midlands had been opened up. Already, pressed by the shortage of wood, such industries as could use coal for fuel were being attracted to the coalfields, for in the inadequate state of transport, unless water carriage were available, coal was too bulky to distribute much further than ten miles from the pit-head. Wherever cheap fuel and practicable transport facilities were present they tended to act as a magnet to industry. Many of these secondary industries, such as sugar refining, which developed near the ports, brewing, glass-making, pottery, brickyards, were no longer domestic trades. The production of iron was also organized on capitalistic lines, though the dependence of the industry on wood for fuel hindered its expansion and the output of British furnaces and forges had to be supplemented by imported supplies from Sweden. Thus, with so much production already organized on a factory basis it is clear that even before the pace of industry quickened there must have been a very considerable class of workers dependent upon a daily or weekly wage for their livelihood.

The textiles, however, which were the greatest exporting industries, and which produced in addition large quantities for the home market, were for the most part still organized on the putting-out system. Here again there were exceptions. The finishing of the cloth was usually done in the employer's workshop. Dyeing was more and more concentrated in small manufactories. In the throwing of raw silk, machinery as complicated as anything later used in the cotton spinning trade, was to be found in Lombe's silk mills, to the admiration and wonder of all observers. Here already the main labour force was supplied by women and children. But despite these exceptions, the mass of workers employed in making either woollen or cotton goods were working in their own homes. Generally all the family was employed. In the cotton trade the women picked and cleaned the cotton, separating it from the bale and beating it on a riddle with switches, a process that can hardly have contributed to the health of the family as the sole living-room must have been thick with the fluff. The cotton was then washed and spun. It was calculated that one weaver could keep three spinners employed, and if the family were small and the wife partly occupied with tending the stock, where domestic industry was combined with the possession of a small holding, or the running of a few animals on the waste, then the spinning had to be sent out. If not only the spinning but all the preliminary work of cleaning and preparing the cotton is also taken into account, one weaver could find employment for six to eight people, though some of these were children or old people whose strength had gone. In those families engaged in cloth-making the nature and character of the work done in the home depended on the degree of capitalist organization that prevailed. In Yorkshire and those districts where the smaller clothier predominated, most of the processes were carried on under the same roof, though the labours of the family were often supplemented by the help provided by one or two hired journeymen. Where the larger clothier dominated there was more specialization, and weaving for the men and spinning for the women was the usual division of labour. Nor was this familiar domestic organization confined to the textiles. Nail-making, dating at least from the sixteenth century, the casting of buttons by the button moulders, and the making of all types of small metal goods were a few of the trades carried on by craftsmen working in their own homes.

By the end of the century great changes in production methods had come about, and more were foreshadowed. In industry after industry the invention of new technical devices and new machinery revolutionized the older methods. Outstanding among these was the increased use of power, first water-power and then, after James Watt's success in perfecting Newcomen's engine, steam. Since a high degree of mechanization was not compatible with the old domestic organization of industry this began to be undermined on all sides. In the place of the merchant capitalist the petty industrialist began to appear in increasing numbers. As technical inventions took branch after branch of industry out of the home these men seized the opportunity to set up tiny works and exploit the new developments. In the eighteenth century, industrial innovation and the industrial capitalist grew side by side; to trace the growth of this new element in the social structure of the period it is necessary to trace first the industrial changes which gave them birth.

It was not only the domestic industries which were revolutionized by the new processes. Perhaps the most characteristic and

Two illustrations from R. Bradley, *Gentleman's and Farmer's Guide for Increase and Improvement of Cattle*, 1729

Sheffield Cutlers

Women Spinning in Yorkshire

important of all the early industrialists were the iron-masters, though a good deal of capital was going into lead and copper mining and the production of brass. At the beginning of the century this would have seemed unlikely. The production of iron laboured under a perpetual handicap owing to its dependence on charcoal, which drove it to those areas where wood was still plentiful and where streams could be used to work the bellows for the blast furnaces. In spite of these difficulties, which were increased by inadequate transport, many small capitalists were operating furnaces and producing pig-iron, which they sold to the forges. These, with much consumption of charcoal, turned it into the bar-iron required by the iron-worker. But at all stages the competition of Swedish iron was keen. The forges bought pig-iron from Sweden as well as the products of English furnaces, the slitting mills and iron-workers used a good deal of Swedish wrought-iron as well as the output of English forges. Strained relations with Sweden in the twenties drove home the inconvenience of this dependence and stimulated the search for methods that, by substituting coal or coke for charcoal, would free the English industry from its reliance on imported iron.

The first step in this direction was taken by the Darbys of Coalbrookdale. The story of their achievement is well known, so well known, indeed, that it is sometimes forgotten that the advance they made, thoughly highly significant for the future, was itself a limited one. Though Darby was able to use coke in his furnace to produce pig-iron that was well adapted for making cast-iron goods, it was unsuitable for turning into bar-iron at the forge. In consequence the contribution of the Darbys was not so much, at least in the first half of the century, to free the older branches of the iron industry from its dependence on charcoal and therefore on Swedish imports, as to open up new aspects by developing a market for pots and pans and kettles and, in time, for the cast-iron cylinders for steam engines, or the structural parts of the new iron bridges. Therefore, as a result of all these activities, both in the more traditional aspects of the industry and in its newer developments the iron-master provided an important element in the new class of industrialist that was emerging.

If the rise of the iron-master was chiefly associated with technical invention, so was that of the small industrial capitalist who found his opportunities in the expanding demand for woollen and cotton goods. So long as the methods remained traditional the merchant capitalist continued to organize production. He supplied the raw material, marketed the finished product, and enmeshed the nominally free 'manufacturers', in the older sense of the word, in a web of credit that ensured his general compliance with the needs of the linen draper or clothier. Here again technical development gave the small industrialist his chance. This came very unevenly, influencing first one section of the manufacture and then another. It is sometimes too easily assumed that the textile industry stood still until the invention of Kay's flying shuttle, followed by the invention of mechanical spinning, and that then progress towards industrial capitalism took place all along the line, accompanied by the fairly rapid building of factories in which to house the new machines. The reality was both a more protracted and less simple process.

Possibly the most significant breach in the older merchant capital domination, which gave the small industrial capitalist his chance, is to be found in what Lancashire always described as the 'Dutch loom'. This loom, sometimes also misleadingly known as an 'engine loom', was an elaborate, though hand-worked, machine for weaving the ribbons and garters and tapes so much in demand by the fashions of the day. It soon replaced the old narrow looms previously used for this type of small-ware since upwards of twelve pieces could be woven simultaneously by the same weaver. But these looms, with their many shuttles, were not cheap to buy, and could not be made, as the ordinary loom could, by a local craftsman. Some were valued at between £6 and £12 each, so that to buy one for his own use was generally beyond the resources of the average domestic worker.[1]

Here then was a opening for the petty industrial capitalist. The first step was to acquire half a dozen or so of these looms, which were housed in a long room or garret. There journeymen could be hired to work them under supervision. The employer, though he owned the means of production and hired the workshop and the labour, could hardly be described as a manufacturer in any but the older sense of the term. He still depended on the small

---

[1] A. P. Wadsworth and J. de Lacy Mann: *The Cotton Trade and Industrial Lancashire, 1600–1780* (1931), p. 105.

wares dealer for his raw material. He was, indeed, simply an undertaker for the merchant, an industrial middleman under whose roof some concentration of the industry was taking place, even though in the Manchester district some of these undertakers claimed to be controlling as many as twenty looms. In the country districts something more akin to a real factory organization was developing. The Philips brothers had a loom-house at Tean and adjacent to it bleach works and dye works, though they were still supplying looms to domestic workers in the vicinity.[1] By the middle of the century in Lancashire, which was the only area in which the opposition of the weavers had not succeeded in defeating the introduction of the Dutch loom, optimistic entrepreneurs were experimenting with the use of water-power to drive the looms. Here, Kay, whose name is more popularly associated with the flying shuttle, invented a device by which several looms could be connected with a wooden beam and the whole driven by water-power.

Like so many inventions in their early stages, this one proved of doubtful economic value. Each loom still required the attention of a weaver, and, whereas by the older hand-controlled process defects could be noticed and remedied almost instinctively by a skilful workman, now much mischief might be done before the loom could be stopped and the necessary adjustments made. So, though the thing was technically possible by the end of the century, it was not so much the Dutch loom driven by power as a more efficient version of the hand-driven one, the so-called swivel loom, which tempted the small capitalist to buy and instal looms and to create what was in essence a miniature factory. In spite of this advance, important small-ware manufacturers, like J. and N. Philips and Company, were not concentrating all their looms until the third decade of the nineteenth century. It was not, therefore, so much the factor of power as the expense of the elaborate looms required in the small-ware factory that encouraged industrial capitalism in this very specialized branch of the textiles.

In the silk-throwing industry both elaborate machinery and the use of water-power speeded the newer type of industrial organization and provided openings for the capitalist who cared to invest in plant and machinery. Here the story is well known. From the

[1] *Ibid.*, p. 289.

beginning the silk industry had relied upon the capitalist to import
the expensive raw material, as well as to market the finished goods,
and by the end of the seventeenth century rather crude wooden
contraptions were foreshadowing the use of machinery for silk
throwing. But it was the introduction of the Italian methods of
throwing the silk by means of elaborate machinery driven by
water, so as to produce the warp for the weaver, which really
opened the way for industrial capitalism in the silk manufactory.
Here the Lombe brothers were pioneers, though as John died
comparatively young it was Thomas who was really responsible
for the success of the enterprise. To the traveller, Lombe's mills on
the Derwent, the first of their kind, were a source of wonderment.
To little William Hutton, apprenticed to the mills while still so
small that he was not able to reach the machinery until pattens
had been strapped to his feet, the whirling wheels must have
seemed less a matter for enchantment!

During the first part of the century, mills of this size were confined to the silk industry and were never very numerous, though
Derby, Stockport and Macclesfield became little pockets of industrial capitalism and provided a good deal of employment of
the factory type, very largely for women and children, but the
most skilled work was still done by male operatives. On a very
much smaller scale, and for reasons akin rather to the concentration of the Dutch looms in the small-ware manufactory than to
those that moved the Lombes to set up their mills on the Derwent,
silk weaving also tended to become concentrated under one roof.
We hear of a silk weaving establishment that contained twenty
looms housed in a narrow shed. Just as the loom was too expensive for the average workman to possess, so the little work-
shops in which they were collected had rarely been constructed
for that purpose. Half a dozen looms installed by a very small
employer, himself usually very dependent on the merchant who
handled his goods, was a common arrangement throughout the
century.

Interesting though these early breaches in the domestic organization of the textile industry are, until technical progress had
forced developments on the spinning and weaving of wool and
cotton there was little chance of the industrial capitalist emerging
in sufficient numbers to create a new element in society. Before

this could happen the preparing of the cotton or wool for the spinner, the spinning and the subsequent weaving would all have to be revolutionized by the invention of machinery inappropriate for use in cottage homes. The transformation of the textile industry therefore depended on the invention of efficient machines for carding and spinning, and on the discovery of a mechanical loom. Only the first two of these had really been achieved by the end of the century. Mechanical weaving, though technically possible before its close, was not adopted, even in the case of the less conservative cotton industry, until the early nineteenth century. The power loom therefore played no part in creating a new manufacturing class of industrialists in the first stages of the Industrial Revolution.

The invention of the carding machine and mechanical spinning were closely connected, and, indeed, two interdependent aspects of the same need: once the process of spinning had been speeded up the older method of carding by hand was plainly inadequate. Hence, once Paul and Wyatt had patented their device for spinning by rollers, they turned next to making some improvement in their apparatus for carding, as it was evident that if the spinning were a success a bottleneck in the earlier stages was inevitable. As is well known, neither device was very satisfactory in use, and the small factory which Paul set up in the Upper Priory in Birmingham, if a converted warehouse can be dignified by the name of factory, functioned for little more than two and a half years, during about half of which the unlucky Wyatt was imprisoned in the Fleet for debt. Edward Cave, the founder of the *Gentleman's Magazine* who had bought up the rights in two hundred and fifty spindles and who had some capital available, was rather more successful. In 1742 he set up the new machinery in a mill at Northampton, where the motive power was provided by water, and he can therefore claim the honour of having been the first mill-owner to spin by water-power. The profits of the enterprise do not, however, seem to have been such as to encourage similar investment. There was also a small mill at Leominster where Daniel Bourn, in addition to having purchased a licence to instal Paul's spindles, was experimenting with a carding machine which he, like Paul, patented in 1748. This met with disaster, being destroyed by fire in 1754, and by 1760 it was widely felt that the attempts hitherto made only illustrated the impossibility of substituting a machine for the traditional technique, which is possibly the reason why other attempts made by Kay, by Laurence Earnshaw and James Taylor received no financial backing.[1]

By the 'seventies the position was completely different. Sometime between 1764 and 1767 Hargreaves invented his spinning jenny, while Arkwright applied for his patent in 1768, and between them they revolutionized the early stages of the spinning industry, though Arkwright did not take out his hated patent for his carding machine until 1775. Both men gave practical proof of the utility of their inventions; Hargreaves and James had a small factory in Nottingham, and Arkwright started his water-driven mill at Cromford in 1771. The change in the structure of the industry for which they were to be responsible was not immediately apparent. Indeed, Hargreaves' jenny at first seemed as it would perpetuate the older forms of domestic industry, since the earlier jennies with less than twenty-four spindles could be driven by hand and installed in the cottages of the spinners. Nor were they so expensive that, like the Dutch loom earlier, they needed to be concentrated under one roof. Arkwright's frame, driven as it was by water-power, was a different matter, and the need to card the cotton rapidly to meet the increasing demand stimulated still further the growth of factories. Here was an opening for the small capitalist, both in the cotton and the woollen areas, and scribbling mills, which prepared the cotton and wool for the spinner, sprang up wherever there was water-power to drive the machines.

As yet such mills were mere adjuncts to the domestic system, merely relieving the clothier from the tedious business of the processes preparatory to spinning which, when done in the home, had been tiresome and time-wasting; and in Yorkshire the woollen manufacturer, even after the close of the century, took his wool to the scribbling mill and received it back in the form of slubbings, just as he had been in the habit of taking his cloth to the fulling mill, paying the mill owner for his services but retaining the control of his own product. It was, however, clearly advantageous for the owner of the mill to branch out into other activities. The man who started by carding soon came to add jennies, driven either by hand or power, and so combined the

[1] Wadsworth and Mann: *Op. cit.,* pp. 431–48.

business of carding and spinning, while the small spinning factory, using Arkwright's frames, found it convenient to do its own carding and slubbing. Here then, even by the 'seventies, there were openings for a man of some technical knowledge to buy the new machines and to start up in a very small way as a manufacturer of yarn; and so from the 'seventies onwards the numbers of the small capitalists grew.

Once the fabric, whether cotton or woollen, had been woven, the finishing processes offered further openings. In the case of wool the cloth had to be dyed, sheared and fulled. In the cotton manufactory the analogous processes were dyeing or bleaching or printing, whichever type of finish was required. These processes in the case of wool were traditional and had not been much altered by technical improvement before the end of the eighteenth century, except that steam-engines were being substituted for the water-wheel in driving the great stocks at the fulling mill or the gig mills in the finishing shops. The fuller was almost always a small independent capitalist owning, or at least renting, his own mill, and working on the cloths sent to him by the local clothiers or merchants. The practice with regard to the finishing shops was more varied. In East Anglia and in the West the merchant capitalist often made himself responsible for these later stages, since it enabled him to secure the standard he required. In such cases accommodation for cloth finishing was often attached to the warehouse. In Yorkshire, with its mass of small clothiers, the small independent cloth dresser or finisher was more common, and boys were apprenticed either to clothiers, or to cloth finishers or to cloth merchants. In these areas, particularly in the early decades of the nineteenth century, when the opposition of the croppers, as the journeymen who handled the great shears were called, was overcome and the mechanical gig mill, widely introduced, was a fresh opening for an enterprising man with a little capital to invest.

In the cotton trade the number of bleach works and printing shops expanded with the industry and made little centres of industrial capital even though the great business of organizing the actual production of the cloth still remained with the merchant capitalist. In the first half of the century these establishments were small, but here, linked as they were with a new and expanding trade, technical improvements were eagerly sought after and hopefully adopted. In 1752 a new bleach works near Manchester, at Collyhurst, was set up by three men who, in partnership, installed the latest machinery and eagerly called attention to the increased speed with which their new process could perform the long and tedious business of bleaching.[1] Such men were typical of many who found ample and profitable employment in handling the growing yardage of Manchester goods. When, therefore, the main branches of the industry became mechanized and production leapt forward the opportunities for the establishment of bleach works increased also, and many Lancashire families owed their fortunes to this source. Those men who went into calico printing had similar experiences.

Calico printing was not, however, originally tied up with the growth of the native cotton industry, but had depended on the imports of the East India Company, whose printed Indian goods had stimulated a demand for such fabrics in the home market. By the beginning of the eighteenth century this competition had become so serious that in 1701 the woollen manufacturers succeeded in getting the wearing of Indian printed goods prohibited. To the chagrin of the clothiers this prohibition merely acted as a stimulus to the growth of the printing of cotton in this country, since the white Indian calico was still available and the home demand large. Even before this date the foundations of the industry had been laid, for the Indian goods were expensive and there was a large untapped market for some cheaper substitute. In an attempt to supply it, France, Holland and England all began to experiment, and it seems probable that by 1678 the industry had been established in all three countries. But in England after 1701, since the Indian prints, but not the English prints on Indian material, were prohibited, there was every encouragement for the industry to forge ahead. That the earliest centres should be at ports like Bristol and, above all, London, with its great import of Indian calicoes, was to be expected. By 1719, when the agitation of the woollen manufacturers to have the prohibition against the wearing of such printed goods extended to the home-produced variety was becoming formidable, there were apparently some thirty printers in London, not counting the smaller job printers

[1] Wadsworth and Mann: *Op. cit.,* p. 306.

whose small scale of business and anxiety to avoid paying the excise on their wares made them difficult to trace.

Even the larger printers were not great employers of labour. One, a Mr. Mauvillion, had printing shops at both Mitcham and Wandsworth, and employed just over two hundred people, but he was an exception, and the common contemporary assumption was that about eight hundred people were employed in this trade[1]. But if the labour force was not large, the printers were typical of the new manufacturing class in their keenness to avail themselves of new technical devices, and the use of new copper plates, in place of the old wooden blocks, improved both the quality of the work and the speed at which it could be done. Miss Mann gives 2,825,200 yards of printed calicoes, linens and stuffs as the figure for the year 1718–19. The printers had indeed been too successful; in 1721 the prohibition was extended to any stuff made of cotton or mixed with it, the only exceptions being muslins, neckcloths and fustians, or calicoes dyed all blue, which were presumably used for smocks and aprons.

From the point of view of the Lancashire cotton industry the exceptions, and particularly that of fustians, which were not clearly described, until the Act of 1736 defined them as material made in Great Britain of linen yarn and cotton wool, were important. Before the advent of cotton, a good deal of linen had been made in the area, and since linen was not included in the prohibited fabrics, and carried a lower excise duty than the home-made calicoes had done, it tended to be used as a substitute by the printers. The combination of the older linen industry with the newer cottons also facilitated the weaving of the fustians, which were of various types and qualities, though all combined a mixture of cotton and flax. These fabrics met the home demand for lighter, gaily coloured materials and were used by the printers in place of the forbidden calico, though it should not be forgotten that it was the wearing, not the making, of Indian prints that was prohibited. Goods made for export, whether to Europe or the greedy African markets could still be made in this country. The effect of this legislation was twofold. The production of fustian was greatly encouraged and printing grew up near its place of production. Though there is little evidence to·show that the printing of

[1] *Ibid.*, p. 137.

textiles was at all widespread in Lancashire before the middle of the century, in the late 'fifties, and even more in the 'sixties small printing works were springing up all over the textile areas of Lancashire, Cheshire and Derbyshire. Here again was another new field for the petty industrialist.

Dependent as it was upon the vagaries of fashion and demand, it was a highly speculative business. Moreover it is likely that many of these small works had insufficient capital behind them, for bankruptcies were common. But where one man failed the prospects of success seemed bright enough to make another come forward. Not only did their numbers continue to grow, but, especially after the impetus the cotton industry received with the invention of machine spinning, some very considerable concerns, employing hundreds of hands, emerged. Like spinning, fabric printing also became mechanized. Just as copper plates superseded the older wooden blocks, so the copper cylinder and the revolving press superseded the older, more laborious hand process. Bell's invention which was introduced in Lancashire in 1785, was not the first attempt made to speed up the process, but earlier experiments had proved less satisfactory. Up to this time most print works had been small independent concerns with a clear line of demarcation between them and the cotton manufacturers. With the coming of machine printing, men already engaged in making cloth, added printing to their other activities. In the same way the printers in their turn branched out into the business of making the cloth they used, and as a result some firms, like that of the Peels, emerged, which were very large by the standards of the time.

To go into every activity that developed in connexion with technical changes, and that gave increased openings to the small capitalist to invest in machinery and plant, would be a wearisome process. Everywhere, though the advance was an irregular one, changes in methods in the textiles and in the production of metals were encouraging industrial capital and substituting the factory and the workshop for the traditional putting-out system, dominated by the merchant capitalist. It might have been expected that a good deal of the capital that financed the transition and went to equip the new factories would have come from those men, who, as clothiers and linen drapers, had been interested in organizing

the work of the spinners and weavers. These men were well acquainted with the details of the trade and familiar with the market.
They were well aware of the bottleneck created by the shortage of
yarn, and they had the necessary capital to sink in the new machinery. Yet in a sense the very fact that they were so intimately bound
up with the older type of organization seems to have prevented
them from experimenting with the new. The old had served them
well, they had the profits of the merchants capitalist, of the entrepreneur; if new men wanted to take the responsibility of providing
them with more ample supplies of yarn that was, or seemed to be,
no real threat to the whole basis of the domestic system. This
point was made again and again as late as 1806 in the evidence
presented to the members of the Committee on Petitions relating
to the Woollen Trade. Thus, Sir Robert Peel declared:

> I was very fearful that something would have come out, during our
> sitting here, which might have afforded an apprehension that the
> Factories would have swallowed up the little manufacturers, but
> everything I have heard has led me to believe that the factory must
> give way to the domestic system, when the Trade happens to be in
> the state the reverse of what is at present, in a depressed state[1];

while another witness stated that having made enquiries into

> their supposed apprehensions that the Factories would destroy the
> domestic system, [after mature deliberation he was] satisfied that, so
> far from injuring them, it must be a very great benefit . . . that the
> domestic manufactory and the factory system are increasing each
> other, and are carried on to much greater advantage where there are
> factories than where there are solely domestic manufactures.[2]

Thus few of the men who were already committed to the old
system saw much advantage in switching over to the new.

The opportunity which they let slip was seized by lesser men.
Some of them came from the older type of small working clothier.
They had started as weavers and, with thrift and hard work, had
managed to save up enough to purchase a few jennies that could
be installed in the cottage and worked by the women and children.
In many cases the connexion between these men and the land was
still very close. Often they owned or rented a little holding and

---

[1] *Minutes of Committee on Petitions relating to the Woollen Industry* (1806), p. 441.
[2] *Ibid.*, p. 444.

were as familiar with agriculture as they were with industry. But, as we have seen, agricultural changes were breaking down the old partnership. Profitable farming was calling for more specialization, more capital, larger holdings, if the new methods were to be followed, and full advantage was to be taken of the rising prices. Also with the growth of population the amount of land in the cloth-making areas was limited. Here the agricultural and industrial changes were closely interlocked. In agriculture the opportunities for the small man were limited in comparison with what industry seemed to offer. To an ambitious man, already familiar with industrial processes, and tempted by the high prices for which he could sell his small property it must have seemed almost the obvious step to concentrate all his efforts in the direction where the openings appeared most promising.

The rise of the Peel family is a classic example of the small landed proprietor who deliberately seized the opportunities that the new enterprise seemed to offer, and concentrated all his resources upon developing them. Like so many of their contemporaries, their interests had originally been divided between farming a small family property, making woollen stuffs and trading in both cloth and hand printed cotton. Then one brother concentrated on spinning cotton by the new processes, while another went into calico printing at Bury. In 1780 the various members of the family were between them employing most of the working population of Bury, either as spinners in the factory or as weavers in their own homes. In 1788 Robert Peel bought land at Tamworth, built a factory there, and began to pile up the fortune which was to make his son Robert eligible for the hazards of a political career, when that was still the preserve of the gentleman. John Fielden, also a Member of Parliament and a leading exponent of the need for factory reform in the nineteenth century, was the product of very similar conditions. His father, Joshua Fielden, had also combined farming with the possession of a few looms, selling cloth in Halifax market, as so many of the Yorkshire clothiers did. Then he became interested in spinning with jennies and, investing in a few, set his family to spin. From these small beginnings came the mill that was to make his son a rich manufacturer.

Not all those who turned to industry and afterwards prospered did so as a result of a free choice deliberately made. As open fields and wastes were enclosed smallholders who were tenants, not owners, might find themselves dispossessed. Their choice lay between staying on the land as landless labourers or seeking an opening in industry. William Radcliffe's father had been driven from the land as a result of an Enclosure Act and had been forced to concentrate on weaving, so that young William had been brought up with a full knowledge of the whole process of cloth-making, and, being ambitious and intelligent, it is no wonder that he should have early set up in business for himself, employing as much of the new machinery as his capital would allow.

The rise of the iron-masters is in many ways very similar. There is the same close connexion with the land, though the social categories from which they were drawn seem to have been more varied than those from which the textile manufacturers came. Possibly this is due to the fact that iron-working, like coal-mining, had been since the sixteenth century one of the methods by which the landed gentry had striven to increase their financial resources; an Elizabethan list of iron-masters operating in 1577 contains an impressive number of noble names. This tendency persisted. It is not difficult to find eighteenth-century iron-masters who had every right to write the word 'gentleman' after their names. Such were the Lloyds, later to be prominent in Birmingham both as industrialists and as bankers. Sir Charles Lloyd, an Alderman and sheriff of the City of London, in 1651 bought the forfeited Manor of Caereinion from the Commonwealth Commissioners and set up a forge near Dolobran. Though the Powys lands, of which this had formed a part, were repurchased after the Restoration the connexion of the Lloyd family with iron-making continued. Not content with making wrought-iron the furnaces at Bersham were started in 1717: when these came into production in 1719 the Lloyds were able to feed their forges with iron of their own making, an early example of integration in the iron industry.

The majority of the eighteenth-century iron-masters, however, started their industrial careers lower in the social scale, though the connexion with land was often still there. For example the father of the first Abraham Darby was a farmer, but as he was also engaged in making nails and in the manufacture of locks, to bind his son apprentice to a malt mill maker in Birmingham was an understandable choice. The stages by which young Abraham's interests were directed towards iron-making are not difficult to trace. First, he extended his ideas to include brass-casting, then became manager for the newly-formed Bristol Brass Wire Company, and from that it was an easy transition to experiment in cast-iron and to the setting up of a small iron works. John Wilkinson, whose name stands almost as a symbol of the iron-masters of his age, and whose private tokens were circulated in the Midlands with as much confidence as coin of the realm, came from very similar stock. His father had been interested in pot-founding, and seeing the possibilities of the new processes had set up one of the early coke-using furnaces. On this foundation John and his brother built, until by 1770 they possessed between them three important works. Then came the development in canals which made it possible to connect the Broseley works with Birmingham, thus linking the plant with the growing demand of the Black Country metal-workers for the raw material of their craft. At his zenith, John Wilkinson represented something new in the economic and social structure of England, for after 1777 his activities were not even confined to this country; he had works near Nantes, and later his brother built the famous Creusot foundry. Though his success was outstanding, his social and economic antecedents were common to many of those men who owed their fortunes to early utilization of the new technical developments in the making of iron and, later, steel.

To accumulate the capital required even for the modest expansion of the eighteenth century, whether in textiles or heavy industry, was no easy task. Few of the founders of those firms whose names were later to become almost household names could command much inherited wealth, though there are more exceptions to this than is sometimes realized, and here the importance of landowners like the Lloyds, or of industrial dynasties like the Darbys, should not be forgotten. Though the father of the first Abraham Darby seems to have been no more than a small farmer, combining, as we have seen, nail-making with agriculture, he left a very solid foundation on which his son could build. By the time the inventions of Henry Cort and Peter Onions had made the use of coal possible in the forge as well as in the furnace such families had ample resources behind them with which to develop the new processes. Matthew Boulton was another prominent manufacturer who had not had to depend on his own exertions for the foundation of his famous Soho works. His father, a prosperous silver stamper, when he died in 1759 left a considerable fortune which his son further augmented in the following year by marrying Anne, the daughter of Luke Robinson, Esq. She, it is said, brought £28,000 with her.

Yet in spite of exceptions most of the men who promoted the new inventions acquired the capital which enabled them to do so, the hard way. William Hutton, attempting to estimate the wealth of Birmingham manufacturers in 1783, calculated that out of the two hundred and nine leading citizens, whom he had selected for this purpose, there were ninety-four who possessed more than £5,000, eighty with above £10,000, seventeen with some £20,000, eight with £30,000, seven with £50,000 and three with more than £100,000. As a commentary on these figures he added:

> I have selected 209 people who take the lead among 50,000 by commanding property of £3,500,999. Of the 209, 103 began the world by their own prudence; 35 more had fortunes added to their prudence, but too small to be taken into account; and 71 persons were favoured with a larger, which in many instances is much improved. Hence it follows that the above sum is chiefly acquired by the present inhabitants.[1]

For most of them these fortunes had been amassed by unremitting toil and frugality. The successful manufacturer of the eighteenth century had extraordinary capacities for work. Thus Joseph Rogerson, the owner of a slubbing mill in Yorkshire, wrote in his diary:

> For those first four years of this mill of ours running I have seen us begin almost every morning sometimes at 5 & 6 o'clock in the Morning & also seen the fires put at Night when we gave over, which was at 8, 9 & 10 & 11 o'clock at night; & we have generally run later in Winter than in Summer, in Winter frequently all night. I have had to go home for Breakfast—Dinner—& Drinking and I generally had got back before they had got theirs, time we allotted Slubbers for Dinner was 1 hour.[2]

[1] Quoted R. K. Dent: *Op. cit.*, p. 261.
[2] W. B. Crump: *The Leeds Woollen Industry, 1780–1820* (1931), p. 110.

Though a craftsman and shopkeeper rather than a manufacturer Francis Place's record is equally impressive. He wrote in his diary:

> I never lost a minute of time, was never on any occasion diverted from the steady pursuit of my business, never spent a shilling, never once entertained any company. The only thing I bought were books, and not many of them. I adhered steadily to the practice I had adopted, and read for two or there hours every night after the business of the day was closed, which never happened until half past nine. I never went to bed until twelve o'clock, and frequently not till one, but I indulged a little in the morning by laying in bed until seven.[1]

As he continued this régime for five or six years it is perhaps not altogether to be wondered at that elsewhere in his diary he notes that Mrs. Place seemed to have lost that cheerfulness of disposition that had once been hers!

The driving force behind this grim austerity and utter devotion to business was doubtless due in part to early circumstances. Few of these men had known ease or leisure or soft living as children. Where their parents had been small farmers combining agriculture, often, Arthur Young averred, of a very slipshod kind, with the following of some craft, from childhood they had been accustomed to helping their parents in one or other of their activities. Life for poor children in the eighteenth century was hard, and that most of their waking hours should be devoted to work the normal lot. There was more, however, than habit and routine behind the 'success stories' of the Industrial Revolution. Because the older social and economic pattern was breaking up, the man who was prepared to work might, and often did, win great prizes, not only in hard cash but in reputation. The apprenticeship laws were almost moribund, and rarely obligatory for newer trades; they provided cheap labour rather than barriers to keep men out of crafts, and for the enterprising, despite the settlement laws, there was great fluidity of labour. This fluidity, more characteristic to-day of the American than the British workman, is well illustrated by the career of John Baskerville, one of the greatest typefounders. He began his working adult life as a gravestone cutter, by twenty had started a writing school, then went over to the

[1] G. Wallas: *The Life of Francis Place, 1771–1837* (1898), p. 35.

A View of the Upper Works at Coalbrook Dale in the County
of Salop, 1758

A View of the Mouth of a Coalpit near Broseley, in Shropshire

View of Scout Mill, 1795

Mill Children in Yorkshire

business of japanning, making snuff-boxes and trays, and gilt buttons. By the time he was thirty-nine he had built himself a house and set up his own carriage. For some years he experimented in printing and type-founding, and by 1758 the reputation of his Press stood so high that he was appointed official printer to the University of Cambridge. When, therefore, there were to be found in combination both a spartan background and great rewards to be won, it is not surprising that the social environment was favourable to the rise of a new class of manufacturer.

It has by now also become something of a commonplace to ascribe their rise as much to religious as to social forces. As Professor Ashton has pointed out, many of the early industrialists bore the names that implied familiarity with and fondness for the old Puritan traditions, traditions which, with their scorn of display and of soft, luxurious living, did much to reinforce the so-called economic virtues of frugality, hard work and an honest performance of the work in hand. By the eighteenth century the driving force behind this Puritan tradition might well have become more formalized and less compulsive if it had not been reinforced by the great growth of the Society of Friends. Though the Toleration Act of 1689 had freed them from the grosser kinds of persecution they still suffered from disabilities sufficient to maintain their unity and canalize their economic activities. They were still, because of the Test Act, excluded from the English universities, and from most aspects of public life. They could still be distrained upon for tithes and Church dues. Such men, prepared to suffer for their convictions, were ready both to preach the old puritan ideals and to live them in their everyday life, and though economic success was no part of their creed, it did in many cases prove to be the by-product of their conscience.

That this should have been so is not surprising: in part it was due to the lack of distractions dissipating time, energy and money. Resources not spent on easy living could be put back in the business, and because money itself was not over-valued the temptation to secure it by quick and sometimes dishonest profits was absent. Men dealt with Quakers because they could trust them. Minds, often trained by first-rate schoolmasters, that were not allowed to fritter their energies away on trivialities, turned naturally to more weighty and scientific topics. That such men should make real

16

contributions to the technical and scientific achievements of the age is understandable, Moreover, as Dr. Raistrick has shown, their social consciences often forced them to be pioneers. No sincere Friend would willingly make money by producing what might injure his fellow men, either materially or morally. In consequence the Quaker iron-masters turned from manufacturing cannon and shot to making pots and pans and firebacks. As their reward they found a great untapped and expanding market, a notable example of the scriptural admonition, 'Seek ye first the Kingdom of God and His righteousness and all these things shall be added unto you'.

This was not the only reason why the standards of the Society of Friends contributed to the worldly success of their members. There is perhaps a tendency to overstress the illiteracy of the labouring poor. The effect of the charity schools and village schools should not be underestimated. It may well be that in the middle of the eighteenth century, before the educational apparatus of the day had been overwhelmed by the deluge of the growing population, the proportion of the people able at least to read was greater than in the dismal years of the early nineteenth century. Even so, it seems likely that the standard of education amongst the Quakers was markedly high. The poorest among them needed at least a degree of education that would permit the easy reading of the Holy Scriptures, while the Quaker habit of examining the conscience led in many cases to the keeping of diaries and journals. Also the Quaker insistence on the most careful and exact performance of personal obligations and responsibilities made the matter of keeping careful accounts almost a religious duty.

Here, then, were a body of men, careful, exact and well educated. They had also all the advantages that came from belonging to a society of like-minded people. A Quaker setting up in business could be sure of the help and advice of the brethren. Wildcat schemes and over-optimistic financial estimates would be discouraged by the monthly meeting, where the Quaker abhorrence of bankruptcy was manifest again and again, but sober, well-thought-out plans would be encouraged; and the young Friend, about to launch out for himself, would receive advice and encouragement that was both well informed and disinterested. Certainly he would not be left to sink or swim alone. This economic unity of the Quaker world was further strongly reinforced by marriage. Partly because marriages outside the Society were frowned upon, and partly because the meeting, where the young folk would automatically mingle, was the great point of contact there was much intermarriage between prominent Quaker families. This was so usual that an air of contrivance was imparted to what were in all probability purely personal preferences. Nevertheless, the economic consequences were important, for Quaker enterprises tended to be joined together by family ramifications. The result was to impart a certain toughness and coherence to the Quaker business world. Capital could be applied where it was most needed. Promising works or experiments could be nursed, unnecessary or uneconomic plant could be scrapped, a degree of competition could be eliminated. The Quaker meeting contributed yet another element of industrial strength in that it also promoted good relations between master and man. Where possible, Quaker employed Quaker, and a common attitude towards life and work knit together the employer and the workman, the one avoiding exploitation and the other giving of his best. Even where the enterprise was large and the pay-roll contained non-Quakers, the tradition that demanded a square deal for the workman made for good relationships, for an honest payment of wages, and for some attention to education, to housing and to sickness. And in consequence the Quaker manufacturer tended to be able to cream the labour force of his locality.

But though the Quakers were an important element in the body economic, the part they played can be overestimated, nor is it safe to assume that what is true of them is true of the other non-Anglican elements that were prominent amongst the rising class of manufacturers. Among the Quakers were to be found men of breeding and some capital who had become Friends in the early days of the sect through the force of conscience and conviction. Later, when persecution was less severe, the proportion of men of education and capital amongst them remained high because the same qualities which made them good Quakers also helped them to attain eminence as merchants, as bankers, and as manufacturers. This seems true also of the Presbyterian community in the early decades of the century, though less so later when the ranks of the wealthy among them were thinned by a drift away to the

Established Church, which was more socially eligible and which freed them from legal restrictions imposed by the Test Acts, on the holding of office and the enjoying of educational endowments by Dissenters. When John Evans, the Presbyterian minister, made a survey of his London congregation in 1715, he found among them one baronet, one esquire, eight men worth £10,000 and more, forty-three 'men of substance', fifty-four Liverymen of London, and twenty-six freeholders. Of the returns that he obtained elsewhere those of Bristol are interesting because of its commercial importance. Here five churches supplied him with information. The first, with a congregation of about five hundred, reported 'very few of them poor. The whole congregation is reckoned worth £100,000'. The second, with about sixteen hundred hearers, also said they had very few poor and were worth, in all, some £400,000. The story from the others is much the same. The third in the list had a congregation of five hundred souls, worth in total between £60,000 and £70,000, the fourth, with a congregation of twelve hundred, was worth about £160,000, and the fifth and smallest, being between four and five hundred, represented wealth to the tune of £50,000.[1] From the county returns, too, come many indications that the Presbyterian Church had not yet been denuded of its gentlemen by the social erosion of the eighteenth century. But if the Presbyterians of the late seventeenth and early eighteenth century were often men of substance, of the Wesleyans this is less likely to be true since so many of Wesley's most sincere and enthusiastic converts were made amongst the lowest and most debauched strata of the labouring poor; his teaching tended to transform drunkards into good workmen rather than to appeal to the more educated class.[2] Nor were Whitefield's successes amongst the fashionable world more likely to swell the numbers of Nonconformist industrialists. Where, therefore, one of the new industrialists was a Wesleyan he tended to be also a self-made, or, perhaps more accurately speaking, a Wesley-made, man.

But to stress the possible importance of the religious factor is not to assume that all eighteenth-century manufacturers were men of strong religious feeling, or that piety and fair dealing were the

---

[1] E. D. Bebb: *Nonconformity and Social and Economic Life, 1660–1800* (1935), p. 51.
[2] W. T. Warner: *The Wesleyan Movement in the Industrial Revolution* (1930), p. 165.

marks of all Dissenters. Many of them were quite prepared to seize any advantage that came their way and to drive any bargain, however hard, that benefited them. The attitude of the manufacturers as a class towards the inventor is not conspicuous for its brotherly love and Christian charity. Though they were ready to seize with avidity on any new device, or process, or machine that increased output and lessened costs, there was an almost universal resentment against paying the licences that the inventor demanded as some recompense for his own contribution towards industry. Only those inventors who could collect enough funds to employ their own inventions got much out of them. When Crompton threw the details of his mule into the common pool of knowledge, being promised a subscription in lieu of patent rights, it only realized the paltry sum of £67 6s. 6d., while Hargreaves, because he allowed his invention to be sold and copied before taking out patent rights, found that these could not then be enforced.

Nevertheless, despite much sharp practice and hard dealing, the example of men like Matthew Boulton, though not himself a Friend, and Josiah Wedgwood, could not be without its influence, if only because of the success which they achieved. To Boulton a hard bargain was a bad bargain. In his opinion, which he gave to one correspondent, 'Patience and candour should mark all our actions, as well as firmness in being just to ourselves and others. A fair character and standing with the people is attended with great advantage as well as satisfaction'.[1] That he practised what he preached is well illustrated from a letter which he wrote to John Taylor in the January of 1769, pointing out, 'I have had many offers and opportunities of taking your people, whom I could, with convenience to myself, have employed; but it is a practice I abhor'.[2] With Wedgwood, too, nothing that fell below his standard 'would do' for him, and his dislike of sharp practice and shoddy workmanship was well known to all in his employ. And many men of no great natural virtue, seeing how business flowed to the Quaker because he was trusted, and how the man of probity built up a reputation for his wares, must have come to the conclusion that in business 'honesty was the best policy', and in this way the religious principles of the few tended to leaven the

[1] S. Smiles: *Lives of Boulton and Watt* (1865), p. 171.
[2] *Ibid.*, p. 178.

lump of business ethics as a whole. Even so, the creed that they preached was a hard one. Relentless in the demands they made on themselves, whether in the name of God or in the name of Mammon, they were relentless towards those who worked for them, and felt no compunction, no injustice, in so being. What they preached was a gospel of work for themselves and for all those who were connected with them. They believed devoutly that he who would not work neither should he eat. Thus, from their efforts came not only the productive drive and energy, but also the accumulation of capital that was to equip England with the mills and machinery on which her economic greatness was beginning to be built.

Thus, by the end of the century, developments both in agriculture and in industry were, in the aggregate, considerable. They were, moreover, of such a character as to threaten what had been for generations an accepted way of life. The new techniques of agriculture could not be applied easily within the framework of the old open-field community, any more than the water-frame could be installed in the domestic worker's cottage. How far, by the end of the century, was the social pattern of the country showing a sympathetic change?

Chapter Seven

THE IMPACT OF ECONOMIC CHANGE ON THE SOCIAL STRUCTURE BEFORE 1800

B
Y THE last three decades of the eighteenth century it is clear to the historian, and might even have been perceived by sagacious contemporaries, that changes of sufficient magnitude in the technique of industry were taking place to affect the traditional social structure of the country. As we have seen, in a brief review of some of the most outstanding among them, they offered opportunities of successful advancement, even of wealth, to the man who could somehow accumulate a tiny capital to invest in the new machines or the new processes. By the close of the century many men, with diverse backgrounds, had thrown themselves with enormous energy and singleness of purpose into developing these possibilities. Already in the areas most suitable for their activities, Lancashire, Yorkshire, the Black Country and South Wales, this new type of businessman was numerous. In these districts, and particularly in growing towns like Birmingham and Manchester, a new kind of society was forming. In this society, though the merchant was still important, he was slowly losing his predominance. More and more his activities were being restricted to those of the mere merchant rather than the wider ones of financing and organizing production. These functions the industrialist was beginning to perform for himself and, as he came to differentiate his interests from those of the merchant, his influence on the new pattern of society became increasingly important. Lastly it was a society in which the town proletariate was assuming a new significance and to some extent a new character, though just what that character was to be, and how it was to differ from the older urban craftsman was not yet clear. In the country the same break with the pattern of the past was occurring. In these last decades all was flux, though it would have taken a very discerning eye to visualize the shape of things to come.

It is not easy to assess the extent to which economic developments had transformed the structure of rural society by the end of the eighteenth century. The greatest and most obvious break with the past was provided by the disappearance of the open-field village and the enclosure of the wastes and commons, which in 1700 still sprawled across much of the less fertile land. Neither was a rapid process. If half the arable land was still in open fields at the beginning of the century, even at its end not all of it had been enclosed, while the reclamation of wastes and commons too some hundred and fifty years before it was reasonably complete. Yet, though the process was a lengthy one, it was fundamental. The society which had grown up within the framework of the open-field village, or whose economy depended upon extensive wastes, could not survive the destruction of the agrarian shell in which it had lived.

Because these changes were definite and concrete and because there was much that the social historian could rightly deplore in the English countryside of the nineteenth century there has been a tendency to blame enclosures for many, if not most, subsequent evils. Both the destruction of the peasantry and the creation of the landless labourer have been attributed to them, and it is often emotionally implied, if not specifically stated, that in the course of a comparatively few years the peasant, happy and prosperous, was transformed into the labourer, wretched and poor. As a corollary it is often argued that misery led to rural depopulation; that the growing towns were fed by unfortunate country folk, driven from the land when it passed into the occupation of large tenant farmers, paying economic rents to greedy landlords. According to this view the manufacturers could offer mere subsistence wages to men and women who, through desperation, had no alternative but to accept. All this it is implied took place in an atmosphere of exploitation, greed and bitter injustice.

On this picture recent research into eighteenth-century agrarian history has cast increasing doubt and suggests that enclosure has been blamed for much for which it was not, in fact, responsible. Some of the confusion has doubtless arisen because of an imperfect knowledge of the complexity, and often of the misery, of earlier rural conditions; there has been an inclination to see the past as a golden age of a prosperous peasantry. In consequence, later suffering has not been balanced against previous wretchedness. Also difficulties have been created by the failure to realize that the enclosures of the century were not all of a piece and did not all produce the same effects. It seems likely that the enclosures of the earlier decades did press hardly on the smaller farmers and were a contributory factor in diminishing their numbers. It is more doubtful whether the later parliamentary enclosures had a similar effect. Indeed, if anything the agrarian re-organization that was accelerated by the pressure of the French wars and the growing population appears to have a contrary result. That enclosure eliminated the open field is obvious; its effect in reducing the number of small occupying owners and modest tenant farmers is more difficult to assess. A change in farming methods does not necessarily imply a change in either the rural population or in the acreage farmed.

The conditions prevailing in the early eighteenth century were such as to encourage the formation of large farms. The low price of grain, combined with the desire to draw as great a revenue as possible from well-managed estates, made the more progressive landowners anxious to consolidate small open-field farms into larger enclosed ones, which could be used for pasture and cattle breeding. Such enclosures, in this period, were only profitable if they could be carried out with a minimum of opposition. If resistance was likely to be widespread, so that recourse to an Enclosure Act [1] was necessary, then considerations of expense seem to have intervened. The legal expenses that were connected with obtaining the required legislation were heavy. When to these had to be added the inevitable cost of hedging and ditching, and the previous charges for surveying the land, the expected profit could seldom appear to warrant such expenses, in view of the price of meat and the rate of interest charged in the first part of the century. Consequently, Enclosure Bills were not common before the middle of the century. Such enclosure as took place was made possible by a combination of consent, pressure and financial inducement. The smaller freeholders were often bought

---

[1] This was a local Act, usually initiated by the largest landowners in the parish concerned. It had the advantage of overriding all opposition on the part of the minority and terminating existing leases.

out : if not numerous this did not present a real problem. Also not all freeholders were occupying owners, though even when a man was farming his own land, if the price offered were attractive enough, he must often have been induced to sell. Nor would a refusal necessarily wreck the scheme. Obstinate freeholders could be conciliated by the offer of a consolidated farm of a size equivalent to their former holdings. Getting rid of small freeholders was not, therefore, too difficult and Davies is of the opinion that in the parishes of 'ancient enclosure' which he examined the occupying owner had all but disappeared from eighty-two per cent. of them.[1] Eliminating the smaller tenants was a simpler process though it might be a protracted one. When copyholds fell in they would not be renewed. Small leaseholders were treated in the same way, while tenants at will could be dealt with even more easily. In such circumstances it seems very likely that some diminution of the peasantry did occur, though, as it took place before the era of increased industrialization and heavy parliamentary enclosure, it cannot be attributed to either of these factors.

The enclosures of the later eighteenth century took place in very different circumstances and had very different consequences. They destroyed the open-field farmer but it is very doubtful if they had an adverse effect on the numbers of small farmers. It is probable that many of these men would have preferred to be left in peace to farm along traditional lines and that Enclosure Bills were sought and reorganization carried out against their wishes; but this does not mean that they were helpless or exploited victims. Irregularities and unfairness on occasion there may have been, but, in the main, the petitions for enclosure which came before parliament seem to have been impartially considered. Investigations into one hundred and seventy-one Nottinghamshire Enclosure Bills, that were discussed between 1743 and 1845, seem to point to the fact that

> Even if injustice were inflicted upon every occasion where there seems to have been the remotest possibility of it, the number of occasions on which enclosures may have been unfairly handled in Parliament because of the members being personally interested

[1] E. Davies: 'The Small Landowner, 1780–1832, in the Light of the Land Tax Assessments'. *Econ. Hist. Rev.*, Vol. I, No. 1 (January 1927).

cannot be more than 16 per cent. of the total. By any fair computation it must necessarily have been very much less.[1]

Nor were the enclosure commissioners the ogres that they are sometimes depicted as being. Claims seem to have been carefully considered and, though undoubtedly high-handed decisions must often have been taken, the average commissioner seems to have tried to show reasonable consideration for all the different interests involved. If there was grumbling and complaint, as undoubtedly there often was, it must be remembered that to make a division of the open fields and the waste in such a way as to meet the conveniences and wishes of all the smaller property owners, many of whom in any case were disgruntled and distrustful, was far from an enviable task.

It was at one time suggested that even though no substantial injustice took place in the allotment of land, the new conditions were very unfavourable to the small occupying owner, and that, in consequence, he must often have been forced to sell the land that had been awarded to him. This supposition is based on two lines of argument. The first is that the burden of paying for the enclosure pressed with undue harshness on such men because they had little in the way of reserves into which they could dip in order to pay their share of the legal charges and, a formidable task, to pay for the hedging and ditching or fencing of their new farm. Secondly, it is argued they lacked the necessary capital and experience to employ the new methods by which alone production could be increased. No doubt the initial outlay was often burdensome but it must not be forgotten that everything they could raise could be sold for a good price. Also, the employment of the new methods, though they called for more labour, more intensive farming, called for no artificial manures, no machinery and for very little that the small farmer could not provide. The day of the large acreage had not yet come; the smallholder, using the labour of himself and his family and experimenting with the new rotation of crops, the use of winter feed, and higher standard of clean farming, could still do very well. It was, therefore, unlikely that economic pressure, due to enclosure, drove many small owners off the land if they wished to remain. Even if they decided to sell and

---

[1] W. E. Tate: 'Members of Parliament and the Proceedings upon Enclosure Bills'. *Econ. Hist. Rev.*, Vol. XII, Nos. 1 and 2, p. 75 (1942).

try their luck in industry their holdings seem to have been purchased as often by men of their own type as absorbed into bigger farms. In the areas which he investigated in Suffolk, Mr. Lavrovsky is of the opinion that 'the enclosures did not lead immediately to any substantial changes in the proportion of land owned by peasant proprietors'.[1] Indeed, in Derbyshire, Leicestershire, Lindsey, Nottinghamshire and Warwick between 1780 and 1802 there was an increase in their numbers after parliamentary enclosure.

It is also probable that the small tenant farmer survived in greater numbers than is always supposed. It is easy to assume that much the greater proportion of the land enclosed belonged to the nobility, gentry and clergy, who had an interest in replacing many small tenants by a few large ones. Here the need for much more intensive local study is apparent. In some counties this many be a true picture, but it was certainly not true of all parts of England. In the parishes examined by Mr. Lavrovsky in Suffolk fifty-one per cent. of the enclosed land still belonged to peasant owners. Nor must it be assumed that every small freeholder was an occupying owner. Many were not, and such men often leased out their small properties to other smallholders. Even in districts where the small freeholder, willing to lease land in this way, was less numerous, there were other factors which helped to make it possible to rent a very modest farm. Many new farms were carved out of the waste. This is too often forgotten. If the population was growing, and more large farms were being built up, the amount of farming land available was also increasing. Nor should it be forgotten that, however anxious the greater landlord might be to let his newly enclosed farms to big tenant farmers adequately provided with the capital to develop them, the numbers of these men were at first likely to be limited. Small tenants were better than no tenants at all, and during the prosperous war years they, too, could afford to pay economic rents. The testing time for them, as for the small occupying owner, came later when, in the second decade of the nineteenth century, prices tumbled and the whole agricultural world was plunged into distress.

If enclosures did not eliminate the small farmer they at least encouraged a new type of capitalist farmer, renting a considerable

[1] V. M. Lavrovsky: *Art. cit.*, p. 202.

acreage. The improving landlord preferred this kind of tenant and gave him every assistance. Men like Coke spent considerable sums on buildings, chose their tenants with care and gave them long leases so that they might have every inducement to put both labour and capital into their farms. The result was a new breed of prosperous farmers. Arthur Young speaks with appreciation and perhaps some envy of the way of life of the prosperous farmer with his

> large roomy, clean kitchen with a rousing wood fire on the hearth, and the ceiling well hung with smoked bacon and hams; a small room for the farmer and his family, opening into the kitchen, with glass in the door, or wall, to see that things *go right*. When company is in the house a fire in the parlour. At table great plenty of plain things, with a bottle of good port after dinner, and at least a hogshead of it in his cellar. . . . Attendance, never anything but a maid, this I consider as one of the lines of separation between different classes of people; the farmer is to have every thing that yields comfort; those who chuse to give up that enjoyment for liveries or *shew* of any kind, arrange themselves with another order of mortals; no farmer who is wise will ever make the experiment of a change for he gives solidity for moon shine. . . . In the stable a good nag, for his own riding, but not good enough for hunting, a recreation too common, as it is apt to lead into a dissipated, idle, drinking and expensive life.[1]

As for his wife, she was to be allowed 'a one horse chaise'.

Not all prosperous farmers were prepared to concentrate on the substance and let the shadow go. There is a certain amount of scattered evidence that indicates that at least some of them were adopting a style of living that had previously been associated with their social superiors, and were beginning to constitute a rural variation of the middle class. Such men aroused Young's wrath. To him the wise farmer was one who, if he increases, 'he does not alter his plan of life, but saves'. However, he concedes that not all farmers are so wise.

> I see sometimes, for instance, a piano forte in a farmer's parlour, which I always wish was burnt; a livery servant is sometimes found, and a post chaise to carry their daughters to assemblies, those ladies are sometimes educated at expensive boarding schools, and the sons

[1] A. Young: *Annals of Agriculture*, Vol. XVII, p. 152.

often at the University, to be made parsons but all these things imply a departure from that line which separates these different orders of beings, let all these things, and all the folly, foppery, expence and anxiety that belongs to them remain among gentlemen. A wise farmer will not envy them.[1]

Arthur Young's disapproval was mild beside the vituperation of a writer to the *Gentleman's Magazine* who, after speaking of men whom he admits are no longer mere farmers, having branched out as graziers, corn factors, mealmen, millers, maltsters, brewers and horse-dealers, described their sons as generally belonging

to some of the numerous corps of volunteers and embodied yeomanry; these dashing bucks we see flourishing their broadswords, and exhibiting their neatly buskined posteriors to the admiration of the misses, their sisters, or neighbours, who display in their turns all the attractive graces of Grecian gesticulations and nudity. Instead of dishing butter, feeding poultry, or curing bacon, the avocations of these young *ladies* at home are, studying dress, attitudes, novels, French and musick, whilst the fine ladies their mothers sit lounging in parlours adorned with the fiddle faddle fancy work of their daughters. With as much rapidity as post horses can convey them, the fashions fly from London to the country towns, and from the country towns to the remotest villages; in so much that the *exhibitions* of girls in the country vie with those in the capitol. As the females of each class imitate those belonging to the class above them, so those below the farmers' daughters must have their white dresses as well as them, even if they appropriate to the purpose the cloth that should make them shifts.[2]

Finally he laments,

We see not now the farmers' wives and daughters jogging to the towns for the purpose of selling the productions of the cartons and dairies; but we see them rattling in their spruce gigs to the milliners and perfumers, in order to lavish on fripperies part of the enormous gains extorted by their fathers and husbands from the groaning public.

Such tirades were obviously exaggerated distortions of the new tendencies, as any one acquainted with farming mentality must realize. In the earlier part of the letter quoted above the writer

---

[1] *Annals of Agriculture*, Vol. XVII, p. 156.
[2] *Gentleman's Magazine*, Vol. LXXI (1801), p. 587.

idealizes the small farmer of the past as grossly as he pillories the successful farmer of the Napoleonic era. Nevertheless, he was probably right in realizing that there was a new tendency abroad. The running of the dairy had meant steady drudgery, and in the cheese-making districts exhausting physical strain. Now some farmer's wives were beginning to leave this more and more to hired servants, and to content themselves with oversight, leaving the actual manual toil to others. Where this happened the rough social equality of the farm kitchen, the 'house place' of the North, began to disappear, and the farmer ate with his family in the small room leading out of the great kitchen. In some areas, too, the number of farm servants who were hired by the year and who lived in decreased. It is often suggested, censoriously, that this was because the new type of farmer's wife was too grand, and too lazy, to undertake the directing, feeding and controlling of so considerable household.

This is less than fair. Even earlier in the century, before the habits of rural England had been seriously threatened by economic change, it was chiefly in the North that the farm servants lived in, as they tend to do even to-day. In the south, as Kalm noted as early as 1744, it was the custom 'that a farmer does not keep many servants, but always employs day labourers, for which reason in every village there live a great many poor, who hire themselves out to work for pence'.[1] Later in the century this tendency was increased by the rising cost of food which made it more profitable for the farmer to sell what he produced and to employ day labour, which he did not have to feed, even though it increased his wages bill. At the same time the increase in population and the enclosure of the wastes, which drove the ertswhile squatters on them to seek more regular work, increased the labour pool available. A still further impetus in the same direction came after 1795 when the sanction given by the Berkshire justices at Speen to the payment of allowances in aid of wages meant that the wage bill of the large farmer was supplemented by parish money. This made the employment of day labour doubly attractive. Contemporaries, bewildered by the rising price of food, were apt to condemn the new capitalist farmer for pride and greed and social pretension without recognizing that economic factors were

Kalm: *Op. cit.*, p. 191.

responsible for much that they deplored. Doubtless, however, the war-time farmer made hay while the sun shone.

This agricultural prosperity was shared by the landowners. Not all their increased rental, it is true, represented clear gain. War taxation pressed with especial severity on land, while, with the rising cost of living, their own expenses were going up. Even so the steady policy of improvements followed by families like the Cokes of Holkham was increasingly effective in raising rents. Most observers would have concluded that the agrarian changes had strengthened the position of the nobility. The squirearchy appeared equally secure. They, too, like the large capitalist farmer, were improving their standard of life as more money flowed into the countryside. The squires of the early eighteenth century were often almost as boorish as the country folk amongst whom they lived. They were devoted to the chase, to the pleasures of the table and the bottle, and had little contact outside the small area in which their estates and their position on the local Bench gave them influence over their neighbours. There were no doubt many exceptions, men who, through family connexion, had access to a wider and more liberal way of life; but the average squires were men of limited experience and limited taste. By the end of the century they seem, as a class, to have become more civilized and to have acquired more polish. Their sons were being sent to the expanding public schools, where they learnt to be something more than the cock on the local dung-heap. Also, due to the prosperity of agriculture, there was more money to spend on adorning their houses and laying out their gardens, so that many old manor houses became minor country seats. Edgeworth, commenting on this new breed of squires wrote:

> The obstinacy of ignorance and of imaginary self importance used to be one of the common ludicrous characteristics of our English squires; but the Sir Wilful of Congreve, the Western of Fielding, and the Tony Lumpkin of Goldsmith, are not now to be found in the most remote part of England. The ignorant, hunting, drunken, obstinate, jovial, freedom loving tyrant is no more to be seen, except in old novels and plays. The ptarmigan, the bustard, the cock of the woods, and the country squire, are nearly extinct. Instead of country squires we now have country gentlemen.[1]

[1] R. L. Edgeworth: *Op. cit.,* p. 255.

Manchester Exchange

The Duke of Bridgwater's Aqueduct

The Port of Liverpool, 1797

By the end of the century most observers would have concluded that the landowners, as a class, had increased rather than diminished both their share of the national income and their general control over society. Both to them and to their contemporaries there was little to suggest that they were, in fact, not so much crowning the edifice of their own power as digging the foundations for a rival class. Yet without the food which enclosure and improved methods made possible, the growing population could hardly have been maintained. It is sometimes confidently asserted that the great landowners not only provided this essential food but, with poetic justice, supplied the industrialists, who were later to break them, with the cheap and docile labour which they employed to such good effect. If, it is argued, the landowner and the farmer had passed on to the rural poor some of their own prosperity, there would have been no exodus to the towns and no cheap labour for the manufacturer to exploit.

The situation was more complex and the evidence more conflicting than such oversimplified generalizations would imply. The country had long been the reservoir of population. As Petty, writing on the Dublin Bills of Mortality in 1681, observed, 'London would in time decrease quite away, were it not supplyed out of the Countrey, where there are about Five Births for Four Burials, the proportion of Breeders in the Country being greater than in the city'.[1] Even if there had been no widespread enclosure of open fields and waste, once the population increased to any marked degree, the surplus would have had to turn to industry for its support. The fact that industry was also facing a period of readjustment and change, and being re-sited on the coalfields, made the exodus to the towns inevitable. More detailed work than has yet been done on the composition of the new town populations and their reasons for being there will have to be undertaken before generalization is possible, but even now not all the evidence points to rural misery as a predominant factor.

Lowe, on his *Agricultural Survey of Nottingham* in 1794 noted that most cottages had their potato patch, and that many cottagers had their cow and a few pigs, while the fact that the average farm remained small seems to indicate that the attack on the old

---

[1] W. Petty: *Observations upon the Dublin Bills of Mortality*, 1681. Edited by C. E. Hall, Vol. II, p. 482 (Cambridge, 1899).

social structure was not yet decisive. In Bedfordshire, too, investigation has shown that 'there is no evidence that eighteenth century enclosure was accompanied by loss of population. Indeed some of it would point to the fact that it was actually increasing a little more quickly in the enclosed than in the open villages'.[1] That this should be so is at least as reasonable an assumption as that misery was driving people into the towns. Certainly up to the end of the first decade of the nineteenth century agriculture was prosperous, new land was being brought into cultivation, more intensive methods calling for more labour were being used. In such circumstances it would have been surprising if rural depopulation had taken place. It may well be that the growing towns were not so much denuding the rural areas of their population as taking off that surplus, due to a declining death-rate, which could not, even under the old conditions, have found employment there. To say this is not to minimize rural misery but merely to suggest that its influence in driving country folk into the towns has been exaggerated.[2]

Though the view that the parliamentary enclosures of the late eighteenth and early nineteenth centuries created a vast pool of landless labourers from evicted small freeholders and small tenant farmers can no longer be accepted uncritically, the belief that the landless labourer, as the nineteenth century was to know him, was the by-product of the enclosure movement is more tenable. Agricultural work, before the days of the large farm, had rarely provided a regular occupation except for the specialist, the skilled cowman, the ploughman and the shepherd. Frequently such men were hired by the year and lived in. Where holdings were small, some twenty or thirty or even forty acres, little labour, except at times of pressure, was required beyond what the family could normally provide. Only the larger farmers required full-time agricultural labourers. For the majority it was only at hay-time and harvest that the need for extra workers arose.

Because it came so unevenly this demand for spring and summer labour could rarely be met locally, even when all the available

[1] L. Marshall: 'Rural Population in Bedfordshire'. *Bedfordshire Historical Record Society*, Vol. XVI, p. 33.
[2] For a fuller discussion of this point, see J. D. Chambers: 'Enclosure and Labour Supply in the Industrial Revolution'. *Econ. Hist. Rev.*, 2nd Series, Vol. V, No. 3 (1953).

man-power was mobilized. The gap was filled by migratory labour. Sometimes artisans came from more purely industrial counties, as to-day the hop-pickers needed in Kent are recruited in the East End of London. Sometimes they came from Wales and Ireland. Kalm describes the way in which

> at the beginning of May there come from Ireland over to England a very large number of Irishmen who go and hire themselves everywhere to the farmers. The whole of this part of England which lies immediately north and east of London, carries on nearly all its hay-making and harvesting work with only these people, who come over at the beginning of May and remain there the whole summer. . . . So it is the case with those from Wales that they earn their money also on this side of England in Kent, for towards the haymaking season, the folk come from thence in very large numbers down to the country parts of Kent to work for wages; but with this difference that instead of only men coming as from Ireland, there come mostly only women and girls from Wales, all well, cleanly and very neatly clad.[1]

With the consolidation of farms that accompanied the non-parliamentary enclosures of the early eighteenth century openings for regular farm workers grew, but until the end of the century rural economy did not call for them in large numbers.

Thus, though even the medieval village had contained a fair sprinkling of landless men, the full-time agricultural worker, living in his cottage and dependent on his wages, was not a feature of rural England until larger farms and more intensive agriculture created a need for his services. In this sense the landless labourer of the nineteenth century was the creation of changing conditions in the eighteenth. Some of these men, as tradition avers, were no doubt the product of enclosures and consolidations which deprived small tenants of their holdings and left them with no alternative but to work for wages for the big farmer who had dispossessed them. But these, for the most part, were drawn from those individual 'hard cases' which always accompany large-scale economic change. It is probable that in reality the rural poor suffered more from the enclosure of the waste than they did from that of the open fields. When the waste was gone the illegal squatter, against whom the Acts of Settlement and Removal had

[1] *Op. cit.*, p. 82.

been directed, had no other resource than to work for what wages the farmers were prepared to offer. Their livelihood had always been precarious and their standard of living low. With the loss of the waste they exchanged one kind of poverty for another, but whether they were really pushed down in the social scale may well be doubted.

Many of the eighteenth-century rural poor were neither squatters on the waste nor full-time agricultural workers but Jacks-of-all-trades, doing work for the farmers when it was available, keeping a little livestock on the waste and working intermittently at some local industry. Few counties and few districts were without their own specialities. Thus Bedfordshire, Buckinghamshire and Hertfordshire were noted for straw-plait making. At straw-plaiting women could earn from six to twelve shillings a week, and even children three or four, particularly after a change in fashion decreed the great Leghorn hats, so often depicted by Gainsborough. Lace-making was also very widespread. 'The town of Bedford', wrote Young, 'is noted for nothing but its lace manufactory, which employs above 500 women and girls. . . . Women that are very good hands earn 1*s.* a day, but in common only 8*d.*, 9*d* and 10*d.*'[1] As a result of the demand for women in these crafts it is said that maid-servants were in short supply. Not all the local crafts depended largely on female labour. In Nottingham the villages were full of stocking-frame knitters; round Northampton they made boots and shoes; in Shropshire they made garden pots at Broseley, fine china at Caughley, chains, ropes and china at Coalport, glass at Donnington, at Lebotwood there were dye works. The illustrations could be indefinitely extended to take in almost every district. Also, apart from every type of light secondary manufacture, so often forgotten or ignored as a part of the traditional pattern of the English countryside, there were very few areas that had not some branch of the textile industry. Cloth-making of every variety was probably the most widely diffused, but a good deal of linen was also manufactured, and in Lancashire cotton spinning and weaving was already a staple employment.

It is these people who have most claim to be regarded as the victims of economic change. In a world of small farmers, ample

[1] A. Young: *Northern Tour* (1770), Vol. I, p. 45.

uncultivated land and scattered industry there was a place for them, though no one would describe them as well off, even at the beginning of the century, when food prices were low. Rural housing was often very bad and terribly overcrowded, food was monotonous, the hours of labour, whether in agriculture or industry, long. The value of common rights has been hotly debated, both by contemporaries and by later historians. It is easy to produce an idealized picture, where every countryman had his pig in the sty and his cow on the common. It is equally easy to pick out the idle, shiftless household that refused to bestir itself because a half-starved beast or two on the waste and a scrap of land provided a wretched minimum existence. Many poor families could not afford the price of a cow, and where they could the pasture available was often so over-stocked that the beast was half-starved. Even so the most over-stocked common was worth something to a poor family. If they could not afford a cow or a sheep or two for wool, at least they could keep a few geese, perhaps some hens, maybe a pig, and above all, they could gather fuel or, especially in the North, dig peat and turf. So long as the price of food was low, so long as there was some local supplement to agricultural work, so that a man was not too dependent on that for his cash earnings, so long as there was some waste available, a country family, unless it were very shiftless or unhealthy or too overburdened with very young children, could just manage. Kalm, it may be remembered, commented on the way in which, when the day's work was done, the labourers would sit drinking in the ale-house with their cronies, or would congregate round the fire, singing and telling tales. Nevertheless even this simple standard was precarious. Not one of a poor man's resources was sufficient by itself to maintain him. Any change in the delicate balance might well prove disastrous.

In the closing years of the eighteenth century that is increasingly what happened. One support after another was knocked away just at a time when an increase in the rural population was swelling the numbers of the poorest families. Many of those who depended most upon the commons had least legal right to do so. In the eyes of the Law commons were not the property of the community as a whole: they belonged to the lord of the manor, to the holders of strips in the open fields, and to those cottagers who were fortunate enough to own a cottage with such rights attached. In very few cases was compensation paid where no legal claim could be established, however disastrous the loss suffered. Even when a poor cottager was able to prove his case, his grazing and other rights were usually so trifling, though not to him, that the land allotted in their stead was rarely of much use. The potato was not yet the common crop that it was soon to become, and the potato patch could not act as a recompense for the loss of the keep of a cow or a pig, and above all, for the loss of free fuel. In consequence the plot allotted was nearly always sold.

Yet had it not been that agricultural and industrial changes went together the position for the rural poor might not have deteriorated so drastically. More intensive methods were creating a demand for more farm workers and more opportunities of earning steady wages. If the wife and children could have supplemented the family income with some industrial earnings, once the family economy had been adjusted to the loss of common rights their position might well have been no worse than it had been before. Unfortunately, just when local industry and by-employments were needed most they began to fail. It is difficult to say how far changes in industry had affected rural life by the close of the Napoleonic wars. The spinning of cotton, and to some extent wool, had gone into the factories. This was a serious loss; everyone could spin, and spinning could be combined with household tasks, or with watching animals on the waste. There were few technical reasons why other local industries should, as yet, have been affected where fuel was not involved; nevertheless, the tide was beginning to run strongly in the direction of concentrating industry in the growing towns. The increasing use of coal as fuel, the increasing use of the steam-engine as a source of power, combined with better transport facilities, provided by improved roads and the new canals, all contributed to this effect. It is possible, however, that fuller investigation of the history of rural areas will show that it was those places which depended largely on the unspecialized preparing of yarn for the textile industries that were worst hit in the closing years of the eighteenth century by the drift of industry to the towns, and that for places which had developed a local domestic industry of their own the difficult years of transition came rather later.

For the rural poor as a whole, however, the last and final burden was the rise in prices, particularly in their staple food, due partly to the pressure of war and increased population, partly to a long series of bad harvests. If the harvests had been good, in spite of the increased pressure of demand, the population could probably still have been fed at moderate rates, for before 1765 we had been exporting on a considerable scale, and therefore had a fair margin in hand. But by the second half of the century a bad harvest could turn this small margin into a deficiency, and when that happened there was always rioting and distress among the poor, as witness the year 1766, before either a very rapid increase in population or the difficulties of war combined to aggravate the situation. Scattered years of bad harvests and high prices followed, but it was not until the war years between 1793 and 1814 that a succession of singularly poor and even disastrous harvests occurred. Between those years there were fourteen unsatisfactory harvests when the yield was below expectations, and in seven of them the situation was very serious. Thus, in spite of better methods and an increased acreage the price of bread remained high. For the rural worker this was a disaster, particularly in those areas where wheaten bread had become his staple food, since the rapid rise in the price of bread coincided with his increased dependence on wages. In purely agricultural districts, where there was little alternative employment and where the new towns were too distant to exert much influence on wages, there was a good deal of distress.

The consequence was a rapid rise in the Poor Rate, which in the long run only increased the misery of the rural poor. The method followed, as is well known, was to use the allowance system to supplement wages. There was nothing particularly new in the device. Poor men 'overburdened with children' as the phrase went, had frequently received some addition to their wages, even when in full employment, as a kind of primitive family allowance. Now the practice was more widely followed. It was not surprising therefore that the Berkshire justices, at their famous meeting at the Pelican Inn at Speen, should have recommended a flexible scale of relief that varied with the price of bread. Nor is it surprising that other counties followed their lead; it must have seemed the obvious thing to do. Two years later, in 1795, an act of parliament clarified the legal position by allowing justices to order out-door relief over the heads of the local overseers. From this date the drawing-up of local scales for allowances, which would be paid to bring wages, otherwise inadequate, up to subsistence level, became a general practice. It must be remembered, however, that the scales were local, not national. They could be increased or cut according to the will of the justices concerned.

The Speenhamland system, as it has come to be called, has been fiercely condemned, and for its effects little good can be said. Yet that some such experiment should have been tried was very much in line with the practice of the past. The employers of 1793 were not gifted with the power to foretell the future, and few men in that year realized, or could have realized, that Britain was entering a period of almost unbroken warfare, combined with an investment in capital goods, that was likely to lead to long inflation. Even less could they have been expected to guess that this time of difficulty was to be cursed with a series of poor and even disastrous harvests. Consequently, they took a short-time view, which the experience of the past had justified. When the harvests had failed, prices had shot up, as they did in 1709, in 1728, in 1766, and, since wages had failed to follow them, there had been distress and rioting and special charitable efforts to deal with what proved to be temporary distress. As has been said, mercantilist policy laid great stress on low wages, partly to spur the labouring poor on to habits of industry and frugality, partly to enable English goods to compete favourably in the export market. To allow wages to rise, therefore, because of a rise in the price of grain that was not expected to be permanent, would not have been considered in the national interest.

The Quaker Lead Company, which was not given to exploiting its workpeople, provides an illuminating example of this mercantilist point of view. In 1728 prices had risen, causing some distress among their workers, so that wages had been increased, but because the price of corn continued to rise, it was decided that other measures must be taken, as the following entry shows.

Whereas our Chief Agent in Flintshire Thos. Baker hath in Severall of his Letters represented to us the Scarcity of Corn & the Hardships of the poor Miners Smelters and others were under by the advanced price thereof & that if they were not Speedily supplied he should be obliged to raise their Wages to allay their great Complaints & keep them Quiet, being at the same time sensible how difficult it will be for us to reduce their advanced Wages hereafter to prevent wch Inconveniency we think it for the Interest of the Company & will redound much to their Reputation to send them a supply of Corn from hence being much cheaper than at their Markets. Therefore we desire the Treasurer that he will give orders for the hiring of a vessell abt 60 Tns & for the buying about 400 Quarts. of Corn vizt: 280 Qurs. of Barley 80 Qurs. Wheat and 80 Qurs. Oats for the relief of the Miners Smelters and others who are Imployed in our severall Works there.

When a company, careful to act towards its workpeople in accordance with the precepts of Christianity, felt that by following this course they were doing something that would 'redound to their Reputation',[1] it is easy to understand why the Berkshire justices also felt that a definite attempt to raise and fix wages, which by the as yet unrepealed statute of 1563 they were legally empowered to do, was not the best way to deal with what they must have considered to be a special emergency. Once the device of supplementing wages via the Poor Law had been embarked upon, particularly as the emergency of high prices continued year after year, it became more and more difficult to change a policy, which had, in a sense, been advocated by no-one but merely adopted spontaneously by many local authorities. Hence the distortion of the Poor Law between 1793 and 1834 and its overdrastic reorganization in that year.

But, however understandable the actions and laudable the motives of the men who saw in charitable relief the answer to high prices, the effects on the rural poor were, in many localities, disastrous. It would not be true to imply that no increase in wages, even in rural areas, took place in these difficult years. The effects of the Speenhamland policy did not freeze wages completely. For example, in Essex, farmers, who in 1800 were paying 10*s*. 6*d*. a week, in 1802 were paying 12*s*., and by 1815 as much as 15*s*.[2] But though wages were going up the price of bread was soaring so rapidly, under the twin pressure of war-time inflation and

[1] A. Raistrick: *Quakers in Science and Industry* (1950), p. 175.
[2] R. E. Prothero: *Op. cit.*, p. 314.

actual physical scarcity, that the gap between them remained. Indeed, it has been calculated that if wages doubled, prices trebled in the same period. In such circumstances the rural worker, where he had little chance of alternative employment, could rarely hope to maintain his family without some help from the parish.

The result of this policy was a vicious circle. Few farmers were willing to pay a living wage at the current rate of prices while they could get a man whose wages were being subsidized. If a man had a little property, if, in spite of enclosure he had managed to retain his own cottage and perhaps kept a pig or a cow, he was not likely to receive an allowance in aid of wages. This made farmers reluctant to employ him, if subsidized labour were available, unless he was a specialized and outstanding worker. Not only was it difficult for a man to raise himself out of the ranks of the semi-pauperized, at the same time new families were being pushed down. The smallholder, especially if he were a tenant with war-time rents to pay, found the burden of the Poor Rates, which went to subsidize the wage bill of the bigger farmers, an almost intolerable load. If he could no longer carry on he, too, had to look for work on the land. In such circumstances it is, perhaps, surprising that the rural exodus was not greater, for after 1793 the parish officers were empowered to remove persons without a settlement only after they had actually become chargeable. But Speenhamland spelt security, even at a wretchedly low level, and while there was work to do on the land the countryman remained there. Only the surplus moved.

With such conditions prevailing it is clear that the pool of rural misery must increase. Such were the circumstances which created the poverty-stricken labourer of the nineteenth century. That his plight was a wretched one few people will deny, but the responsibility was one that must be shared between the mistaken Speenhamland policy, the high prices and difficulties of the war years and the undermining of rural industry by the new competition of the towns. Commercial farming, larger units, the enclosure of open fields and wastes created the need for more specialized agricultural workers, a need which the growing population could have met without serious strain. It was other fortuitous circumstances which created the misery for which agrarian reorganization has been blamed.

If in rural England the sign of economic change was to be found in the disappearance of the open field and unimproved waste, in industry its symbol was the mill and the concentration of population in urban areas. These changes also had their repercussions on the social structure of the past. Hitherto it had been the merchant, able to provide credit and secure markets, who had dominated production. Now, as the opportunities for industrial investment grew with the growth of the new techniques, the industrial capitalist became an important element in the society of the manufacturing areas. Though few of them were wealthy the ploughing back of profits meant that industry began to accumulate enough capital to finance its own production. When this stage had been reached it is possible to speak of the manufacturers as constituting a new class in the society of the day.

Gradually a tendency to act together began to emerge, as they became conscious of their common interests and common identity. Informally, almost haphazardly, groups of men drifted into consultations on their joint interests. Out of consultations came committees, at first *ad hoc*, but later more permanent in their organization. At the beginning these committees were strictly economic in their purpose. For instance, in 1764, the employers in the Lancashire worsted industry formed a prosecuting committee to prevent the embezzling of the raw material by their employees.[1] These committees were empowered to appoint inspectors and to prosecute offenders at the common cost. Manchester, with its increasing population of new manufacturers, was a natural centre for such experiments. In 1774 a meeting of some of the more prominent amongst them, both merchants and manufacturers, was called at Compton's coffee-house 'to consider the proper measures for the security and encouragement of the cotton, linen and other manufactures of the town and neighbourhood'.[2] After discussion it was decided to appoint a committee of nineteen members. This, in itself, is evidence of the widespread interest taken in the matter of increasing production. The committee, presided over by a chairman and assisted by a secretary and treasurer, was to meet regularly. As a result of its deliberations it was later decided to set up a still more permanent body to be

[1] In 1777 a statute conferred legal powers on these committees.
[2] A. Redford: *Manchester Merchants and Foreign Trade* (1934), p. 2.

known as 'The Committee for the Protection and Encouragement of Trade'.

It was a sign of the times that after 1776 one of the questions which most interested the committee was that of patent rights over the new mechanical inventions. This was a matter on which the manufacturer and the inventor were constantly clashing. The new industrialist was anxious to make use of the new ideas and to instal the new machinery in his mill, but he disliked paying the fees to which the inventor was entitled by his patent. Many signs of dramatic struggles are embedded in the files of the business papers of the time. Many are the stories told of the bitter feuds between these two sets of men. Among the Gott papers is the record of one such episode. Lawson an engineer employed by Boulton and Watt, while fixing an engine in Gott's mill at Bean Inge, heard rumours that Bowling, an iron-master at Low Moor, was using an engine similar to Watt's without having paid fees for so doing. Direct investigation was impossible as the engine-house was closely guarded. However, as Bowlings were casting some new wheels for an engine Lawson was erecting at Leeds, he paid a surprise call at the works. Then, having primed his mechanic, he sent him to the engine-house, ostensibly to ask the way to the office, but in reality to see if he could get a glimpse of the offending machine. Once his identity was discovered he was hustled away at some speed, but the ruse was successful, and as far as a hasty glance could reveal, Lawson's suspicions were con-firmed. That was the beginning of a long struggle between Boulton and Watt and Bowling. Bowling put up the usual de-fence, namely that though similar in many ways the engine they were using was sufficiently different in detail for it to be no in-fringement of Watt's patent.[1]

Arkwright, a man of business and an adapter of other men's ideas, tried to protect himself against similar tactics by taking out patents so vaguely and loosely worded that they might seem to cover all those small changes that a manufacturer, attempting to dodge payment, might make. It may also be that he hoped, less excusably, that patents so wide might block genuine improve-ments made by other inventors to Arkwright's original machines. It was to protect themselves against this kind of sharp practice,

[1] W. B. Crump: *Op. cit.*, pp. 188–9.

and possibly to protect their own sharp practices, that 'The Committee for the Protection and Encouragement of Trade' operated. The fight grew more intense when in 1781 Arkwright served writs on some manufacturers for infringing his patents. The better to defend their interests the committee reconstructed itself on a wider base, bringing in representatives of the cotton, linen, silk and small wares manufacturers. After a bitter struggle Arkwright's patents were declared void in 1785. Though fighting Arkwright was perhaps one of their major and more spectacular achievements, the committee showed itself active in protecting all the economic interests of the new manufacturers, whether it was by fighting combinations of workmen, dealing with the embezzlement of goods, or striving for an easier importation of raw material. This committee, important though it was, did not exhaust the organizing activities of the Manchester merchants. In addition there were separate committees for many of the smaller industries such as fustian manufactures, calico dyers, printers, etc.

These early experimental attempts at common action were not confined either to Manchester or to the textile industries. They were to be found, in a more or less developed form, in most of the industrial centres that were springing into mushroom growth. Among the iron-masters of Shropshire and the Midlands they were much favoured: under the guise of Trade Associations, and even of convivial meetings and dining clubs, a good deal of common policy, often concerned with price fixing, took place among the more prominent of them. At first this rising class of manufacturers do not appear to have been alive to the usefulness of concerted political action and, unlike the merchants, they had still to discover the importance of a parliamentary lobby. It was the proposal to allow Ireland to trade directly with the colonies and to remove the galling restrictions on her commerce that seems to have taught them this. Irish discontent threatened, in view of the possibility of a French invasion in the April of 1778, to become dangerous. In consequence Lord North succeeded in persuading the House of Commons to pass five resolutions favourable to Irish trade. The response of the threatened English and Scottish interests was immediate, and petitions, both from merchants and manufacturers, against the tenour of the resolutions poured in. The government, 'only too conscious of its weakness'[1] drew back, though next year, fearing that Ireland might go the way of the American colonies, substantial concessions were made. Ireland was to be allowed a share in the colonial trade and to export her woollen goods elsewhere than to England.

A most serious threat to purely industrial interests was provided by Pitt's programme of commercial and financial reform. Driven by the financial stringency of the post-American war period, Pitt contemplated introducing a new excise, by which the taxes on dyed stuffs made of cotton or cotton and linen mixed, were much increased. This in itself would have been unpopular enough, but in order to work it administratively bleachers and dyers would be forced to take out licences. Moreover, there was a strong and justified dislike of any attempt to confine the new, and often flexibly experimental, processes of the cotton industry within the rigid regulations of an excise system, which required all kinds of specifications to be laid down and followed. Indeed, by the very nature of his proposals it was clear that Pitt was very far from being aware of the latest developments within the industry. To the Lancashire cotton manufacturers it was a matter which touched them very nearly, which they could not afford to let go by default. A committee was appointed which sent delegates, Mr. Thomas Richardson and Mr. Thomas Walker, to London, and the local press recorded their activities with the keenest attention. On the 8th of April it was reported that Mr. Garrow, counsel for the fustian manufacturers, spoke for two hours at the bar of the House, and hopes in Manchester ran high. When on the successful completion of their mission the delegates returned on the 21st of April, a large crowd that had gathered to meet them chaired them triumphantly through the streets. Next day the ladies and gentlemen of the town, or those whom the local press regarded as such, appeared wearing favours to celebrate the occasion. Not content with this display of gratitude, next month both men were presented with a silver cup and a public procession took place. Nor did the gratitude of the Manchester manufacturers stop here. In August a public dinner was given to

---

[1] H. Butterfield: *Op. cit.*, p. 79. For a full account of the way in which the question of Irish Commercial restrictions became a part of the tangled politics of the 1779 crisis, see pp. 69–177.

Thomas Stanley, M.P., as an acknowledgment of his help.[1] Parallel suggestions for taxes on coal, iron, and copper brought similar, though less well organized protests from the manufacturers concerned, though Matthew Boulton reported after an interview with Pitt, 'I fear our young Minister is not sufficiently aware of the importance of the subject'.[2]

Fresh fears were aroused by Pitt's proclivity towards Free Trade. Cotton and iron manufacturers were alike seriously perturbed by the sympathetic reception of the Commercial Propositions put forward by the Irish Parliament in the February of 1785. If Irish goods could compete freely in this country with their own the lower level of Irish wages would, they argued, lead to serious under-cutting. Personal and local protest seemed too weak in face of such a threat and the manufacturers came to realize that 'whilst the *landed* and *funded interests*, the East India, and other *commercial bodies*, have their respective advocates in the great council of the nation, *they* alone are destitute of that advantage'.[3] Perhaps they may have been influenced by the recent petitioning activities of the Yorkshire Association. Certainly they were conscious that ministers were 'unacquainted with their real interests'. It was in these circumstances that Wedgwood suggested that a committee from the main English and Scottish centres of manufacture should be elected to watch over their common interests. From this suggestion came the General Chamber of Manufacturers, in itself another affirmation of the fact that another stratum was emerging in English society.

This committee acted as a central organizing body. As a result petitions against the obnoxious proposals poured in, at least sixty from different local bodies being received by the House of Commons. This demonstration was sufficient to convince Pitt that the interests he had minimized and flouted were sufficiently formidable to command his respect. In consequence the Irish treaty was modified to such an extent that it was no longer acceptable to the Irish. It was a significant victory. Nor was its lesson lost on Pitt. When he came to negotiate a trade treaty with France he moved with extreme care. Eden, who was sympathetic

---

[1] W. A. Axon: *Annals of Manchester* (1887), p. 111.
[2] H. W. Dickinson: *Matthew Boulton* (1937), p. 130.
[3] T. S. Ashton: *Iron and Steel in the Industrial Revolution* (1924), p. 169.

to the interests of the manufacturers, was entrusted with the negotiations, and took care at all stages to sound their feelings. Indeed, so tender and heedful of their interests did Pitt now become that Arthur Young, commenting on a speech of Pitt's in the House in the February of 1792, declared that the agricultural interests of the kingdom had never found themselves in so contemptible a position. Twenty years had indeed made a difference.

It is doubtful, however, if this new class had got beyond an *ad hoc* interest in politics. When their immediate interests were threatened they took action but it was defensive rather than aggressive. They had, as yet, no constructive policy to put forward. Probably their interests were still too divided for that. The older manufacturers, makers of silk and ribbons, clocks, hats, leather goods, the smaller, more traditionally organized, industries clung to the idea of protection, but the more progressive industries, the makers of cotton, were beginning to realize that their real interests could best be forwarded by an expansion of trade: if that meant making concessions to foreign competitors in order to win entry into foreign markets even so the advantage would lie with them, because of their lower costs and greater technical skill. Such enlightenment, even with regard to their own interests, was still far from general. Just as the woollen manufacturers had long secured the prohibition of the export of wool, so that the home manufacturers might enjoy the advantage of abundant raw material, so now there was a very real attempt to prevent the export of British yarn. To some extent, therefore, the cohesion of the newly growing class of factory-owners was retarded in the political field by the fact that they by no means spoke with the same voice or wanted to press the same line of action upon the government. In consequence, and except in special cases, where enough industrial interests were threatened by the same piece of legislation to induce something like a united front, the political action of most manufacturing groups was confined to *ad hoc* petitions upon specific points. Nevertheless, the fact that towns like Manchester and Birmingham, which were the strongholds of the new class, could look to the formation of any organization, even as permanent as the Chamber of Manufacturers, was significant of the part that they were to play in the not very distant future.

The Theatre in Manchester, 1805

Preparations for the Tragedy of Hamlet, or a Green Room in the Country, 1790

The Assembly Rooms, Newcastle

Masked Ball at Wanstead Assembly by Hogarth

Just as the manufacturers were beginning to sort out their own interests from those of the merchants and were looking to their own organizations to protect them, so they were beginning to take their place in the society of the day, though quite what this place was to be was not, even by the end of the century, very clear. As a class they were not really numerous, though each year saw a steady increase, and they were still concentrated in little pockets in or near the industrial towns. The eighteenth century was marked by a steady growth of social amenities. It is interesting to notice that, just as the economic wealth of the merchants preceded that of the manufacturers, so there is some evidence that seems to point to the fact that the towns in which the merchants predominated, such as Bristol and Liverpool and Newcastle, developed the appurtenances of civilized urban living before towns like Birmingham or Manchester or Leeds, whose prosperity was more closely dependent on the new technical changes in industry, and which, therefore, were more likely to be inhabited by the small industrialist.

The pattern in most of the new towns was much the same. As the citizens grew in wealth and education they came to demand not only a higher standard of cleanliness, with adequately paved, drained and lighted streets, but also such things as a convenient assembly hall, a subscription library, possibly a printing press with a local newspaper, certainly book shops, and often a Literary and Philosophical Society. Newcastle, much of whose original wealth came from the coal trade, was, as early as 1761, raising subscriptions for the levelling and enclosing of St. Nicholas's churchyard, and town planning schemes were in the air. The great problem was that of improving communications within the town, still bottled up inside its walls, and by 1784 plans to connect the northern gates and Quayside, Pandon Gate and Westgate, were afoot. By 1789 the Lort Burn, a deep ravine, described variously as 'a vast nauseous hollow' and 'a place of filth and dirt', was filled up and levelled and the additional ground so obtained used to relieve the congestion of traffic by the provision of new roads. Another sign of prosperity was the building of new, commodious houses, sometimes still within the walls, as, for example, Charlotte Square and Hanover Square in Newcastle, but more often in the suburbs. By the 'eighties, the merchants of

18

Bristol were moving out into the western suburbs, and the building of Berkeley Square had begun, though it long remained unfinished, possibly due to the French wars, for in 1799 several half-built houses were being offered for sale.

Nor were bricks and mortar and a higher standard of living the only improvements sought. The Assembly Hall was a prominent feature in the social life of the eighteenth-century town, and its erection, usually by subscription, is, therefore, a landmark of some importance. Bristol was raising money for this purpose in 1753, a subscription committee issuing a hundred and twenty shares of £30 each, while even earlier, in 1736, Newcastle exchanged the occasional assemblies held in the long room of the Turk's Head for permanent quarters in the Groat Market. Forty years later these, too, were considered inadequate, and in 1776 William Newton designed new Assembly Rooms which, when finished, were described as being 'the most elegant and commodious edifice of the kind in the kingdom, except the House of Assembly in Bath'.[1] The facilities provided included the grand saloon, a card-room, coffee-room, a news-room and a library. Arthur Young apparently thought well of the Assembly Rooms at Hull, which he described as 'handsome and well contrived.'[2] Liverpool, too, acquired Assembly Rooms, which Derrick, Boswell's quondam friend, who had succeeded to Nash's throne at Bath and who, therefore, might be expected to speak with some authority, was gracious enough to describe as 'grand, spacious and finely illuminated', adding, with a touch of condescension, 'here is a meeting once a fortnight to dance and play cards; where you will find some women elegantly accomplished and perfectly well dressed.'[3] Perhaps, in this, Liverpool showed the superior polish of a port as against that of an industrial town, for Major Floyd, visiting Manchester in 1780, wrote to Lord Herbert, 'I am not much enamoured of Manchester, yet it is not quite so bad as I had expected. We had a fine Assembley here last night; there were some very tolerable pretty tits, but they don't look like gentlewomen, a circumstance,' he added, 'I set great store by.'[4] In addition to its Assembly Liverpool had its subscrip-

---

[1] S. Middlebrook: *Newcastle upon Tyne* (1950), p. 154.
[2] A. Young: *A Six Months Tour Through the North of England,* Vol. I, p. 178.
[3] Ramsay Muir: *A History of Liverpool* (1907), p. 186.
[4] *Pembroke Papers*. Edited by Lord Herbert, p. 72.

tion library. Starting with a little informal group, by 1758 it had
a hundred members, charged a subscription of five shillings a year
and possessed four hundred and fifty volumes. By the close of the
century such libraries were common; even small country towns
often boasted one. It may be remembered that the Bennet sisters
considered the changing of their library books as much a matter
of routine as the modern reader. Where such libraries are to be
found one may presume the presence of a middle class reading
clientele.

Literary and philosophical societies were more solid affairs and
in consequence less common. They seem to have found their
most congenial soil where modern industry, with its technical
problems and mechanical conundrums, flourished. Newcastle,
which combined both commercial and industrial activities, early
showed an interest in both literary and scientific discussion.
Since the sixteenth century its civic life had been dominated by
the Lords of Coal, but by the eighteenth its industrial enterprises
had become more diversified. Though salt-making was declining
in face of the competition of the Cheshire rock salt the number of
its glass workers had increased, soap making was carried on after
1770, and pottery was manufactured. In view of this background
it is interesting to notice that there was an audience for a course
of lectures on astronomy in 1768, and that the earliest of its de-
bating societies, the Philosophical Society, was founded in 1775.
The more famous Literary and Philosophical Society did not
follow until 1793, by which time industry was well established.

Everywhere, too, there was a great demand for actors, whose
audiences were drawn from all classes. In country towns, the
centres of local society, they played in whatever building was
available, from the 'long room' in the local inn to a convenient
barn. Where the middle class were considerable and the population increasing, permanent theatres were built, and these indicate
in some measure the changing composition of urban society.
Where the players, when they first came to Liverpool, performed
is not certain. There seems to have been a small theatre in the Old
Ropery of Fenwick Street in 1745 and one in Drury Lane by 1749,
before Mr. Gibson succeeded in getting Letters Patent for the
Theatre Royal. His application was apparently approved by the
councillors on the understanding that Mr. Gibson would pay the

expenses of procuring the necessary Letters Patent and also those of providing a suitable building! The circuit in the North-east, too, was well served, and theatres multiplied rapidly. Durham got its first theatre in 1771, and between then and 1796 Newcastle, Sunderland, Berwick and South Shields all acquired permanent buildings, the Theatre Royal at Newcastle being built in 1788. Nor did the entertainment which the theatres provided suffice for the new urban middle class. The eighteenth century was also a period of concerts and musical festivals. Charles Avison, soon after his appointment as organist at St. Nicholas's, Newcastle, organized public subscription concerts, held either in the Assembly Rooms or at that useful 'long room' at the Turk's Head. Nottingham, at its Musical Festival in 1772, saw the performance of *The Messiah* and *Judas Maccabaeus*; Liverpool was holding a festival by 1784. Such then were the outward signs of the growth of a sufficiently prosperous and intelligent class within the towns, men and women who demanded not only some increase in material comforts but entertainment of a social character and some food for the mind.

By the last three decades of the eighteenth century even a cursory survey of the history of those towns where the new manufactures were being concentrated reveals a similar process at work to that which had marked the development of a social life in the ports. As an illustration of this, the rise of Birmingham is interesting. By the end of the century it had become the centre of a diversified industry, japanning, button-making, buckle-making, and metal trifles of all kinds. Of it, St. Fond, regarding it with the tourist's eye, wrote,

> From the activity of its manufactures and its commerce, Birmingham is one of the most curious towns in England. If any one should wish to see in one comprehensive view, the most numerous and the most varied industries, all combined in contributing to the arts of utility, of pleasure, and of luxury, it is hither he must come.

And he goes on to speak of

> the vast works where steam pumps are made . . . the manufacturies in constant activity making sheet copper for sheathing ships bottoms . . . those plate tin and plate iron, which make France tributary to

England . . . the extensive hardware manufacture which employs to so much advantage more than thirty thousand hands, and compels all Europe and a great part of the New World to supply themselves from England, because all ironmongery is made here in greater perfection with more economy and with greater abundance, than anywhere else.[1]

Birmingham, perhaps more than most contemporary towns, was the creation of the new manufacturer. What sort of a way of life was emerging there?

It is interesting to contrast the amenities which the town could provide at the beginning and at the end of the century. In 1700, Birmingham consisted of one long straggling street, neither drained nor paved, unlighted at night and littered with heaps of refuse and the waste products of its industries. Its fifteen thousand inhabitants were not sufficiently interested to support a single book-seller, and a weekly stall supplied all their literary needs! Amusements were brutal. There were no Assembly Rooms, no regular theatre, no intelligent and cultivated society. By the middle of the century the position was improving. A large room belonging to the same Mrs. Sawyer whose school Catherine Hutton attended, and whose son was a dancing-master, was used to house an occasional assembly; and that by this time Birmingham could at least support the services of a dancing-master is perhaps some proof that the graces of life were beginning to penetrate even there. By 1772 there was sufficient support to make the provision of regular Assembly Rooms possible. Hutton records that 'a building was erected by Subscription upon the Tontine principle, at the head of Temple Row, and was dignified with the French name of Hôtel. From a handsome entrance the ladies are now led through a spacious saloon, at the extremity of which the eye is struck with it a grand flight of steps, opening into an Assembly-room which would not disgrace even the royal presence of the Duke's brother.'[2]

The drama was also receiving more public support. In the first part of the century performances were still given in converted

[1] B. Faujas de Saint Fond: *A Journey through England and Scotland to the Hebrides in 1784*. Edited by Geikie, (Glasgow, 1907) Vol. II, pp. 346–8.
[2] W. Hutton: *History of Birmingham*, p. 13.

buildings because Birmingham had no regular theatre. As only one of these had secured a licence for the presenting of dramatic performances the other two had to adopt the usual expedient of charging for a concert and throwing in a play free between the first and second halves. It was the arrival of a company from the Theatre Royal in London which appears to have created a new interest in the stage, and a theatre was actually built in King Street. It was not, however, until 1774 that the Theatre Royal was built, and by this time there were enough citizens of sufficient discernment to afford an audience to such players of renown as Kemble and Mrs. Siddons when, during the summer months, they played in the provinces. Byng, who visited Birmingham in 1792, partly for the pleasure of seeing Mrs. Siddons act, recorded that 'In the High Street there was an amazing crowd before the play house door, striving for entrance, and, near them, in pleasing contemplation, stood Mr. Siddons; (for it was Mrs. Siddons benefit).' For Birmingham, which he described as 'this hourly increasing town', he had little liking, exclaiming as he left next morning, 'How eager was I to get from the insolence of Birmingham—a town wherein I should be crippled in a week for want of flagstones. Tell this to a buckle-maker and he would stare and say "That he never remark'd it." Even Manchester has a flat stone footpath.'[1] Byng was often a petulant witness but no such charge can fairly be levelled against William Hutton, the historian of the town, yet he noted, 'It is remarkable, that in a town like Birmingham, where so many houses are built, the art of building is so little understood. The style of architecture in the inferior sort, is rather showy than lasting'. The Birmingham manufacturer was apparently reluctant to spend money on such luxuries as good buildings for Hutton adds the comment, 'We have people who enjoy four or five hundred pounds a year in houses, none of which, perhaps, exceed six pounds per annum'.[2]

It is not surprising that John Byng found so little in the town to please a man of taste but it is surprising that to his condemnation he should have added 'No booksellers!' Possibly he did not know where to look, for by 1780 Birmingham had acquired its first subscription library. Priestley, who had had experience of a

---

[1] J. Byng: *The Torrington Diaries*, Vol. III, pp. 148–50.
[2] W. Hutton: *Op. cit.*, pp. 50–1.

similar experiment in Leeds, where he had been prominent in starting a library in 1768, was useful in advising upon the rules to be adopted but it is perhaps significant that its first steward, Jon Lee, was a button-maker. Until 1782 he housed the volumes in his own dwelling; then the whole library, which by that time amounted to some five hundred books, was moved to Swan Yard. There they could be borrowed every day. For this convenience members paid a subscription of eight shillings a year, plus one pound entrance fee. By the end of the century, as well as a subscription library Birmingham had its local press, Baskerville's, with a reputation for fine printing. It ran its local newspapers and even, in the person of William Hutton, whose *History of Birmingham* was published in 1782, its local historian. It had in addition a permanent theatre, pleasure gardens and entertainments for the lesser fry, while on the outskirts were to be found the small estates and dignified houses of those manufacturers who cared enough for the amenities to leave the dirty town.

By the end of the century something was being done to secure greater cleanliness within the town. An attempt to get a Local Act in 1765 failed, largely because the idea of a new rate was unpopular, but in 1769 powers were obtained for appointing local improvement commissioners. In 1773 their powers were further enlarged. Apparently less was effected than had been hoped. The commissioners, of whom there were some seventy-six, were too busy with their own affairs to deal adequately with the problems of Birmingham. Hutton described them as 'irresolute'. It was difficult, despite the seventy-six commissioners, to get a good attendance, and sometimes even a quorum was lacking. Even so something was done to remove the obstructions caused by projecting bow-windows and the dangers of open cellar flaps after dark. In 1791 feeble attempts were even made at paving the main streets and providing a footpath[1], attempts of whose success Byng seemed singularly unconscious when he visited the town! But until the end of the century Birmingham, though by now containing some 74,000 persons, housed in some 1,600 dwellings, must have been a dirty, slackly organized place. The machinery for the removal of nuisances was still far from effective. Before 1789 there were no night-watchmen, and even until 1801 they

[1] S. and B. Webb: *Statutory Authorities* (1922), p. 254.

were only to be found in the wealthier parts of the town, where the inhabitants were willing to subscribe to pay them. Though the wealth of the town was increasing every year its new industrialists still seem to have been unmoved by the squalor around them. Perhaps this was because it was becoming fashionable to live outside the town. Hutton, in his *History* said that already about thirty-six men were keeping carriages for their own use, and that at least fifty, when he wrote in 1781, had houses outside the town.

Across the Pennines in Yorkshire there is the same evidence of a new class coming into social prominence. 'I can remember the time', said James Graham, while giving evidence on the woollen manufacturers, 'when there were not seven carriages kept in Leeds, and now, I dare say there are a hundred'.[1] The keeping of carriages implied more than just a piece of idle display, an aping of the gentry. It indicated a new way of life, a new standard of living. As the towns grew more and more congested the more prosperous merchants and manufacturers moved into the suburbs. It was happening everywhere. Byng noted that 'the avenues to Birmingham are mark'd by citizens houses', and observed that around Stoke on Trent there were 'numberless new buildings, and many pleasant villas for the principal merchants'.[2] Catherine Hutton, writing to her brother in 1801, made the same comment on the approaches to Liverpool, declaring that 'At a distance of five miles from the town we perceived ourselves in its environs; elegant houses, the retreats of merchants rose on every side'.[3] For the business man, who was anxious to move away from the counting-house or the workshop, at a time when no public means of local transport was available, a carriage was a necessity. Their increasing number is but one more piece of evidence of the growth of a new and materially prosperous urban society. Of real elegance of living among them there is little sign, and Catherine Hutton was doubtless justified when she wrote to a friend in 1783, 'I have laughed twenty times at your enquiring after fashion at Birmingham, a place celebrated for neither fashion nor taste. We are showy enough but nothing more'.[4] Yet that she, considering

---

[1] *Minutes of Committee on the Woollen Industry* (1806), p. 445.
[2] J. Byng: *Torrington Diaries*, Vol. III, p. 126.
[3] C. H. Beale: *Op. cit.*, p. 131.   [4] *Ibid.*, p. 35.

her parents' background, should make this comment is in itself revealing; 'showiness' to her was already something that called, at best, for tolerant amusement. John Byng certainly would have passed the same judgment on most of the industrial towns which he visited on his tours, being stirred up by the poor standard of most of their inns, to declare that: 'In places where wealth is procured, it is ignorantly spent; for the upstart man of riches knows no better; the inns therefore are bad, dear, and presumptuous; but on roads where gentlemen travell and scold there will be a reform'.[1]

His view of Manchester was also an unfavourable one. 'Oh! what a dog hole is Manchester!', he wrote: 'For the old town is like Wapping; and the upper, the new town like Spital Fields— in the same gloom and dirt—', and described, after having collected his letters at the Post Office, 'my best and only treat'; how he 'then wander'd about the town till dinner time, without seeing anything that I should ever wish to see again'.[2] It is interesting to notice that this year, 1792, was the year in which Manchester and Salford procured their Police Act, which enabled commissioners to take over the cleaning, lighting, watching and regulating the streets, lanes, passages and places, and for the widening of many of them. Up to the end of the century, however, Manchester, like Birmingham, showed indifference and slackness in the use of the powers which it had now obtained. Since the property qualification for the new commissioners was to own or occupy premises of £30 a year or more, the new powers were essentially vested in the middle class inhabitants, whether industrialists, merchants or professional men; indeed any householder occupying premises of less than £4 10s. 0d. annual value was exempt from paying even the one-and-sixpenny rate which was authorized to provide the necessary funds. Moreover, any person who subscribed £10, though not one of the full commissioners, might become one for that part of the act which concerned the widening, improving and opening of the streets.

Despite the urgency of the problem in the early period very few people thought it worth their while to subscribe £10 to this very necessary work. Early meetings even of the full Police Commissioners were badly attended and unenterprising, and John

---

[1] J. Byng: *Op. cit.*, Vol. III, p. 117.   [2] *Ibid.*, p. 116.

Cross, the Steward to the Court Leet, in his charge to the Jury in 1799, described eloquently how

> during many wet and dark winter months, the streets have remained uncleansed and without lights; for some time no watchmen or patrols were appointed . . . and none could pass through the streets in safety. Escaping personal violence, they were still in imminent personal danger, from the numerous unguarded cellars, pits and various obstructions that everywhere interrupted their passage . . . the streets are still crowded with annoyances . . . not a street has been widened or laid open; not one yard of land has yet been laid into them, for any of the proposed purposes of improvement.

He had, however, to concede that, of late, 'A few respectable and active persons have directed their attention to these public concerns'.[1] But though the town was still dirty and dingy the same interest in cultural activities which was to be found in Birmingham was apparent there also. In 1770 a 'Subscription Library for Promoting General Knowledge' was established, and in 1781 the Manchester Literary and Philosophical Society was founded. Entertainment, too, was provided by the licensing of a theatre in 1775, though this was done with some misgivings as it was thought it might be a temptation to idleness to the poorer sort.

From the course of events in both Birmingham and Manchester it would seem as if both the contributions and the interests of the new manufacturers were distinctly limited. As a class they can hardly be blamed for the squalor of the new industrial towns. Their insanitary streets and overcrowded houses were things which contemporary opinion, at least in the first part of the century, took for granted as part of the normal pattern of urban life. Certainly apart from some attempt to safeguard property by better lighting and more watchmen, and apart from some attempts to facilitate transport by removing obstructions, they were uninterested in the state of the towns that were becoming the background of their activities. Such interest as they had seems to have been exhausted by the procuring of a Local Act for Improvements. It should not be assumed too readily, therefore, that the demand for more cultural amenities, for assemblies and literary societies came from the industrialists. With the growth of towns

---

[1] A. Redford and I. S. Russell: *Op. cit.*, Vol. I, p. 206.

and with prosperity there was increasing scope for the new professional classes, for doctors, for attorneys, for teachers, and to claim that every cotton-spinner or iron-master was an enthusiastic member of the local Literary and Philosophical Society would be patently absurd. Many, possibly most of them, put back every penny not needed for the essentials of life into their business and left it to their sons to ape the ways and accomplishments of gentlemen. If, however, the majority of manufacturers were still pouring their not inconsiderable energy into the extension of their business they were at the same time creating the wealth that made other, less material, activities possible, and attracting professional men, more calculated to enjoy them, to the new urban centres. But if the manufacturer had little time for the cultivation of more gracious living, his wife and daughters and even his sons were less oblivious of the attractions of the theatre, the concert hall and the Assembly Rooms. It is surely not without significance that in those towns where the new industrial activity was to be found, this new, active, urban social life was already emerging. Crude it may have been, but by the end of the century it was certainly not unimportant.

But though to the historian looking back the eighteenth-century manufacturer may seem already to be constituting an element new in English society, contemporaries seem to have been, in many cases, less aware of the emergence of a new, socially important, class. Even in those areas where they were becoming numerous, the manufacturer was rarely recognized as being socially acceptable. Yet by the close of the century there were exceptions to this rule. Some men were engaged in enterprises so extensive and so well known that they were obtaining reputations not so much despite their manufacturing activities as because of them. Though Wedgwood would never have claimed to be a gentleman, the force of his character, the charm of his mind, and the wide reputation of the wares he made, had gained for him the friendship of many men of birth. Matthew Boulton, too, found the ownership of the renowned Soho Works no impediment. Catherine Hutton, writing to her brother Thomas, while she was on a visit to Sutton in Arden in 1779, recorded a less eminent instance of a family which was still actively engaged in the cotton manufacture, but whose younger members had already started to climb the social ladder. 'Mr. Unwin's house,' she told him, 'is built of stone and on the outside seems fit for a nobleman; but the best rooms are occupied as warehouses and counting-houses for the cotton manufactory'.[1] They apparently lived in considerable comfort, for she describes the gardens in some detail, and then went on,

> Mr. and Mrs. Unwin, Miss White's grandfather and grandmother are plain and worthy people, who visit all the families in the neighbourhood, even the Duke of Portland's and yet retain something of their original manners. Their carriage is studded with brass nails; their horses are heavy and bob tailed and their coachman's hair in a state of nature. Miss Unwin is genteel, agreeable and about thirty years of age. Mr. Samuel Unwin, the hope of the family, is making a tour along the southern coast. I see his books and his prints, his elegant dressing room. I drink his old Hock, and I hear of his Swiss servant and phaeton and pair of horses; so I suppose he is a fine gentleman.[2]

That even a few of the new industrialists should be able to surmount the social barriers of their age was significant for the shape of things to come, but they must be ranked with the solitary swallow that heralds but does not make the summer. The majority remained unrecognized. Such social power as they had was local. Where a grasp of affairs and a command of money had combined to equip and run a large plant, whose products were in national, and even international, demand, its owner was a man who could not be ignored when matters of local import had to be discussed. If a new turnpike were mooted or a canal suggested his own economic needs were likely to implicate him deeply in the project, while the neighbouring gentry and landowners were glad enough to have the benefit of his advice and the advantage of his capital. Social relations may not have been close but they were at least civil and in some cases formally cordial. The reality of the social gulf was, nevertheless, apparent from the fact that it was being bridged for business reasons only by men. In the great majority of cases their wives and daughters still lived and moved in different worlds. Queen Charlotte might behave with a simple and friendly courtesy to Boulton, the Duke of Bridgewater might co-operate warmly with Wedgwood's plans for canal construction; their

[1] C. H. Beale: *Op. cit.*, p. 22.   [2] *Ibid.*, p. 23.

womenfolk were rarely on such cordial terms. Men may leap over class barriers, it is only when women do not find them an impediment to social intercourse that they can be said to have lost their importance. In the eighteenth century this was seldom the case.

Nor should it be forgotten that the mass of the new manufacturers were not men of the calibre of Boulton, Watt, Wedgwood and Peel. However important they may have been in the place in which they lived, however great the power they wielded over both those in their employ and over local tradesmen, they hardly existed in the consciousness of the neighbouring gentry and their ladies. It is, indeed, very likely that a visiting foreigner, like St. Fond, was more impressed by the new plant and factories and more conscious of the emergence of the new industrialist than the English gentry.

Even so, however little recognized or welcomed by those who reckoned themselves his superior, the manufacturer was already leaving his mark on those towns where his economic interests predominated. Already he was both shaking off the control of the merchant and copying his manner of living. A man like Hutton might start life as a frame-work knitter, or, like Arkwright, as a barber: both ended by buying land, by building, so passing into the propertied class. It was the old familiar ladder which once the merchants had climbed. And as an outward sign of their new social claims, in their new gardens they, too, now erected busts and vases and pedestals, and ordered the construction of temples and grottoes and all the trappings which the elegance of the age demanded, so that what had once been the contribution of the individual artist to one individual setting declined into being a mass produced art to meet a conventional demand. In the same way, too, the Grand Tour was modified to meet the needs of a class which believed in combining business with pleasure. If Benjamin Gott the younger visited Athens in search of culture he had earlier visited France and Belgium, devoting himself not to the cultivation of the arts but to business connected with the firm, and the visiting of foreign mills. Thus, by the early nineteenth century the manufacturer, however much he was considered an upstart, and however crude by the standards of the civilized cultivated society of the day his manners and his outlook might seem, was rapidly attaining an importance which was soon to show itself capable of challenging effectively that of the merchant and the landowner alike.

One of the fruits of industrial progress was the rise of a new class of manufacturers powerful enough to challenge the control hitherto exercised by the landowners and merchants. To the same source is often ascribed the growth of a town proletariate. Yet just as there had been industrial capitalists before the Industrial Revolution so, too, many workers in industry had been dependent upon their wages long before a single lump of iron had been smelted with coke or a single spindle had been driven by water or steam power. Even in rural areas craftsmen who were dependent solely upon their wages were often to be met with, though it was in the towns, because of the lack of alternative resources, that the majority of those who relied solely upon a wage were to be found. On the coalfields, too, there had been a tendency for a wage-earning industrial population to thicken. But while the major part of industry was still organized on the domestic system and the textile manufacture was to be found in half the villages and small towns in England, the necessary conditions to foster a large growth of the urban wage-earner had not been created. Here the coming of power-driven, and in particular, of steam-driven, machinery was the decisive factor. True, by the close of the Napoleonic Wars only cotton spinning and the production of iron were sufficiently advanced in the new techniques to be forcing their workers into the growing towns on the coalfields. But already the mushroom growth of these new centres was impressive. In 1801 Manchester had a population of 94,000, and with the turn of the century concentration was rapid wherever the new factories were to be found. Thus here also the end of the eighteenth century saw a beginning of what afterwards was to be a radical change in the structure of English society. The man in the street was replacing the countryman as England's representative type. With this change came drastic alterations in the way of life and standard of living of the mass of the people. The new siting of industry and its urban character had made this inevitable.

To build factories and re-house the large numbers that, at a time of growing population, were being attracted to the towns was a formidable task. In addition new and better transport facilities had to be provided. All this could not but be a heavy drain on the resources of the country. Whenever it had been undertaken some temporary rise in prices and shortage must have occurred until the new investment in industry had begun to make its contribution towards lowering costs. The pressure of an expanding population on home produced food, even though supply had been increased to some extent by more efficient methods, was another inflationary factor. Moreover, the need to build the new towns with the least possible delay was likely to make for poor housing, while failure to build rapidly enough must lead to overcrowding, though this to the eighteenth-century worker was no new thing. It is not surprising that conditions were often deplorable. There were, even so, some benefits to balance these disadvantages. Wages were higher and, as the products of the new industry became available in the form of consumer goods, an increased standard of living became possible. As the home and the workshop became different the possibility of more domestic comfort grew.

The switchover from a rural domestic economy to an urban factory one could never have been easy but in cataloguing the miseries of the age it is too often forgotten, or ignored, that the transition took place under the pressure of war. Because the peak of the first wave of social change coincided with the long struggle with France potential benefits were delayed and evils prolonged. War expenditure and its diversion of resources from more productive uses drove prices far higher than the investment in capital goods would have done before increased production was reflected in lower prices. As a result real wages fell and the worker was hard put to retain his standard of wheaten bread. In many cases he was driven to eke out his food with the still suspected potato, that despised stand-by of the Irish peasant. What the rise in prices meant to the rural poor, particularly when they were coming to depend as never before on agricultural wages, the budgets collected by Eden and Davies show.

The hardships inflicted by the dramatic rise in prices were not confined to the rural poor, or even to the wage-earner in the towns. Minor civil servants and government officials were hit in the same way. In 1796 the Excise officers, whose salaries had been revised in 1788, petitioned for a further increase to meet the cost of living. To support their claim they presented specimen budgets based, they said 'on the actual experiences of a frugal family (containing five persons) and consisting of such things only as are deemed necessaries of life by the poorest mechanic', and they estimated the annual expenses of such a family at something between £103 2s. 0d., which was the figure sent in by Liverpool, and £86 3s. 6d., though the standard figure, obviously arrived at after some kind of consultation, since eighteen places sent in the same, was £92 16s. 2d. As the items included ten pounds of beef per week, the standard was probably in excess of that of the 'poorest mechanic', and certainly in excess of the country labourer, but most of the items are very moderate both in variety and quantity. Half a crown was allotted to tea, 6s. 6d. for meal, 5s. 0d. for meat, only 9d. for potatoes and greens. A pound of cheese and a pound and a half of butter made up most of the other foodstuffs bought, though the consumption of milk was fairly heavy at 2s. 0d., while beer cost 1s. 6d.[1] If these figures were accurate and genuine it is difficult to see how a footwalk officer with £65 a year, a ride officer with £60, and an assistant with only £45 remained both solvent and moderately honest. Not, however, until 1800 were increases granted, and these fell short of the claims which had been put forward. Thus to those difficulties of transition which could hardly have been avoided were also added all the complications of a long war. As a result, in the past, historians have blamed the industrialization that marked the close of the eighteenth century for evils which, as is now widely recognized, were often due to the strain of the Napoleonic wars.

Of the urban worker, caught up in the life of the growing towns, it is difficult to get a very clear picture; the types were too diverse and the reactions of contemporary commentators too varied. Matthew Boulton wrote with pride, 'I have trained up many, and am training up more, plain country lads into good workmen, where ever I find indications of skill and ability I encourage them'.[2] One form which his encouragement took was the provision of decent living conditions for them. As he explained to one correspondent, he had, 'built and furnished a house for the reception of one kind of apprentices . . . fatherless children, parish apprentices and hospital boys'.[3] On many occasions he was asked

[1] E. Hughes: *Economic History*, Vol. III, No. 2 Supplement of the Economic Journal (1936).
[2] S. Smiles: *Op. cit.*, p. 180.   [3] *Ibid.*, p. 178.

Dr. Syntax disputing his bill with the Landlady by Rowlandson

Englishman at Paris, 1767

Hall's Library at Margate

to include the sons of gentlemen among his apprentices, for the reputation of his works was high, but his policy was to refuse. He preferred his plain country lads, pointing out sensibly that 'gentlemen's sons would probably find themselves out of place in such companionship'. Where they possessed the necessary ability these young apprentices had the chance of developing into skilled mechanics, the aristocracy of the new working class.

With new skills came the possibility of higher living standards. Robert Peel, speaking in 1806 of the advantages which had followed the introduction of machinery in the cotton manufactory, declared: 'They have given rise to a new population, they have promoted the comforts of the work people to such a degree that early marriages have been resorted to and a great increase in numbers have been occasioned by it and I may say that they have given birth to an additional race of men'.[1] On this point Peel may be considered a somewhat prejudiced witness. It must not be forgotten that the incidence of the new prosperity did not fall evenly. Much of the less skilled work in the new factories was done by juvenile and female labour whose wages were much lower than those paid to the skilled male. In consequence, though women and children were employed in large numbers, the demand for male labour was intermittent and patchy and provided one of the problems of the new manufacturing areas. Men were wanted to build the new factories, to make the machinery with which they were equipped, and to care for it when erected. They were wanted in the mines in increasing numbers as the demand for coal grew. They were wanted in the iron works of the Black Country and South Wales and Shropshire. In the cotton areas they were required for weaving and for bleaching and printing, but in the new spinning mills, of which Peel spoke so favourably, two-thirds of the labour force was provided by women and children.

This lack of balance in the demand for labour was serious and in studying the effects of industrialization on the urban worker it should not be ignored. In the eighteenth-century phase of the Industrial Revolution the necessary child labour was met by an extension of the old principle of apprenticeship,[2] and since local

---

[1] *Minutes of Committee on . . . Woollen Industry*, p. 440.
[2] For a fuller discussion of this subject see A. Redford: *Labour Migration in England, 1800–50* (1926), Ch. II.

supplies were often inadequate the pauper children of London were used to fill the gap. That their lot was often cruelly hard cannot be denied. Hours of work by modern standards were unbelievably long; the worst mills worked from five in the morning to eight at night, and food and living conditions were only too often disgusting and inadequate. Nevertheless, there were millowners who took some care of the young labour they employed. Samuel Oldknow's Apprenticeship House was solidly and well built, and his children were given good food in which fruit from his orchard and pigs from his farm played their part, while on Sundays some attempt was made, by a varied programme of schooling and chapel, to cater for their less material needs. Nor should it be forgotten that the workhouses from which they came were often little hells of debauchery and misery where their chances of survival were small. Perhaps one of the grimmest comments on the age is the fact that, whether as victims of the Poor Law or the new factories, pauper children had very little chance of surviving or becoming useful citizens if they did.

But though children were brought in from London, local labour was used where possible, and the changes produced on the social and economic structure of the rapidly industrialized areas is a fascinating, if fragmentary, story. With the growth of the cotton industry, even before any of the new mills had been built, population had thickened. Probably most of the smaller farmers added to their incomes by spinning and weaving, while, except for hay-time and harvest, cottagers and landless folk were regularly employed in this way. Such at least was Ratcliffe's opinion in 1770. The next stage took place when a mill was erected locally. At first, as at Mellor, the demand was for male labour, for the building and equipping of the mill, but after that it was mainly women and, even more, children who were required. In such circumstances single men had little inducement to stay, but for men with large families the state of the labour market faced them with something of a dilemma. Though there was a steady demand for child labour, no family, apart from the social and psychological difficulties involved, could live with fair comfort only on what the children earned, though they might eke out a bare existence.

Whether male labour was redundant or not depended on local circumstances. Weaving was as yet unmechanized and remained a domestic industry which continued to give employment to many men. Sometimes, too, subsidiary building operations, or enterprises such as the lime kilns that Oldknow set up when his Mellor works were in operation, absorbed surplus male labour. Another determent inseparable from the new conditions was that the factory with its new discipline of hours and fines was not popular, and men, even when they could have obtained employment, preferred if possible to stay outside. As a result it was the women and children rather than adult men who represented the largest element in the new industrial population. The men, for the most part, in the textile areas at least, remained domestic workers and craftsmen. Nevertheless, some were being absorbed. Stockport had its Friendly Society of Cotton Spinners in 1785, and the Manchester Friendly Associated Cotton Spinners were drawing up their regulations ten years later, though they were probably a mixed society comprising workers who were using jennies in their homes as well as men employed in the cotton mills.

It is not easy to know what these new industrial workers were like. The Hon. John Byng is perhaps no very impartial witness, but the town proletariate of Manchester filled him with horror. 'In what a lawless state of indecorum', he wrote in the June of 1792, 'must these great manufacturing towns exist; when, from a want of hands, character, and good behaviour are unnecessary; masters wanting servants, not servants wanting masters; so the workman demands excessive wages, is insolent, abandon'd, and drunk half the week.' A little later he commented again on the fact that 'Amidst all this crew of artisans, you may search in vain for healthy looks; for, alas! they are all squalid from unwholesome toil, and relaxing debauchery', and bewailed the fact that 'Instead of clean, jolly husbandmen, strutting about, the 'lean unwashed artificer" here rôles alone to the dismay of modesty'.[1] That his reactions were not baseless may be surmised from the notice which Oldknow felt constrained to put up in his works in the December of 1797 to the effect that,

Whereas the horrid and impious Vice of the profane CURSING and SWEARING—and the Habits of Losing Time,—and DRUNKENNESS,— are becoming so frequent and notorious that unless speedily

[1] J. Byng: *Torrington Diaries*, Vol. III, pp. 115, 118.

checked they may justly provoke the Divine Vengeance to increase the Calamities these Nations now labour under,[1]

he forthwith instituted a tariff of fines to stem such deplorable habits! James Graham, too, while of the opinion that within the last ten years (he was speaking in 1806), the general good behaviour of the semi-rural worker had much improved, thought it 'a deal better than that of people in the towns, where they live together; in towns I think they have increased in idleness and wretchedness'.[2]

Many factors and much history had gone to produce this oft-expressed distrust of the industrial worker. As early as the sixteenth century Cecil had been conscious that the craftsman, dependent on industry, presented new and difficult problems in government. That the poor would be lazy and thriftless if they could was an accepted maxim of eighteenth-century economic writers, and many were the devices and stratagems suggested or employed to drive and keep them in the way of virtue. There was nothing new in the attitude of the Clifton Vestry which in 1787 ordained that 'As the poor of the parish do not frequent the service of the church, but loiter in idleness and are most probably guilty of offences during the time of such services',[3] they were at least to attend prayers every Friday before receiving their weekly relief! Nor basically was there anything new in the anxious debates which took place as to the propriety of licensing a theatre in the new manufacturing towns. That amenities in the form of Assembly Rooms and Libraries and Literary Societies should be provided for the growing numbers of the urban middle classes was accepted as something that called for commendation and civic pride, but distractions that might lure the craftsman and the factory hand into wasting time were a very different matter. When the question arose in connexion with the licensing of a playhouse in Manchester the bill was opposed by the Bishop of London on the ground that Manchester was a manufacturing town and that such distractions would be destructive of its welfare. The Earl of Carlisle, who favoured the project, was in this case ready with an

---

[1] G. Unwin, A. Hulme and G. Taylor: *Samuel Oldknow and the Arkwrights* (1924), p. 198.
[2] *Minutes of Committee on . . . Woollen Industry*, p. 447.
[3] J. Latimer: *The Annals of Bristol in the Eighteenth Century* (1893), p. 481.

argument calculated to appeal to his ecclesiastical colleague, and pointed out that since Manchester was full of Methodists a playhouse might have its uses! 'I know not', declared the noble lord, 'of any way so effectual to eradicate that dark, odious, ridiculous enthusiasm as by giving to the people cheerful, rational amusements, which may operate against their methodistical melancholy'.[1]

The bill was passed, but not without misgivings. Two years later a similar bill to provide Birmingham was under discussion and Sir William Baghot, dwelling on the pernicious effects of theatres in manufacturing towns, drew attention to the examples of Manchester and Liverpool. In both these places he affirmed they had introduced dissipation, checked industry and increased the Poor Rates. His argument was in line with current mercantilist thought but he was answered by a greater man than himself, Edmund Burke, who replied with some justice,

> I do not know that Theatres are Schools of Virtue. I would rather call them Nurseries of Idleness; but then, Sir, of the various Means which Idleness will take for its amusement, in Truth I believe the Theatre is the most innocent:—The Question is not, Whether a Man had better be at Work than go to the Play? It is simply this— Being idle, shall he go to the Play or some Blacksmith's Entertainment.[2]

But if the attitude towards the urban worker was not new the uneasiness which these debates revealed illustrates the growing realization that the new town populations must be disciplined and controlled if they were not to be a threat to the accepted economic and social structure of the day. In the days before adequate and trained police forces were available mobs were dangerous. No politician had any doubts on that. Sometimes, when food prices soared suddenly and intolerably, and angry workers erupted almost spontaneously, any incident such as the sudden appearance of a cart loaded with the high-priced grain was sufficient stimulus to direct action. And when this happened local authorities were helpless. They could persuade, conciliate, or be overwhelmed; they could not control or quell until the military arrived, even though later, when authority had reasserted itself, ring-leaders

[1] Quoted W. A. Axon: *Op. cit.*, p. 103.
[2] Quoted R. K. Dent: *Op. cit.*, p. 173.

might be transported or hanged. But while towns remained small the threat to public order, except in London, was not great. In the new towns, however, the potentialities for mob action were considerable and had, on more than one occasion, been demonstrated. True, the riots in Manchester, directed very largely against the Nonconformists, and the violent doings on 14 and 15 July, 1791, in Birmingham, when property of at least £35,000, and by some estimates £50,000, was destroyed, were engineered by the adroit use of political and religious rumour and suspicion, but they demonstrated very effectively what a mob could do when it got out of hand. If the point needed underlining, what was happening in France was pertinent. There, property was being confiscated and heads were being cut off, and contemporary Englishmen were more conscious of the mob that roared approval beside the guillotine or looted and burned the châteaux than of the more subtle forces that were directing the movement. In England, therefore, it was felt necessary to keep the new urban worker in the place to which mercantilist theory had assigned the labouring poor. That the rural poor would challenge the limits assigned to them was unlikely; they were too scattered, too disunited, too steeped in the traditions of the past. The new town workers were more dangerous.

In consequence, every claim that seemed to hint at equality was sternly discouraged, unless it was accompanied by an accession of riches adequate to palliate the presumption. Francis Place, even when he had attained some degree of prosperity, was very well aware that his intellectual and literary accomplishments would not endear him to his wealthier customers, and might, indeed, cost him their patronage. He wrote bitterly in his autobiography on one occasion:

> Had these people been told that I never read a book, that I was ignorant of everything but my business, that I sotted in a public house, they would not have made the least objection to me. I should have been a 'fellow' beneath them, and they would have patronized me; but . . . to accumulate books and be supposed to know something of their contents, to seek friends too among literary and scientific men, was putting myself on an equality with themselves, if not, indeed, assuming a superiority; it was an abominable offence in a tailor, if not a crime which deserved punishment. Had it been

known to all my customers that in a few years from 1810–1817 I had
accumulated a considerable library, in which I spent all the leisure
time I could spare; had the many things I was engaged in during
that period, and the men with whom I was associated been known,
half of them at least would have left me, and these, too, by far the
most valuable customers individually.[1]

And in another place, stressing the same theme, he wrote,

The nearer a common tradesman approximates in information and
manners to a footman the more certainly will he please his well bred
customers; the less he knows beyond his business the more certain,
in general, will be his success.[2]

Place's comments are interesting because they reveal the
strength of the disapproval to which attempts to change the social
structure of the past were subjected, but he himself cannot be
regarded as the product of the new industrial ferment. Between
the craftsman of London and the factory worker in a northern
town the gulf was very wide. Intellectual triumphs such as those
which he and men like Hutton achieved belong as much to the
pattern of the past as to that of the future. For the individual,
progress had always been possible, though in the field of scholarship the Church rather than the shop had been the more usual
road by which such a goal had been achieved. If the workers in
the new manufacturing districts are to be considered as a novel
element in the society of their day then it is probably safest to
regard them as having as yet very little influence within it; a
potential rather than a present challenge. Contemporary gentlemen, with the excesses of the Paris mob fresh in their memories,
may have looked askance at the disorderly, shabby, indisciplined
workers that thronged the growing towns, as something undesirable and new, but the factory hands were, perhaps, even by the
end of the eighteenth century, more the components of a new
class than a class that had already gained some coherence. Nevertheless, by the time that peace came again to Britain the raw
material which was to organize itself under the Owens and the
Dohertys of the future was there. But though in existence in em-
bryo, it was still the craftsman working in his own home at the
loom, or the hard toil of the nailer, or the unrewarding drudgery

[1] G. Wallas: *Op. cit.*, p. 37.   [2] *Ibid.*, p. 38.

of the stocking frame that typified the industrial worker of the day.

How then is the impact of the new economic developments on the older social structure to be assessed? In rural England, particularly where the open-field village had hitherto survived, much that was traditional had clearly been swept away. With the open fields had gone the type of rural community they had made possible, while the new dependence of industry on coal and power and machinery had encouraged a return to the specialization of the Middle Ages; agriculture in the countryside, industry and trade in the towns. The rift between the countryman and the town worker, so characteristic of the nineteenth century, had already become perceptible. But what had not yet become clear was that the latter was to gain so large a predominance. James Graham, in his evidence given to the Committee on the Woollen Industry, could still say in 1806, 'the domestic manufacturers have increased in number as well as in wealth, if one may judge from appearances they are now, instead of living shut up in narrow streets, in towns extending themselves into the middle of a field, you may see two or three manufacturers' houses in almost every field in Armley'.[1] Therefore, to contemporaries, until at the end of the Napoleonic Wars prices collapsed and the landowner found himself faced with very considerable difficulties, it must have seemed as if whatever changes were taking place the position of the Landed Interest was still unshaken. Not till the repeal of the Corn Laws in 1846 did it suffer a major defeat. Until then, though there were considerable alterations in the lower ranks of the rural hierarchy, as the numbers of the agricultural labourers grew and those of the smaller copyholders, farming in the traditional way, declined, the landed gentry and the great proprietors were apparently still capable of maintaining that position which in the eighteenth century had been unquestionably theirs.

If in the world of industry not a great deal that was old had been swept away much that was new had already become apparent. The number of smallish industrial capitalists was every year growing, and with their growth in numbers came a new social and political coherence that was becoming marked in those areas where manufacture was concentrating. To the ranks of the

[1] *Minutes of Committee on . . . Woollen Industry*, p. 444.

merchant, the shopkeeper, the professional man had now to be added a new figure, the manufacturer. Though the term might in 1700 have implied no more than its literal meaning, a man who worked with his hands, by 1800 it was acquiring a very definite connotation and was becoming associated in men's minds with cotton and with iron, with machinery, with power and with factories. The manufacturer, as the nineteenth century was to understand the term, was already in being. So, too, was the new industrial town. Manchester and Birmingham were already becoming, if not household words, at least well known and a curiosity to be visited by foreign as well as English travellers. And in them the new type of urban workers lived and moved and had their being.

The influence of this new industry was not, and could not be, confined to the propagation of new classes. It was equally important in creating a demand for better transport. The new towns had to be fed, the new mills supplied with raw materials, their finished goods had to be distributed. Newer turnpike trusts, often inspired and controlled by industrialists, were replacing the older inefficient ones. On these new roads traffic could move smoothly and fast even over the clay belt and even in bad weather. In consequence the stage coach and the Mail were linking parts of the country with a speed and certainty that they had never known before. People were travelling more widely in their own country, rural isolation and the predominance of the local town were alike beginning to break down; Somerset and Sussex, Lancashire and Warwickshire, were fast becoming England. And to this consolidation, particularly on the economic side, the canals, like the roads, the product of industrial changes, were making a great contribution. If the needs of industry were improving communications, so, too, its products were making a general rise in the standard of living possible. Despite the diversion of resources to the needs of war, despite, too, the amount of capital absorbed in the development of transport and in the equipping of industrial plant, the increase in consumer goods was perceptible even by 1800. Textiles, particularly the cheaper cottons, domestic utensils, from pots and pans and firebacks to the products of Wedgwood's potteries were all affected. Moreover, much of this flow of goods was available to persons of very modest means. If

Wedgwood produced the finest china that the collector could desire, he also recognized that profit was to be made in supplying the ordinary needs of everyday people. The Darbys, too, and kindred manufacturers were busy catering for the same humdrum needs. It is easy to be appalled by the condition of the new industrial towns, by their drabness and dirt and the overcrowding in their unlovely houses, but men like Francis Place, who had known the old way of things, were well aware that the standard of living of the labouring poor had improved as a result of this new productivity. The wills of even prosperous craftsmen of the early eighteenth century reveal how few and how simple were the household and personal possessions of most people before the effects of the age of inventions began to make themselves felt.

Therefore, even if it is unwise to overestimate the change in the social structure and the way of life that the economic developments of the late eighteenth century effected, it would be equally rash to underestimate it. Much, probably most, of what was old remained, but much that was new had already appeared. Perhaps what was happening can best be compared to a northern mountain stream, whose waters come from two separate sources and for a time flow side-by-side in the same bed. Just as the watcher on the bank can distinguish between the brown peat-impregnated water and the grey-green of the slate stream until, as the channel widens the waters mingle and take on a common hue, so the historian can say, 'This is old, this new', until both flow together to form the England of the nineteenth century.

INDEX

ACTORS—social background of, 138; Dr. Johnson's opinion of, 140

Agriculture, improvements in, 203; developments in stockbreeding, 205

Aix-la-Chapelle, Peace of, 16

Ale Houses, 193

Alleghanies, 15

Allowance system, 247; reasons for, 248–9; results of, 250

Amusements in small towns, 130

Apothecaries, history of, 134; training of, 135

Apprentices, in Bedfordshire, 64; in eighteenth century, 184; as affected by Poor Law, 188; pauper, in cotton mills, 274

Architecture, standards of, 127

Arkwright, Richard, 214, 252–3, 269

Aristocracy, Ministers chosen from, 117 and the land, 120; in trade and industry, 119; as patrons of art, 121

Assemblies at Nottingham, 131; Newcastle, Liverpool and Manchester, 258; A. Young at, 130

Attorney, social position of, 57, 133

Austen, Jane, on social distinctions, 57

Authors, growing number of, 137

BAKEWELL, Roger (stock-breeder), 205

Bankers, social position of, 55–6

Bannister, Charles (actor), 139

Barclay, Mrs. (actress), 140

Barresford, Mrs. (actress), 140

Baskerville, John, 224–5

Bath, 131

Bedfordshire, occupations in, 64

Birmingham, growing industries in, 145, 260; Blue-coat school in, 152; cellar dwellings in, 169; clothing and rent clubs in, 177; condition in early eighteenth century, 261; acquires an Assembly Room, 261; acquires a theatre, 262; poor architecture in, 262; new subscription library in, 263; Hutton's *History* of, 263; improvements in, 263

Bishops, political functions of, 95–6; struggles for translation by, 97; dangers of political opposition for, 98; of business, 100

Bishoprics, revenues of, 97

Blackpool, Catherine Hutton's opinion of, 133

Bleach works, 215

Boroughs, electorate in pocket, 71; control of pocket, 73–4; judicial powers of, 88

Boswell, James, 3, 81, 105, 118, 140

Boulton, Matthew (iron-master), 223, 229, 252, 255, 267–8

Braunt, William (merchant), 54

Briant, William (carpenter), household possessions of, 166

Brighton, 131

Bristol, economic activities in, 63, 258; House of Industry in, 153

Burke, Edmund, 74; on the Middlesex magistrates, 89; on theatres, 277

Burlington, Lord, 121, 126

CALICO printing, history of, 216–17; legislation against, 217; speculative nature of, 218; new inventions in, 218

Canada, 12, 15–17, 37

Cape Breton Island, 12, 17

Capital, accumulation of, 222

Carding machines, 213

Carriages owned by manufacturers, 264

Carter, Thomas (attorney), 141

Cave, Edward (journalist and farmer), 213

Cecil, William, Lord Burleigh, 19, 23, 53

Charity schools, supported by the middle class, 152; provide education for the poor, 161; importance of, 163

Charles I (of England), 23

Charles II (of England), 10, 70, 87

Charles II (of Spain), 10

Chesterfield, Lord, on Westminster school, 110; on the effects of the Grand Tour, 116; on pleasure and business, 117; on Lord Burlington, 121